# Germany's Colonial Pasts

# Germany's Colonial Pasts

Edited by Eric Ames,
Marcia Klotz,
and Lora Wildenthal
Foreword by
Sander L. Gilman ∾

University of Nebraska Press : Lincoln and London

© 2005 by the Board of Regents of the University of
Nebraska. All rights reserved. Manufactured in the
United States of America. Set in Quadraat fonts by Bob
Reitz. Book designed by Richard Eckersley. ⊗

Library of Congress Cataloging-in-Publication Data
Germany's colonial pasts / edited by Eric Ames, Marcia
Klotz, and Lora Wildenthal; foreword by Sander L.
Gilman    p. cm. – (Texts and contexts)
Includes bibliographical references and index.
ISBN-10: 0-8032-4819-9  ISBN-13: 978-0-8032-4819-9
1. German literature – 19th century – History and
criticism.  2. German literature – 20th century – History and criticism.  3. Nationalism – Germany –
History.  4. National characteristics, German, in literature.  5. Imperialism – History – 19th century.
6. Germany – Foreign relations – 1918–7. Colonies in
literature.  8. Nationalism in literature.  I. Ames, Eric,
1969–  II. Klotz, Marcia, 1961–  III. Wildenthal, Lora,
1965–  IV. Texts and contexts (Unnumbered)
PT363.N27G47 2005  830.9'358 – dc22  2005009426

In memory of Susanne Zantop (1945–2001)

# Contents

# Foreword

In my series Texts and Contexts I have published a number of distinguished books over the past decade, their subjects ranging from European and Jewish culture to human psychology. Never have I felt compelled to write a foreword to one of these books, as I believe that they should stand on their merits without any attempt on my part to argue for them. Many of these books have entered into the marketplace of ideas in the most extraordinary manner. They have increased my own reputation much more than I could have puffed theirs.

Writing this foreword is very different. It is an act of homage to a colleague whose work I admired from the beginning of her academic career and whose murder (together with that of her husband Half) shocked the nation. Susanne Zantop was a rare scholar. She was imbued with an enthusiasm for Spanish American as well as German culture because of her lived experiences in both. Early in her career she invited me to speak at a small Heine conference in Hanover, where I had a chance to talk at great length about our mutual love of Mexico, Mexican culture, and Spanish literature. My engagement with her was heightened when she published her major scholarly study *Colonial Fantasies*, in which she took on many of my own early views on German attitudes toward Africa and the Africans in a critical way. Good scholarship surveys the terrain of existing scholarship, building on it, rebutting it. Her scholarship certainly did this in such a way as to further the creation of a field – that of German colonial studies.

Over the past decade, as a result of the current interest in postcolonial studies, much of the work that I did in the 1960s and '70s in response to the civil rights movement as well as my own study of stereotypes have undergone radical reassessment. What was earlier a taboo subject within German Studies, undertaken only at its very fringes, became a bridge between German Studies and the rest of European Studies. There was a search for the meaning of the German colonial experience, for the implications of that moment when the first German chancellor, Otto von Bismarck – against his own sense of what the new Germany should be – decided that engaging in the "scramble for Africa" (to use the contemporary phrase) was a necessary element in the future of the German Reich. The short period of three decades saw the creation of a German colonial experience unlike that of the Dutch and the Portuguese in the sixteenth and seventeenth or even the French and the British in the eighteenth and nineteenth centuries. The German experience had a duration similar to the Belgian one that fulfilled the promise Léopold II made to his foreign minister (engraved on a piece of the Parthenon that Léopold gave him when he appointed him) that "I shall give Belgium its colony." So, too, in Africa, the South Pacific, and China, Germany created a colonial world that mirrored its status as a new nation. Germany and Belgium – nations created in the nineteenth century – built very different colonies but ones that mirrored their need to shape a new national identity as much as it reflected the economic imperatives of colonialism. Both Zantop's project and the project of this volume are to trace a particular version of the German *Sonderweg*: the uniqueness of German colonial practice and imagery. As much as this discussion has been abandoned within German social and cultural history over the past decade, it is vital in understanding the idea and image as well as the practice of the colonial experience in Germany.

Each of the colonial experiences is clearly unique; the culture of France is not that of the United Kingdom (which is in an odd way not England), and neither is close in any way to the cultures of Spain, Portugal, and Holland. While there are striking similarities between Belgium and Germany, the corporate nature of the Congo Free State was a far cry from the eventual colonial rule of the established German colonies. This is even more true because the myth of the "lost colonies" seized under the League of Nations' mandate after 1919 became part of the memories of Weimar and the Third Reich as well as the shadow of memories in both postwar German states, where much of the initial scholarly work was begun. This odd, fuzzy memory of a lost colonial world has shaped German scholarship, and it is this that Susanne Zantop was interested in explaining. This volume is in memory of a great scholar, murdered at the peak of her career by two young Americans wishing to escape their mundane reality to a mythic world of "Australia," as much a myth as that of Africa in German fantasy. The volume is a fitting tribute to Susanne Zantop's life, which was spent explaining the meaning of such worlds.

SANDER L. GILMAN

M A R C I A  K L O T Z

# Introduction

This project began as a workshop, organized by Susanne Zantop over the summer of 2000, that was to bring together a number of scholars who were currently working on German colonial history and literature. The goal was to offer the various historians and literary theorists who had taken an interest in the field a chance to share their work in a relaxed setting. If the exchange proved fruitful, she hoped that an anthology might come of our efforts, much in the spirit of *The Imperialist Imagination*.[1] The authors represented in this volume are those whom she originally invited or planned to invite to that workshop, scheduled to take place in June of 2001. With the news of Susanne's tragic and untimely death, the plans for the workshop were cancelled. Yet as June of that year came and went, those of us who had been involved in the project found that we could not simply leave her plan unfulfilled. It seemed only fitting that we should honor Susanne and her work by holding the workshop she had envisioned a year later, using it as a forum to commemorate her pioneering study of German colonial fantasies and the profound influence she had on all of us. Thus was this project born.

Unlike most of the essays collected in this volume, Susanne's own major contribution to the study of German colonialism, *Colonial Fantasies*, did not focus on the body of colonial literature that was written during the period when Germany actually held colonies. Instead, she examined the two hundred years that preceded Germany's direct involvement in the "age of empire." Moreover, she looked at texts situated in the New World rather than the regions in Africa, Asia, or the South Pacific where Germany actually established territorial rule. For her, the final establishment of German colonies "marked not so much the beginning as the end in what Mary Townsend termed a 'distinct colonial cult,' a cult that had characterized much of German public discourse during the two previous, 'precolonial' centuries" (2). She was thus not concerned with how German colonial literature represented – or even misrepresented – concrete colonial practice, but rather with a body of literature that had no relationship to any existing colonial policy nor even to a German nation-state that might have aspired to become an imperial power. For this reason her texts

xi

functioned quite differently from most of what is taken as "colonial literature," whether in German or in other languages: "By virtue of existing in the 'pure' realm of the imagination, 'untainted' by praxis, German fantasies were not only differently motivated, but had a different function: to serve not so much as ideological smokescreen or cover-up for colonial atrocities or transgressive desires, but as *Handlungsersatz*, as substitute for the real thing, as imaginary testing ground for colonial action" (6). It was thus the very lack of German colonies that made the fantasies she investigates so compelling. Unsullied by any colonial practice on the ground, Germans were free to imagine that they would be better, kinder, gentler colonizers than the Spanish or the Portuguese, the British or the French.

Methodologically, she was interested in the concrete (if sometimes latent) content of conquest fantasies, reading them in a manner similar to Freud's analyses of dreams, which is to say, as expressions of unconscious or half-unconscious desires. This was of course not a strictly Freudian project, for, as she stated in the introduction, she was "less concerned with the fantasies and the unconscious of individuals than with a collective mentality of a nation in the making" (4). Together, these fantasies come to suggest a collective individuality, "producing not just a 'family' of like-minded readers, but the illusion that when it came to colonial expansion, the nation was driven, like an individual, by one will, one desire" (4). In this sense her book also follows in the tradition of Benedict Anderson as a study of one venue where the German "nation" came into being as an imagined community, at a time when there was no state or government in which that "nation" might find political representation.

In her analysis the main content of these narratives revolves around a singular theme: Germany – understood as a loosely formed community of German speakers – developed a kind of ego-ideal through these colonial fantasies, coming to view itself as a kind and benevolent community dedicated to the well-being of colonial peoples and lands everywhere. Though sadly and unjustly excluded from participation in the civilizing mission, Germans would (if only allowed to do so!) behave as loving fathers to native children and as doting husbands to colonial wives, rather than the abusive and rapacious tyrants the Spaniards had turned out to be.

It is this function of constituting an imaginary, idealized understanding of the German national community, differentiated both from those colonized peoples of other lands and from other colonizing nations, that has been most influential to the group of scholars represented in part 1 of this volume, "Identifications of Self and Other." Woodruff D. Smith, in his essay, argues that the familial fantasies that served to contrast hypothetical German colonizers with those of other countries had everything to do with what he calls a cult of respectability. He is interested in the "framing concepts" of historical accounts of modernization, which have traditionally focused on the rise of bourgeois society and culture on the one hand and on a growing discourse of liberalism on the other. While these narratives are not necessarily wrong per se, they are incomplete. He focuses on the rise of the discourse of respectability in its relation to these more familiar historical narratives, examining its centrality to German colonial history. Like Smith, Bradley D. Naranch is also interested in the historiographical framing concepts that have been brought to bear on histories of German colonialism. He follows Zantop's lead in situating his study in the period before Germany actually acquired colonies, looking at a gradual shift that took place in the way Germans who left their country for other regions were represented between the 1840s and the 1860s. He shows how that twenty-year period saw the term *Auswanderer* (emigrant) slowly become replaced by *Auslandsdeutsche* (German abroad). This shift demonstrates a growing sense of national identity over those two decades: the latter term, in contrast to the former, implies a deep, organic connection that linked those who had left the homeland with those who remained there. Vanessa Agnew's essay brings us into the colonial period proper, the time when Germany maintained its own overseas empire. She focuses on the relationship between comparative musicology, a new scientific field in the 1880s, and anthropological studies of race. Looking specifically at representations of Pacific Islanders, Agnew finds, like the subjects of Zantop's study, numerous representations of the "noble savage" type. Music was understood to be a marker of the "advanced" status of a people, proving, for example, that the Polynesians were the "most deserving of the fruits of our civilization." The familial metaphor that Zantop so deftly analyzes is played out here on a cultural level. Comparative musicologists traveled throughout the world recording the music of peoples "destined for rapid extinction." Upon closer examination, however, Agnew finds that their fears have less to do with the people's actual "extinction" than with the loss of their "pure" musical forms, as they came in contact with and were influenced by German music and came to influence that music in turn. Cultural mixing, symbolically celebrated in the family metaphors of Zantop's study, is here decried as the extermination of native culture.

In the earlier texts of Zantop's study (most of which were written in the seventeenth and eighteenth centuries), the familial metaphorics of cultural mixing are less abstract and tend to follow a common narrative structure. The colonizer is inevitably represented as a European male, the colonized as an indigenous woman. The familiar sexualized metaphor of the Conquest casts the lands of the New World in the figure of a woman who, after an initial period of resistance, eventually relinquishes her virginity to the conquering European soldier, symbolizing her people's welcoming acceptance of his legitimate rule over themselves and their lands. Zantop identified three stages in this narrative: first, the "bride" is familiarized and domesticated, in order that she might belong to the same human species as the European; second, she is assimilated into the European family and becomes, in the process, subject to patriarchal control; and finally, the land that she symbolically represents is cast as depopulated and dehumanized, becoming an empty space in need of inscription.

Part 2, "Orders of Colonial Regulation: Sex and Violence," focuses on how this narrative both changes and remains the same during the period when Germany lays claim to overseas colonies. Sara Lennox's essay on Hans Grimm's *Südafrikanische Novellen* (South African novellas) shows that a similar narrative is at work in the short stories that represented German colonial activity in German Southwest Africa in the years preceding the First World War. The colonizing man is again tempted by an all-too-willing indigenous woman, who clearly and immediately prefers his charms to those of her own countrymen. Here, however, a new element comes into play: "race mixing" is viewed as a deadly threat to the future of German rule in the colony, for which reason it becomes imperative that the colonizer resist the native woman's seduction. Yet this resistance creates a dilemma. On the one hand, the sexual freedom and gratification that the native woman personifies is precisely what draws any truly virile man to the colonies; he resists temptation only by voluntarily emasculating himself, sacrificing the very masculine strength that might allow him to survive in the colonies. On the other hand, if he succumbs to temptation, he quickly finds himself drawn "down to her level"; in a word, he "goes native." Kristin Kopp outlines a very similar narrative structure operating in the *Ostmarkenroman* (novel of the eastern marches) – a genre often used as propaganda for the German cause in colonizing the Polish east. These novels typically feature a young, inexperienced German male colonist whose erotic obsession with a Polish woman leads to precisely the same consequences as the union with a native African woman in Grimm's texts: he becomes idle and loses his self-respect, which ultimately leads to his doom. The hapless colonizer of the eastern marches "goes Pollack," just as the overseas colonist who intermarries with a local woman "goes native."

Two elements are striking in the narratives analyzed by Lennox and Kopp. First, there is an extraordinary similarity between these narratives about overseas colonialism and those thematizing the struggle for cultural supremacy in Germany's own eastern regions. Clearly, the kinds of racial distinctions one usually associates with colonial discourse, marked by a binary between "white" and "nonwhite," could easily be applied to distinctions between various groups of "whites" as well. Second, these narratives resemble those earlier colonial fantasies Zantop discussed and yet are very different as well. True, colonialism is portrayed through the trope of seduction: native women quickly and freely choose the occupying colonizer over their own masculine compatriots, indicating that colonizing men possess a natural, virile superiority that is immediately obvious to all. Here, however, that choice has dire consequences for the colonizer. The female native's culture has become more powerful in the years that separate Zantop's sources from Lennox's and Kopp's; indeed, it is assumed to vanquish in any cultural conflict. Yet it would be too hasty to find here an expression of power for the colonized or to see this as a strategy of colonial resistance; it marks, rather, a developing fear on the part of the colonizer, one often linked to ever more repressive strategies of control. One might attribute this shift to the difference between the utopian colonial fantasies Zantop studied, which operated as a substitute for concrete colonial activity in the world, and the anxious fantasies that dominated once colonial policy had become a reality – when real people had to explain their own actions, and failures, in narrative terms.

The third essay in this section focuses less on colonial regimes of desire and sexuality than on issues of colonial law. David Simo offers a Foucauldian interpretation of the history of German annexation and colonization of Cameroon, understanding colonialism as an attempt to export to the colonies the modernization process that Foucault critiques. That process includes the practice of power through the imposition of a system of rules that appears, on its surface anyway, to transform chaos into order. For example, Simo looks at the Berlin Conference of 1884–85, in which the indigenous peoples of Africa were repeatedly described as "legal minors," incapable of acting on their own behalf in the modern world. Nevertheless, the various European claims of sovereignty were generally supported by treaties that were negotiated with the leaders of local ethnic groups. Simo points to a contradiction in the logic of colonial rule: in the final analysis German officials claimed colonial rights in Cameroon based on the sovereign will of the Cameroonian people – the very ones who were simultaneously cast as legal minors. What interests Simo in general is the way in which a legal system that purports to create order out of chaos ultimately turns out to spread a culture of utter lawlessness throughout the land. Hannah Arendt and Aimé Césaire, and more recently Paul Gilroy (among others), have argued that this development ultimately was to have consequences for Europe as well; once a political culture was constituted in which even the most severe crimes – including genocide – remained unpunished, there was nothing to keep this culture from "coming home" to Europe, specifically to Germany.[2]

The possibility of a connection between Germany's colonial campaign and the development of German Fascism was a topic of great interest to Zantop, though she resisted the overly facile links that other scholars have sometimes made. As she put it, "There is always a danger of reading German history backward from the Holocaust. By the same token, the Holocaust has taught us to take the first stirrings of racism seriously, and to look for powerful ideological undercurrents even in times of relative tolerance and stability, undercurrents that can be activated in times of crisis. While the Holocaust was certainly not the only possible outcome of German eighteenth- and nineteenth-century history, it is the outcome with which we must contend" (16). She clearly believed that there *was* a link between the fantasies she uncovered in her study and the development of the kinds of racist thinking that led to the Holocaust. At the conclusion of her work, she asks whether such fantasies had to end in Nazi expansionism and racial extermination and concludes that they did not, finding evidence in the numerous critics of the colonial fantasies she describes. She finds counternarratives in the works of Gottfried Keller, Heinrich Heine, and Heinrich von Kleist – proof that resistance was possible even if it did not, in the end, carry the day. In concluding that these writers, who posed counterfantasies to those she describes, might have pointed history in a different direction, she implies that the narratives that form the bulk of her study did in fact contribute to Hitler's rise. But what exactly *was* the link between such colonial fantasies and the development of National Socialism? She no more answered this question than that of the nature of the connection between the fantasies generated by a Germany without colonial holdings and the concrete policies of colonial expansionism that developed in the late nineteenth century. These broad and deeply intriguing questions, which remain unanswered, are precisely what has made her work so provocative for other scholars and so influential.

The essays in part 3, "Colonial Racism and Antisemitism," address the nature of the relationship between these two forms of racism in German history. Pascal Grosse argues that there was indeed a connection between the two. He does not trace it, as Zantop had implied, through the genealogy of specific colonial or racial fantasies, but rather (not unlike Arendt) as the development of a "racial order" in the colonies that later became central to the establishment of Nazism. He argues that we should see Germany's continental and overseas expansionism as complementary, based on the same racial logic, in which "culture" was seen as an expression of race. He argues that a racialized understanding of citizenship developed in the colonies and was then implemented at home. This "racial order" was part of a wider biologization and militarization of society in the period from 1900 to 1919; the Nuremberg Laws only made that order much more explicit.

While some scholars have argued that the genocidal order, for example, of General von Trotha in German Southwest Africa (now Namibia) establishes a clear precedent for the extermination of the Jews under Hitler, Grosse is more circumspect, asking why such colonial policies did not lead to genocide in other colonial metropoles. He concludes that the Weimar era is crucial to explaining how German colonialism led in a unique way to racial extermination, for that was the time when Germany practiced "colonialism without colonies." After losing its overseas empire at the end of the Great War, a difference emerged between Germany and other powers. There was no concrete reality to the German colonial idea, hence no need for negotiations with the colonized or with other colonizing powers, no check on an ideological framework that could grow in a completely unrestrained atmosphere. The German experience of decolonization occurred in isolation and not as a result of compromise or negotiation with the colonized. As Zantop had argued in the context of Germany's precolonial period, the very lack of colonial practice makes the fantasy life associated with it that much more powerful. Yet while her work is filled with perfumed imaginings of German colonizers as altruistic and benevolent, the colonial fantasies of the Weimar years are gloomy and violent; here, Germans cast themselves as defenders of the white race, the final bulwark against the forces of degeneracy, miscegenation, and corruption of the human spirit.

Marcia Klotz's essay works within a similar framework, looking at the ways in which the colonial world that had shaped the past two centuries of Europeans' understanding of the globe continued to provide the dominant paradigm for how people made sense of the experience of the Great War and how Germans made sense of the political order that came to take its place. What Grosse terms "colonialism without colonies," Klotz describes as Germany's position as a "postcolonial nation in a still-colonial world," a position that allowed fears of reverse colonization to run rampant. She links these anxieties

– fears that Germans were now to become the victims of colonialism rather than its perpetrators – to Hitler's mass appeal. Hitler, in her analysis, did not simply portray the Jews as *Untermenschen* who were racially inferior to "Aryans" and hence existed on a parallel plane with Africans, Asians, and other non-whites. Rather, he portrayed the Jews as colonizers who had entered Germany, along with the rest of Europe, long before and were now exploiting the continent's wealth while setting the European nations against one another using the "divide and conquer" strategy that had proved so immensely effective in guaranteeing colonial rule around the globe.

The third essay in this section finds a more abstract, general link between anti-Semitism and colonialism in the world view of Protestant theology itself. Susannah Heschel makes the bold claim that "Christianity was well-suited to serve as a religious justification for colonialism . . . because at its heart, Christian theology is a colonialist theology." She argues that the genesis of Christianity lies in a colonial relationship to Judaism – a religion whose cosmology, deity, and religious teachings it came to adopt, while denying that they continued to be valid for Judaism itself. Hence, Judaism functions as an internalized Other within Christianity. Her paper focuses on the various attempts made by German Protestant theologians to contain, redefine, and eventually exorcize this internal Other from the mid-nineteenth century into the Nazi era. She discusses, for example, how Protestant theologians under National Socialism countered the revival of Teutonic myths and rituals by offering their own version of a "dejudaized" Christianity.

Part 4, "Nazi Visions of Africa," examines the relationship between colonialism and National Socialism from a different angle by foregrounding the Nazis' own representations of the colonial past in Africa, along with what they hoped would be their return to its colonial future. Elisa von Joeden-Forgey is interested in "the enduring impact of subtler ideas and institutions that emerged as a result of formal colonial engagement." She illustrates this continuity by examining the German Africa Show, a traveling exhibit in the Third Reich that employed black performers, some of whom were German citizens and almost all of whom had spent many years in Europe, but who played the part of "Africans" for German crowds. The show offered a means of survival to a number of black Germans who found it nearly impossible to find employment under the repressive regime established by the Nuremberg Laws. In exchange, however, they were forced to voice the political message of colonial revisionists: German colonizers had not been brutal to their colonial subjects, as the victors of the First World War had proclaimed, but had rather been especially benevolent and caring, for which reason Africans wanted nothing more than for Germany to recolonize their continent. The show thereby "provide[d] a moral economy of race, in which the potentially incendiary racial policies of the Nazi regime – those that became publicly known – could be positively presented, and the brutal, criminal treatment of groups it claimed were inherently degenerate and valueless could be legitimized." The second essay in this section, by Robert Gordon and Dennis Mahoney, interprets a 1939 documentary by Karl Mohri, *Deutsches Land in Afrika* (German land in Africa), which, like the German Africa Show, polemicized for the return of Germany's colonial holdings in Africa. The film documents a journey taken from Tanganyika, part of Germany's former colony, German East Africa, to German Southwest Africa. Like the traveling German Africa Show, the film aims to prove that German colonial subjects were especially well treated and Germany's previous colonial holdings exceptionally well developed, reflections of a history of benevolent ardor whose traces still remained in 1939. The efficient, well-organized plantations founded by Germans were still functioning, the roads Germans laid still operating, and so forth. Mohri presents German Southwest Africa as the "Sleeping Beauty" of Africa, a country rich in natural resources that would surely blossom under the proper colonial authority – which is to say, if and when German rule returned. Both of these essays illustrate the reemergence of the central fantasy of Zantop's study in the National Socialist era: the myth of Germans as the "better" colonizers, a rebuttal of the Allies' contentions that they had actually been worse than others.

The fifth section of the book, "Colonial Legacies: The Racialized Self," brings us to the present moment, looking at contemporary perceptions of race in German-speaking areas and how these are influenced by the colonial legacy. Nina Berman writes about two recent German best sellers: Corinne Hofmann's *Die weisse Massai* (The white Masai), an autobiography of a Swiss woman who travels to Kenya and marries a Sambusu man there, and Miriam Kwalanda's *Die Farbe meines Gesichts: Lebensreise einer kenianischen Frau* (The color of my face: Life-journey of a Kenyan woman), which recounts a voyage in the opposite direction, tracking the journey of a Kenyan woman who marries a German tourist and embarks on a journey to Germany that concludes with her ultimate self-emancipation. Hofmann's marriage ends when she abandons her husband and moves back to Switzerland with their daughter; Kwalanda's likewise ends in divorce. Both narratives, according to Berman, serve to reinforce German stereotypes by neglecting the impact of colonization and modernization on Kenyan societies. Patrice Nganang's essay is similarly concerned with autobiographical accounts that foreground racial relations, but he focuses on two recent depictions of what it means to be black in Germany. Hans Massaquoi's *Destined to Witness* looks back at a youth spent in Nazi Germany, while Chima Oji's *Unter die Deutschen gefallen: Erfahrungen eines Afrikaners* (Among the Germans: An African's experiences) describes a more recent period. Nganang focuses on a point in each autobiography when the author "discovers his race," a key to autobiographies of blackness in Germany. Both Massaquoi's and Oji's works begin with a description of a peaceful childhood, quiet and harmonious. Awareness of racial identity breaks in on this idyll as a trauma. Both narratives depict a time when the author discovers his own body as a racialized entity that is not his own, a kind of doppelgänger. Blackness unites the parts of the figure in the mirror, ending its fragmentary status, but its unity is defined in the fictional terms of race. Nganang concludes that the unity of the black self, that which makes it possible for the autobiographical narrator in each text to employ the first-person pronoun "I," only comes from "inside the accepted fiction of the racialized body." Blackness positions both autobiographers as at once outsiders and insiders in Germany.

The essays collected in this volume thus span a time frame from the mid-nineteenth century up to the present moment, yet all reflect a deep interest in the approach to race, gender, and national identity that Susanne Zantop's book developed. We have missed her at every stage of this process: we missed her leadership and guidance in organizing the conference, her wit and sense of humor while we were holding it, her inimitable ability to respond to work from inside its own logical paradigm during the workshops, and her extraordinary editing skills while we were putting the manuscript together. We hope that this volume will serve as a tribute to her memory and as a token of gratitude for all that she and her work brought to us.

We would like to express our profound gratitude to those individuals and institutions who made this collaborative project possible. Professor Jonathan V. Crewe and Margaret Robinson generously agreed to host the conference on the Dartmouth campus, and their hard work and impeccable organizational skills, with the support of Leo Spitzer and Marianne Hirsch, allowed us to meet under truly optimal circumstances. We thank Sander Gilman, who generously accepted this volume for his series and wrote a foreword for it. Finally, we are very grateful to Dartmouth College's Office of the Provost, Associate Dean of the Humanities, Department of German Studies, and Jewish Studies Program as well as to the Graduate School at the University of Washington for their generous financial support for this project.

### NOTES

1. An anthology coedited by Susanne Zantop, Sara Friedrichsmeyer, and Sara Lennox (Ann Arbor: University of Michigan Press, 1998).

2. Aimé Césaire, *Discourse on Colonialism*, trans. Joan Pinkham (New York: Monthly Review Press, 1972); Hannah Arendt, "Imperialism" in *The Origins of Totalitarianism*, new ed. with added prefaces (New York: Harcourt Brace Jovanovich, 1973), 121–302; Paul Gilroy, *Against Race: Imagining Political Culture Beyond the Color Line* (Cambridge: Harvard University Press, 2000).

# PART 1

# Identifications of Self and Other

WOODRUFF D. SMITH

# Colonialism and the Culture
# of Respectability

In recent years a new generation of scholars has taken up the subject of German colonialism. Their work has been distinguished by the adoption of a variety of novel interpretive approaches and research directions. The contributions to this volume testify to the sophistication and vigor of their work, which is heavily influenced by the methods and aims of poststructuralist criticism, by cultural analysis, and by gender and postcolonial studies. A large proportion of the people currently doing German colonial history (indeed, a large proportion of the people doing colonial history in general) are not, formally at least, historians at all, but rather scholars in the various fields that make up culture studies. They have particularly emphasized the importance in historical explanation of constructed understandings, imaginings, and fantasies.

This is all to the good. It is particularly appropriate for comprehending modern imperialism, and perhaps especially German imperialism, because it allows us to get at the constructed, imagined character of that phenomenon in a way that older approaches were never really able to do. Nevertheless, there seems to be a reluctance in recent work on German colonialism to apply cultural, linguistic, and gender criticism as radically as might be desirable. New directions are taken and new insights are revealed with regard to the specifics of particular events or situations – the roles, for example, of colonialist women and biological scientists in the development of a racialist ideology in the German colonies, which Lora Wildenthal and Pascal Grosse have explicated brilliantly.[1] But there seems to be less willingness to challenge, or at least to interrogate, the framing concepts within which nineteenth- and twentieth-century imperialism has been explained for the last few decades. By this I do not mean that one should aim at eliminating all framing concepts through deconstruction, as some poststructuralist critics of historicism have suggested. Rather, it is desirable to be more critical of the ones to which we regularly refer as the backdrops or contexts of our interpretations.

Two sets of such conventional concepts in need of criticism and alternatives stand out. One is the "master narrative" of history since the sixteenth century as the story of socioeconomic modernization, with industrialization as the leading character, which privileges certain sets of changes as the core of causation and presumes that others (changes in colonialism, for example) are primarily to be explained as products of the core. The modernization narrative has come under close scrutiny in recent years, but it still tends to be assumed fairly uncritically by many people studying colonialism from a cultural-studies standpoint. [2] The second framing concept, often presented as a subnarrative of the first, is the story of the development of the bourgeoisie, bourgeois society and culture, and bourgeois liberalism as products of and concomitants to modernization. Here as well, the ambiguities that have always made this sub-narrative problematical have been discussed very forcefully in recent years, but it, too, still informs the background to many cultural studies of imperialism. [3] It is not that these framing concepts are wrong. It is rather that they are incomplete, that they were created in order to answer questions that were rather different from the ones many scholars are asking today and, most important, that they contain within themselves presumptions about what is significant and what is not, about what causes what, that are simply that: presumptions. We need to construct alternative framing concepts, at the very least in order to elicit convincing defenses of the conventional ones and perhaps also to develop a more satisfactory understanding of the past. It seems to me that the study of modern imperialism would be an excellent workshop in which to create such alternatives. [4]

I have recently been working in another, although not distant, field. In this essay I present – in the barest of outlines – an alternative framing concept that I have developed in that field and then suggest ways in which it might be relevant to German colonial studies. The subject of my research, embodied in a recently published book, is the broad and extremely important cultural construct to which nineteenth-century Europeans and Americans referred when they used the term "respectability" (or its several equivalents in languages other than English). [5] My work on this subject has focused thus far on the seventeenth and eighteenth centuries. It arose from an attempt to explain in a comprehensive way the changing nature of the demand in Europe in those centuries for goods produced overseas. In the course of my research, it became clear that many of the changes in which I was interested were the result of the formation of a culture of respectability, a process that culminated in the late eighteenth century. Because respectability remained the principal context for consumption after 1800, I have been led to investigate the history of respectability in the nineteenth century, which is my current project. In extending my research, I found that significant links to nineteenth- and twentieth-century colonialism appeared. I will discuss some of these shortly, but first we must have some idea of what is meant by respectability as a constructed cultural context.

The culture of respectability was created by western Europeans and North Americans in the second half of the eighteenth century, largely by connecting several more or less distinct contexts that already existed. A "cultural context" is a set of quite varied phenomena (cognitions, words, discourses, practices, behaviors, material objects, even institutions) that are conceived of as belonging together in what is held, by convention and presupposition, to be a meaningful way.[6] A cultural context (of which respectability was a sort of grand, aggregated example) constitutes one of multiple, parallel frameworks existing in people's minds in certain geographical areas and at certain times that provide a matrix of meaning, that allow people to value what they and other people do as being significant. Cultural contexts and their elements are similar to *mentalités*, except that they are usually products of conscious construction and are consciously recognizable by the people who incorporate them into their daily lives. They are not in most cases overtly political or ideological, but they can have political implications. They are not normally programmatic, but they constitute a storehouse of imagined meaningful relations that give significance to the terms in which programs are stated. They often have the peculiar quality of being recognized not only by historians but by the people in whose heads they largely reside as well – though not usually recognized as the comprehensive frameworks that they actually are.

In the case of respectability, it is almost impossible to read a nineteenth-century English novel or a modern book dealing with some aspect of nineteenth-century society without frequently finding the words "respectable" and "respectability" used in such a way as to denote a distinct set of attitudes, discursive practices, moral assumptions, behaviors, and material objects. And yet, the terms are almost always employed as matters of common understanding, without the need for special marking or any kind of analysis – except late in the century, when their use as terms of irony, as code words for hypocrisy, becomes increasingly common. Apart from the latter usage, what this suggests is that they touch upon an array of meanings that is simply assumed – that, despite contradictions among them, these terms are thought of as possessing such obvious coherence and reality that they are not normally subject to analysis.

Nevertheless, respectability was a very real, complex, and important thing, and it possessed a real history. As far as words are concerned, "respectability" was a creation of the 1780s. "Respectable" was a much older term, but it was again in the 1780s that its use became common and the meanings it would possess in the nineteenth century came to predominate. This was more or less the same time that *anständig* and *Anständigkeit* acquired their equivalence to the two English words – in part, through their very frequent use in this way by Goethe. The long-existent French words *honnête* and *honnêteté* received similar primary meanings in the late eighteenth century. [7] Even more significant is evidence that, with national and regional variations, the adoption of the terminology of respectability was matched by the formation of a cultural framework to which the terminology was attached, a framework constructed from a number of already existing, more limited cultural contexts. Neither the process of formation nor the constituents of the new framework of respectability can be detailed here, but the nature of the whole can be outlined by discussing some aspects of the contexts that were aggregated to form respectability.

One of the key elements of respectability was a set of factors having to do with social status. This can be envisioned as modifications of the older (but not immensely old) context of gentility, which had the effect of creating a largely moral definition of status. [8] The process did not lead immediately to the elimination of older forms of gentility, but rather to a set of parallel constructions that co-opted, and to some degree subverted, the terms of gentility. In Britain, for example, "gentleman" and "lady," without wholly losing the sense of being dependent on birth and on upbringing largely available only to the aristocracy, also acquired the sense of being something that depended on the moral virtue manifested in a person's actual behavior. Such behavior included not just exemplary actions rewarded because they were unusual, but also a broad range of everyday practices, including adherence to certain dress styles, adoption of polite manners (which were themselves redefined in moral terms), and other forms of interpersonal behavior. It also came to involve evaluation of a person's public stances on the basis of whether or not they were appropriately virtuous. This, of course, had major political implications, as demonstrated in Britain by the abolitionist movement's success in defining support for the slave trade as something that most respectable people did not evince. Moreover, the status of respectability cut across class lines defined in other ways. Although there were important contradictions in usage even within the repertory of practices belonging to particular individuals, it was generally true that one could be counted respectable regardless of the class in society to which one belonged according to any other social hierarchy. In English usage the term "respectable" was often applied to people in the middle classes, but it could also be used for workers and for members of the gentry and aristocracy. Indeed, in nineteenth-century political discourse, the notion of the "respectable working class" was of vital importance and was a major element of debates over franchise extension in the 1830s and 1860s. The growth of an ironic usage of the term "respectable" was to some extent a response to a growing tendency to hold the aristocracy, indeed, the entire political elite of Britain, up to the criterion of respectability as a test of moral fitness for high public status – to find the pre-Victorian culture of aristocracy wanting in this regard. By the mid-nineteenth century, it became acceptable even for members of the nobility to be accounted respectable, although by no means all of them were.

Another element of nineteenth-century respectability was a context that had developed in the late seventeenth and eighteenth centuries as a way of practicing, understanding, shaping, and justifying sensuality as an aspect of social, cultural, and economic life – what might be called the "context of luxury." [9] It developed around both the new aesthetic of "taste" and an approach to sensuality that emphasized the permissibility – indeed, the desirability – of a wide range of sensual experiences within the limits of conventional moral and institutional frameworks. Among these frameworks were families, certain kinds of markets for commodities, and "nature" redefined for the purpose. The context involved a redefinition of "luxury" – a redefinition that reduced (but did not entirely eliminate) the term's traditional negative moral connotations. The aspect of "taste" was aggressively aristocratic at first, but it was quickly accommodated to a wider social perspective essentially at the same time as its incorporation into the culture of respectability.

The aspect of morality through which the contexts of gentility and luxury were modified in the eighteenth century, and which facilitated their integration into the larger framework of respectability, was primarily supplied by yet another constituent context – one that had emerged in the seventeenth and early eighteenth centuries around ways of thinking about and practicing virtue in relation to physical things. [10] These things included both human bodies and material objects, usually in the form of commodities. The "context of virtue" was in some ways the most fundamental element of respectability – the glue that held it together. One of its central cognitive features was the notion that the way in which a person displays, uses, and takes care of physical objects (especially his or her own body and those of family members) is a principal indicator of that person's moral standing and, as such, is also an indicator of the extent to which the person can be relied upon to perform community responsibilities satisfactorily. Virtuous relations with the material sphere were not the only important aspect of the context of virtue, but they were highly significant because they strongly influenced the kind of behavior that we have come to call "consumerism." The context of virtue as a whole was also essential to the connection between respectability and the "bourgeoisie" – about which I will say more shortly.

The remaining elements of the culture of respectability were two gendered contexts that were constructed mainly in the eighteenth century. One of these linked masculinity to all the contexts mentioned above by defining it according to assumptions of inherent male rationality and sociability. [11] The conscious forms of male behavior that were a significant part of this context constituted a significant aspect of – and to a considerable extent derived from – the "public sphere" that emerged in western Europe in the early modern period. It framed the famous notion of "separate spheres" for men and women. The other context, one that featured domestic femininity, was not actually equivalent to the feminine side of the "separate spheres" dichotomy, but rather a much more extensive, complex cultural construction put together at least as much by women as by men. [12] Its focus was the family and the supervisory responsibility of women within a family for the education, the well-being, and, very explicitly, the continuous civilizing of the other family members. At its most formal level, the context of domestic femininity represented women and families as the basis of civilization itself. It was consciously used as a framework for women's participation in public affairs and therefore existed in more or less permanent tension with the limitations on that participation embodied in the context of rational masculinity that was also incorporated into respectability.

Thus far my research has been primarily concerned with showing how the various elements of respectability, especially when they were connected, shaped consumption in the eighteenth century. Domestic femininity, for example, when embodied in the ritual of English tea, generated demand for tea, sugar, and the other appurtenances of the ceremony. Rational masculinity, manifested in the ethos of the coffeehouse, created demand for coffee and, more generally, influenced an identification of tobacco smoking with male moderation and reasonableness. Linkages among the contexts of revised gentility, luxury, and virtue structured much of the demand for cotton products that helped to drive the early Industrial Revolution. Many of these same features of respectability influenced consumption in an ever-increasing area of the world (and an ever-expanding segment of the European population) throughout the nineteenth century. But along with the shaping of consumption, itself a vitally significant aspect of modernization and the creation of the global economy, went a number of other important phenomena. For example, many of the practical meanings of political reform and of democracy in North America and western Europe were supplied by the culture of respectability. One of the reasons that a widening of the franchise (especially one that excluded the poorest classes from the vote) became the central feature of reformist activity in Europe in the first half of the nineteenth century was that it was perceived as a validation of the respectable status of those added to the voting rolls. This can be seen in the almost universal argument that such people deserved the vote because they were, in fact, respectable; that is, based on the virtue manifest in the behavior of the large majority of the group of people to be enfranchised, it could be predicted that they would vote responsibly.[13] A good deal of the force behind democracy as a political movement arose from the belief on the part of people who had come to think of themselves as "respectable" that their social betters did not accept that assessment – a situation symbolized by denial of the franchise.

These examples bring up one of the most important aspects of the culture of respectability: the relationship between respectability and class. So far I have mostly avoided using the word "bourgeois" as a modifier of "respectability." To be sure, scholars usually connect the two terms, not only as though respectability were an integral part of what it meant to be bourgeois in the nineteenth century (which it was), but also as though respectability were in some sense a product of the bourgeoisie as a class (which it was not – at least not if we use "bourgeoisie" according to any of its accepted social-class definitions) or an exclusive possession of one particular class (which it most certainly was not, unless – and this is a crucial "unless" – you define the bourgeoisie as the class of people who think of themselves as respectable). In fact the elements of the culture of respectability were constructed in the seventeenth and eighteenth centuries by people belonging to a wide range of social categories defined in a number of different ways. Many of these elements were plainly created by and for aristocrats, while the central work of putting the pieces together was clearly performed by people attempting to define their own status as individuals in some satisfactory relation to the aristocracy. Given the way in which the culture of respectability has been described here, it would be very surprising if something as complex and nuanced could be ascribed in a straightforward way to any single class. Similarly, although there are a great many obvious links among respectability, the market economy, industrialization, and many of the things that we associate with capitalism, these links are complex and can be considered determinative only by presupposition – by a theoretical orientation that privileges supposedly "objective" social and economic phenomena as the "causes," and thus the ultimate sources of meaning, in history. There is no space to pursue this subject further here, except to say that my book suggests that the formation of respectability was a central – perhaps the central – part of the bourgeoisie's formation as a cultural as well as a social entity. The bourgeoisie did not first emerge as the result of impersonal forces of economic change and then construct the culture of respectability as a manifestation of its own existence. Rather, the bourgeoisie constructed itself – to a large extent, around the culture of respectability. [14] Moreover, although people of the middle classes in European societies adopted respectability in the late eighteenth and early nineteenth centuries partly as a way of claiming status for themselves, they did not do so in order to create distinctions between their own class and others, but rather so as to participate as fully as they could in a society and value system in which they could feel respected – by other people and by themselves.

To summarize, what we have is the following: a broad cultural construction aggregated from many sources in the eighteenth century in western Europe, the possible significance of which has not in the past been recognized in large part because respectability and the elements of which it was composed were so pervasive that nineteenth-century people, while generally aware of its existence, did not perceive it as something sufficiently problematical to require formal discussion or presentation. It was by no means an "underlying" factor in Western social existence, or a cultural manifestation of some unitary subterranean social force or historical tendency, but rather an autonomous factor in almost all areas of life. In terms of politics, respectability was essentially outside of ideology. That is, it constituted a well-understood basis of reference for political discourse and a source of practical meanings and examples, but it was not organized in ideological form and was not presented or thought about as a subject for political dispute. It did, however, have distinct political implications, as has been suggested above and as we shall see when we come to its relationship to colonialism. More broadly, respectability linked and provided meanings to practices throughout Western societies, acting as an important cultural framework for nineteenth-century modernity.

Let me now suggest some ways in which looking at colonialism, particularly German colonialism, from the standpoint of the culture of respectability might provide us with a new understanding both of colonialism itself and of its meanings in connection with other historical contexts. To do this, we will focus on recent work in German colonial studies. Nothing could be more appropriate than to begin with the research on the cultural prehistory of German colonialism, of which Susanne Zantop's book, *Colonial Fantasies* been the chief example.[15]

*Colonial Fantasies* makes a compelling case for the formation of a set of imagined colonial roles for Germans and for Germany – a colonial "imaginary" – during the century and a quarter before the actual establishment of the German overseas empire. These roles formed a constructed context for the organized, public colonial movement of the 1870s and 1880s, one that could be readily aligned with significant aspects of the constructed context of German nationalism. By looking at a wide variety of texts, ranging from plays and novellas to German versions of *Robinson Crusoe* to late eighteenth-century anthropological and historical writings, Zantop was able to reconstruct a discrete cultural context that, in one form or another, became part of the cognitive makeup of *Deutschtum* in the nineteenth century. This context was multifaceted, but three aspects are especially important: the relationship between families and colonialism in the imagined colonial world of nineteenth-century Germans; the peculiar qualifications for colonial activity that Germans assigned to themselves; and the nature of the connections that Zantop revealed between imagined German colonialism and German nationalism. The culture of respectability played an important role in all three.

Zantop emphasizes the family as a model for several types of imagined relationships between colonial rulers and colonial subjects, as well as relationships among Germans themselves. Fathers and sons, husbands and wives, and extended families taken together constitute the primary cognitive framework for imagined colonialism. For example, in her analysis of the "family" formed by Robinson Crusoe and Friday in Joachim Heinrich Campe's German version of that story, Zantop shows that the image incorporates a "natural" hierarchy (superior European and inferior non-European) within a notion of mutual regard and moral equality that, she argues, is central to many German conceptions of the ideal colonial relationship.[16] In several other instances she describes ways in which texts use familial images (especially the loosening of the colonial man's ties to his mother and his taking of a non-European wife to establish a colonial family) to build (or in some cases, to subvert) an imaginary colonial world invested with moral meaning.[17] Significantly, Zantop identifies the 1780s and early 1790s as the time at which this tendency became pronounced in the construction of German colonial fantasies. She explains the timing as a result of the American Revolution and of growing awareness of the imminent dissolution of the Spanish colonial empire in America, which made that empire potentially open to the activity of supposedly better qualified colonizers – namely, the Germans.[18] This is reasonable from what one might call an ideological perspective, but it suggests that the family image is essentially a conscious metaphor for political intentions, which, given the depth and complexity of the images Zantop discusses, is likely to be only part of the story. One could also argue that the familial images result from the articulation, in the late seventeenth and eighteenth centuries, of the structure of the modern nuclear family – a "real" structure in a sociological sense, with "real" gender roles built into it and an ideology of "separate spheres" imposed on top of it. This, too, makes sense, if one accepts the now-conventional, undeconstructed narrative of the history of the modern family, but it would be difficult to pinpoint the precise period of the 1780s and 1790s as especially significant in this regard.[19]

As indicated earlier, however, that period is quite significant in the formation of the culture of respectability. It is the time at which the word itself originated and at which, in several languages, many of the terms associated with respectability took on the specific meanings they would retain for at least the next century.[20] The formation of what I have called the context of domestic femininity and its incorporation into the new culture of respectability were what made the imagery of the family so meaningful and so heavily nuanced in the last quarter of the eighteenth century. Among the most important aspects of respectability in this regard was its emphasis on the family as the primary locus of education, of building and supporting a rational morality in its members, and therefore of underpinning civilization. The family model was applied to colonial situations and became a significant aspect of imagined colonialism (in Germany and elsewhere) because it legitimated not just hierarchical power relations, but also the colonial enterprise itself as an educating, civilizing venture, in which the process of civilizing worked in several directions. As in a respectable European family, so also in a respectable colony, it should be not only the subordinate but also the superordinate members whose education and civilization are continually reinforced. That is precisely what is happening when one looks, for example, at Zantop's presentation of the German Crusoes: the European character becomes more self-aware, more capable, perhaps more ethical – in short, more civilized – as a result not only of his position as colonial master, but also and more particularly as a result of his involvement in a familial relationship with Friday.[21] One might argue that it is the presence of the respectable familial model that differentiates, for example, Campe's version of *Robinson Crusoe* from Defoe's original, in which Robinson first learns to master himself, then the island, then Friday, and then assorted unlikely and involuntary colonists, rather than forming an interactively supportive moral community.

The model was, in fact, not peculiarly German, but rather one that became prominent in Western cultural commentary in the late eighteenth and early nineteenth centuries as part of a general adoption of the culture of respectability.[22] What was peculiarly German was the emphatic claim, which Zantop describes, that Germans were particularly suited to conduct colonial enterprises oriented around the familial model.[23] It was not just that Germans had preserved themselves from the moral embarrassment of having enslaved and partly exterminated non-European peoples by "virtue" of not having engaged heavily or successfully in the initial phases of official European empire building. It was also that their reasons for wanting to become colonists were inherent in the desire to found families – respectable, moral, civilizing families abroad as replicas of such families in Germany – in contrast to the earlier colonizers, who were rapacious, footloose, and irresponsible men. This remained an essential feature of German colonialism into the twentieth century, one of the key reference points for the settlement or emigrationist variety of colonial ideology that was so strong in Germany.[24]

Zantop also noted that the image of Germans as good colonizers was a constitutive element of the larger image of Germans as members of a nation, even though that imagery changed substantially between the late eighteenth century and the time of Germany's unification.[25] One of its consistent aspects was a strong connection to the culture of respectability, partly (but not exclusively) through the model of the respectable family. German nationalism teemed with blatant male fantasies, but they were legitimated and made consistent with the idea of an orderly, lawful world by being placed in various contexts of respectability. One particularly significant feature of nationalism in Germany, as in other countries, was its incorporation of self-respect. Part of a citizen's self-respect arose from his membership in the nation. Full participation in the affairs of the nation was not only a source of his own self-respect, but also something that was considered by many Europeans and Americans to be a right that they possessed primarily because they displayed, or believed they displayed, the kind of everyday virtues implicit in respectability. In most German states, which developed the institutions of representative government and therefore a meaningful franchise somewhat later than several other countries, the image of overseas or colonial settlement as a means of displaying respectability and gaining full participation as citizens was especially pronounced. As Wildenthal has shown, during the period of the overseas empire itself some German women made an effort to gain full participation in the public sphere by associating themselves with colonialism, and it was in large part the universally accepted essential role of women in maintaining and extending respectability that they used as the central justification for their efforts. [26]

To extend Zantop's arguments, then, I suggest that one of the factors that gave colonialist thinking and colonialist "fantasies" their continued legitimacy and meaning in Germany through the 1870s was their close connection to the culture of respectability. I also suggest (although a full discussion will have to await another occasion) that this paralleled the development in several different countries of the "humanitarian" imperialist tendencies that derived from the abolitionist movement. Groups advocating imperialism as a means of removing moral evils aligned themselves so exactly with the full range of elements of the culture of respectability that they acquired great public force – regardless, in some cases, of economics, government policies, or the aims of political parties. The history of nineteenth-century British imperialism is replete with examples of this force in action, but they were not absent in Germany before the 1880s. [27]

The culture of respectability can also serve as a framing concept for understanding significant aspects of German colonialism during the period in which the colonial empire actually existed. Respectability clearly played an important part in the domestic politics of German colonialism, informing, for example, much of the heterogeneous and intermittent demand for colonial reform. Attacks on the administration of individual colonies emanating from the Social Democratic Party, the Catholic Center Party, and the liberals tended to focus on abuses of authority by colonial officials, especially the exploitation of indigenous labor, corporal punishment, and sexual misconduct. [28] Couching criticism of colonialism in this way had the obvious advantages of appealing to the prurient interests of newspaper readers and of deemphasizing the very considerable differences over the economics of colonialism that existed among colonial critics, but there was more to it than that. It placed colonial policy within the context of respectability – that is, within a well-established, widely held cognitive framework that featured adherence to ethical rules as a requirement not only for social standing, but also for political legitimacy. Colonial administration should meet the test of respectability in its actions, and it should promote respectability in colonial subjects, whether European or non-European. Without the cultural framework of respectability, criticism of official behavior would have had much less resonance than it did, and it would have been much less easily connected to criticism of the exercise of authority within Germany itself. Colonial critics managed to place on the colonial authorities the onus of showing why the peculiarities of the colonial situation permitted or required deviation from the norms of respectability, which often put the defenders of colonial policy in a difficult (although not impossible) position. To some extent the more positive approaches to colonial reform that developed in the decade before the outbreak of the First World War can be interpreted as attempts to change the direction of colonial policy so as to make it conform more clearly to patterns of respectability – not only in terms of the behavior of colonial officials, but also of the private conduct of Europeans in the colonies and of the treatment and behavior of non-Europeans. A respectable German colonial empire was supposed to strengthen the image of Germany as a respectable world power. [29]

Wildenthal has shown very clearly the political uses to which respectability could be put in German colonial politics. As the image of German colonial settlement, especially in German Southwest Africa (Namibia), was closely connected to images of stable, moral (and hence respectable) German families as the distinctively German form of colonization, the fact that the actual settlers in the colonies deviated considerably from those images constituted a major political problem for a wide range of colonial interest groups. The settlers were overwhelmingly male, they sometimes displayed patterns of behavior unsuitable for the supposed vanguard of the German "civilizing" mission, and they tended to marry or (more frequently) to establish extramarital relationships with indigenous women. The fact of such marriages and relationships became, after about 1900, a significant issue of colonial politics – one in which respectability played a very important part in particular cases. For example, in defending themselves and their families against new policies in German Southwest Africa aimed at removing official recognition of interracial marriages, some German settlers made the argument that their marriages were entirely proper and respectable and that, for precisely that reason, it was inappropriate for the authorities to move against them. [30] Such issues provided, according to Wildenthal, an important opening for the women's colonial movement in Germany, which was able to some extent to break through the pattern of male dominance that had previously restricted it by becoming the leading organized advocate of German women in the settlement colonies and of establishing systems of strict racial segregation there. [31] In so doing the women's colonial movement aligned itself with the biological racialism that was becoming an increasingly significant part of colonial politics in the early twentieth century.

This alignment was consistent with a general tendency toward racialism in matters having to do with imperialism that Grosse has examined in his recent study of the relationship between German colonialism and eugenics.[12] Grosse places this tendency in the context of change in bourgeois society in the late nineteenth and early twentieth centuries. It might also be worthwhile to look at the same developments in the context of the culture of respectability as one of the primary factors in the constitution of bourgeois society.

The liberal, bourgeois worldview that Grosse and others describe as dominant in the West in the late nineteenth century incorporated most of the cognitive aspects of respectability. The main behavioral signifiers of bourgeois status were the practices of respectability. But respectability was never the sole property of any particular class (or nation, race, or gender, for that matter). In theory anyone could be respectable if he or she (and his or her family) acted respectably. Large segments of the European working class adopted much of the culture of respectability in the course of the nineteenth century – a phenomenon that strongly affected the way in which working-class political parties and labor unions defined themselves and their goals. While criteria of respectability were regularly employed by people who thought of themselves as middle-class to differentiate themselves from the working class, they were also employed by self-consciously working-class people to define themselves and their values and thus to subvert the bourgeois attempt to establish class hegemony. One reason for the great attractiveness of respectability was that it afforded a claim not just to the respect of other people, but also to self-respect as well as to full participation in society as a whole. It is not surprising that in the late nineteenth and early twentieth centuries groups at the margins of social acceptability in Europe – not just workers, but ethnically defined minorities such as the Irish in the United Kingdom and the Jews in central Europe – should have been especially drawn to the cultural patterns of respectability. Respectability was seen as a certificate of self-respect and a ticket for full admission to the wider world.

One of the many reasons for the movement toward biologically based racialism in Western social discourse at the beginning of the twentieth century lies in a recognition that the criterion of respectability was no longer a satisfactory way to justify exclusionary social practices precisely because respectability could be so readily adopted by the excluded. There was little that racialism could do about the increasing ineffectiveness of the "separate spheres" ideology in excluding women from full social participation or about the demands of the working class for respect – except, perhaps, to devalue the cultural assumptions on which gender and class had previously been constructed. But racialism could be used to justify the exclusion of others who could be placed in "racial" categories: the Irish in Britain, Jews in Germany and Austria-Hungary, African Americans in the United States. It could also be used to counter the subversive effects of claims by colonial subjects for fuller acceptance into the societies of the imperial powers on the grounds of those subjects' adoption of the culture of respectability.

Throughout the colonial world in the late nineteenth and twentieth centuries, segments of indigenous colonial populations with access to education, economic resources, and political influence rapidly appropriated the practices of Western respectability. This process, directly or indirectly encouraged by many of the policies of the colonial powers and accelerated by the integration of colonies into the global economy, was nevertheless looked upon with less than full favor by Europeans concerned with imperialism. It was not just that "Westernized" colonial subjects could become a political threat to colonial rule. It was also that manifestly respectable colonial subjects, respecting themselves and insisting on the respect that their behavior justified, posed a threat to the whole framework of exclusion upon which colonialism was based. In Germany as in other countries, a wide variety of responses emerged around the turn of the century, including humorous denigration of non-European attempts to be respectable (a staple of popular colonial literature). They also included the mobilization of science for the purpose. Andrew Zimmerman has described the efforts of German anthropologists, museum directors, and managers of popular colonial shows to impose racial and cultural categories on colonial subjects that prohibited the latter from participating in the rituals of respectability, at least while they were in Germany, and also the resistance of African visitors to having such prohibitions placed on them.[33] The increasingly strident adoption of racialism in German colonial discourse and policy reflected a similar tendency.

These are but a few of a number of ways in which our comprehension of German colonialism and imperialism could be increased by adopting alternatives to some of our standard framing concepts for interpreting the nineteenth and early twentieth centuries. By treating the phenomenon of respectability as a cultural construct, as an autonomous historical fact that not only was shaped by elements of the process we call "modernization" but was also itself a major contributor to defining that process, and by using it to interpret some of the best recent research into German colonialism, I have tried to show how specific aspects of colonialism can be connected to a richer, more varied and nuanced array of explanatory contexts than is possible through reference to modernization alone. I have attempted to do the same thing with regard to the bourgeoisie as a framing concept. German colonialism, like most modern political and cultural phenomena, was not just the product of a few massively determinative "underlying" causes derived from a single process of economic change, but rather it was a set of attitudes, ideas, actions, modes of discourse, and social structures derived from a wide range of phenomena – some (not all) of which can be encompassed under the heading of "modernization." Obviously, this does not mean that either modernization or the bourgeoisie should be dropped as tools for interpretation, but it does suggest that we should use constructions such as respectability to capture some of the immense complexity of human behavior and historical causation – complexity that tends to be overlooked or too easily explained away in interpretations based on the larger, broader frameworks.

### NOTES

1. Lora Wildenthal, *German Women for Empire, 1884–1945* (Durham: Duke University Press, 2001); Pascal Grosse, *Kolonialismus, Eugenik und bürgerliche Gesellschaft in Deutschland 1850–1918* (Frankfurt: Campus Verlag, 2000).

2. In the historiography of modern Germany, attempts to criticize and partially deconstruct the modernization narrative (as well as the narrative of the bourgeoisie to which it is connected) have been heavily influenced by David Blackbourn and Geoff Eley, *The Peculiarities of German History: Bourgeois Society and Politics in Nineteenth-Century Germany* (Oxford: Oxford University Press, 1984).

3. For a radical critique of "class" as a unit of analysis (and of the bourgeois class in particular), see William H. Reddy, *Money and Liberty in Modern Europe: A Critique of Historical Understanding* (Cambridge: Cambridge University Press, 1987).

4. Work on the construction of new frameworks is clearly under way. See, for example, the contribution of Marcia Klotz to this volume.

5. Woodruff D. Smith, *Consumption and the Making of Respectability, 1600–1800* (New York: Routledge, 2002).

6. Smith, *Consumption and the Making of Respectability*, 5–24.

7. Smith, *Consumption and the Making of Respectability*, 189–91.

8. Smith, *Consumption and the Making of Respectability*, 25–62.

9. Smith, *Consumption and the Making of Respectability*, 63–103.

10. Smith, *Consumption and the Making of Respectability*, 105–38.

11. Smith, *Consumption and the Making of Respectability*, 139–69.

12. Smith, *Consumption and the Making of Respectability*, 171–87.

13. This argument is made in Woodruff D. Smith, "The Great Reform Act and the Politics of Respectability" (paper presented to the Northeastern Conference on British Studies, New Haven CT, October 2002), and in Woodruff D. Smith, "Respectability and Politics in Early Nineteenth-Century Britain" (paper presented to the New England Political Science Association, Providence RI, April 2001).

14. These matters are discussed in Smith, *Consumption and the Making of Respectability*, 57–58, 118–21, 128–30, 221, 243–45.

15. Susanne Zantop, *Colonial Fantasies: Conquest, Family, and Nation in Precolonial Germany, 1770–1870* (Durham: Duke University Press, 1997).

16. Zantop, *Colonial Fantasies*, 102–20.

17. Zantop, *Colonial Fantasies*, 121–40.

18. Zantop, *Colonial Fantasies*, 136.

19. That is, the narrative in which European women, after experiencing substantial autonomy in the seventeenth century, were increasingly restricted by the articulation of specialized gender roles in the modern nuclear family and by the ideology of separate spheres. For the case of England, this narrative is comprehensively presented in Anthony Fletcher, *Gender, Sex and Subordination in England 1500–1800* (New Haven: Yale University Press, 1995).

20. Smith, *Consumption and the Making of Respectability*, 189–221.

21. Zantop, *Colonial Fantasies*, 108–15.

22. The significance of the model can be seen, for example, in its centrality in abolitionist argumentation. See William Wilberforce's 1823 pamphlet, "An Appeal to the Religion, Justice, and Humanity of the Inhabitants of the British Empire, in Behalf of the Negro Slaves in the West Indies," in *Slavery in the West Indies* (New York: Negro Universities Press, 1969), 13–16, in which Wilberforce focuses his arguments not on the physical mistreatment of slaves but on the ways in which the slave system prevents the formation of marriages and families, which are the key to the processes of civilizing and of developing permanent affective attachments among people. He describes as an alternative to the existing system a colonialism that supports family relationships.

23. Zantop, *Colonial Fantasies*, 81–97.

24. See Daniel Joseph Walther, *Creating Germans Abroad: Cultural Policies and National Identities in Namibia* (Athens: Ohio University Press, 2002), 46–63.

25. Zantop, *Colonial Fantasies*, 191–201.

26. Wildenthal, *German Women for Empire*, 1–11, 54–78.

27. See Andrew Porter, "Trusteeship, Anti-Slavery, and Humanitarianism" in Andrew Porter, ed., *The Oxford History of the British Empire*, vol. 3, *The Nineteenth Century* (Oxford: Oxford University Press, 1999), 198–221, and the editor's introduction to Klaus J. Bade, ed., *Imperialismus und Kolonialmission: Kaiserliches Deutschland und koloniales Imperium* (Wiesbaden: Steiner, 1982), 1–28.

28. Wildenthal, *German Women for Empire*, 69–74.

29. Woodruff D. Smith, *The Ideological Origins of Nazi Imperialism* (New York: Oxford University Press, 1986), 144.

30. Wildenthal, *German Women for Empire*, 91–93; Walther, *Creating Germans Abroad*, 33–45.

31. Wildenthal, *German Women for Empire*, 131–71.

32. Grosse, *Kolonialismus, Eugenik und bürgerliche Gesellschaft*.

33. Andrew Zimmerman, *Anthropology and Antihumanism in Imperial Germany* (Chicago: University of Chicago Press, 2001), 15–37.

BRADLEY D. NARANCH

# Inventing the *Auslandsdeutsche*

## Emigration, Colonial Fantasy, and German National Identity, 1848–71

The study of German national identity has rarely strayed far from the familiar geographic confines of central Europe, just as the study of German colonialism has tended to stay within the formal period of overseas imperial rule, 1884–1919. With the publication of *Colonial Fantasies: Conquest, Family, and Nation in Precolonial Germany*, Susanne Zantop broke decisively with both of these scholarly conventions. [1] In the years that followed, Zantop and a number of her colleagues proceeded to outline innovative approaches to the study of race, colonialism, and national identity in modern Germany. By drawing on a variety of analytical methods and theoretical approaches to identify and interpret new historical artifacts and textual sources, they succeeded in revitalizing older traditions of German colonial historiography and in attracting new participants to what had long been a peripheral topic.

Some of the preliminary results of their efforts were on display in the 1998 edited collection, *The Imperialist Imagination: German Colonialism and Its Legacy*. [2] In contrast to Zantop's interest in German colonial fantasies set in South American landscapes of the late eighteenth and early nineteenth centuries, however, the majority of contributors focused on events and issues drawn from Germany's postcolonial history after 1919, while others covered topics from the pre-war colonial period. Only the concluding essay, on colonial tropes in the philosophy of Immanuel Kant, addressed the Enlightenment era that Zantop had so thoroughly investigated. [3] The chronological distribution of the articles in *The Imperialist Imagination* is a telling indication of the direction and objectives of recent work on German colonialism. While not uninterested in Imperial Germany and its colonies, these writers devote considerable attention to the cultural consequences of Germany's colonial past after the loss of its overseas territories. This postcolonial approach, its advocates contend, promises to make colonial history relevant for larger narratives of the German past by offering new perspectives on topics of long-standing interest such as National Socialism, anti-Semitism, and the Holocaust as well as on issues of race, collective memory, and cultural identity. [4] By focusing on the historical processes and discursive patterns that helped shape Germans' perceptions of cultural difference and imperial power, practitioners of German colonial studies treat the period of formal colonial rule as an important episode in a larger story of social modernization, cultural change, and international conflict rather than a self-contained account of conservative social imperialism, middle-class aggressive nationalism, and short-lived colonial expansion that ended in failure during the First World War. [5]

Yet it remains unclear what kind of impact the emerging field of German colonial studies, with its affinities for postcolonial and poststructural theory, will have on more traditional historical narratives of the German past. Zantop's early work on identifying chronologically specific colonial fantasies from Germany's "precolonial," "colonial," and "postcolonial" periods was to be part of a much bigger project connecting German colonial history more closely to the histories of Weimar and Nazi Germany. [6] More recently, Sebastian Conrad has urged his colleagues in Germany to include the study of colonial and postcolonial fantasy in transnational approaches to the German past, for example making the study of race an integral part of class- and gender-based cultural and social historical analysis. [7]

In this essay I consider discursive linkages between the fantasies of colonial conquest that Susanne Zantop studied and contemporaneous debates over mass emigration in precolonial Germany. As historians have recognized, public interest in the patterns of German overseas mobility led to the formation of organized political movements that sought to redirect at least some of the departing migrants toward parts of the globe that might become German colonies. In the late nineteenth century this form of "settlement colonialism" gave rise to a more radical imperialist ideology of aggressive territorial expansion in search of new "living space" (Lebensraum) for a biologically defined national community. [8] While the intellectual history of this transformation in colonial ideology has been well documented, there has been less research on how eighteenth-century colonial fantasies and the emigration debate after 1848 affected German national identity prior to unification.

The next section of this essay discusses the work of historians of German emigration in light of the study of colonial fantasy. Reading Zantop's work in tandem with these historical accounts, I argue, offers a framework for exploring the ways in which global landscapes, real and imagined, affected local constructions of German national identity before unification. In the third section I use this framework to explain the emergence in the 1850s and '60s of a new image of national identity that attempted to capture the global nature of German overseas mobility in a period marked by unprecedented European migration, colonial expansion, and transport and communications technology. This image was that of the *Auslandsdeutsche* or "German abroad," who was part of a cultural diaspora living outside of central Europe yet was connected to the imagined community of Germans "at home" by bonds of language, ethnicity, and ultimately, racial heritage. At that time colonial fantasies of overseas settlement in tropical landscapes coexisted with debates over the impact of mass emigration of Germans on the future national community. Taken together, they remind us that constructions of German national identity prior to 1871 were neither restricted to the geographical area of central Europe nor based exclusively on local customs, regional loyalties, or religious traditions. As the concluding section notes, Zantop recognized that questions of German national identity overlapped at times with questions of race, imperialism, and patterns of global change. Historians of modern Germany have only recently begun to study the complicated processes through which local and global images of national identity emerged and interacted. Their project holds great promise for understanding the relationship between cultural fantasy and political reality in the history of German imperialism, at home and abroad, in the nineteenth and twentieth centuries.

## Emigration "Fever" and Colonial Traditions: Three Perspectives

Zantop's work can be read alongside that of Klaus Bade in order to better understand connections among colonial fantasy, emigration, and German national identity. Bade is now known for his studies of European migration, but his early research focused on the German colonial movement.[9] Bade has examined from a number of angles the impact of increased personal mobility, international economic expansion, and armed conflict on the cultural and social contours of the German people over the past two hundred years, and his research highlights the fundamental reorientation of nineteenth-century German society from mass emigration toward immigration.[10] Despite these changes, the colonial fantasies and racial stereotypes that Zantop located in precolonial years have remained firmly entrenched. As Bade's most recent scholarship shows, obsolete notions of Germany as an *Auswanderungsland* still figure in German politics today. This turn-of-the-twenty-first-century debate was clearly one of Zantop's own motivations in uncovering and analyzing the layers of German colonial fantasy from the past. [11]

Zantop's findings should also be read alongside the work of Hans Fenske. In a series of articles on unrealized imperialist agendas, including overseas settlement initiatives, Fenske documented German colonial activity in Central and South America that predated the better-known colonial movement of the late 1870s. [12] Despite repeated failures, supporters in Germany continued to press for overseas outposts that could absorb some of the German emigrants who left for the United States each year. In their propaganda for settlement colonies, they used the same tropes that Zantop found in literary sources from the time: the idyllic preindustrial community of German farmers in an exotic location, for example, or the middle-class explorer domesticating undeveloped lands and native populations. Fenske's and Zantop's works, read together, help to delineate the impact of Germany's precolonial experiences on its colonial and postcolonial periods. Fenske and Zantop point out the contrast between precolonial Germany's lavish colonial fantasy worlds and its modest, failure-prone experiments in overseas imperial conquest.

The dissonance between fantasy and reality in the context of emigration, colonialism, and overseas mobility also emerges in Mack Walker's history of German emigration in the nineteenth century. [13] Like Fenske, Walker spends little time elaborating the analytical categories and theoretical premises that structure his historical narrative, which explores how small-town residents in southern Germany weighed the risks of emigration against the cyclical threats of crop failure, famine, economic stagnation, and political instability at home. What begins as a tale of German families caught up in episodic waves of "emigration fever" develops into an account of the politics and economics of the 1860s and '70s, the decades in which trans-Atlantic emigration came to be linked to the establishment of German colonies in Africa. [14] The long-running emigration debates in nineteenth-century Germany reveal the deep impact that the exodus of millions of Germans had upon their fellow citizens at home, who sought to explain the reasons for their departure. Economic transformation, political reform, and social modernization in central Europe strengthened liberal beliefs in reason, individual freedom, and progress but also spawned anxiety about Germany's ability to unite its diverse population at home and maintain ties with emigrants. In this conflicted cultural climate of hope and despair, where the distance between fantasy and reality appeared tantalizingly short at one moment and immensely vast at the next, the colonial fantasies described by Zantop were created, retold, and passed on to succeeding generations of

German readers. Zantop's interest in the domestic impact of the European colonial encounter on the presence of fictional overseas landscapes in the intimate local worlds of Heimat-bound German readers fits well with the work of historians such as Bade, Fenske, and Walker.

## Tales of Triumph and Tragedy: The German Diaspora, 1850s–1860s

During the 1850s and '60s there were neither overseas possessions nor a unified state to limit the colonial and national fantasies circulating in German society.[15] Latin America, prominent in Zantop's work, was only one of many sites proposed for the creation of German overseas communities. In the 1840s, for example, the Danube River basin and the steppes of southern Russia were as likely as tropical locales to figure in the colonial fantasies of German readers and writers.[16] The obsession with the rising number of Germans leaving their homelands in search of better living conditions overseas fed German colonial discourse. Here, the German national body – not the non-European native body – was the source of intense cultural anxiety. In the 1840s the clearest manifestations of public interest in this issue were the debates in the Frankfurt National Assembly on regulating trans-Atlantic flows of German emigrants who departed for North America each year.[17] In the spring of 1849 the debate over the "emigration question" led to legislation in the assembly designed to monitor the movement of emigrants, protect them from abuse at the hands of emigration agents, and maintain consular information bureaus to assist them in their destination countries.[18]

The dissolution of the National Assembly and restoration of aristocratic authority later that year dealt a severe blow to the early colonial movement. Political action on a national emigration policy was now virtually impossible. However, the events of 1848–49 provided a political arena for a wide range of ideas and initiatives on emigration and national policy making, leaving behind a mixed record of colonial fantasy and practical, if unrealized, measures designed to connect the fatherland to its disparate communities of "nationals" abroad.[19] After the early colonial movement failed to secure any German state's backing for its plan to redirect German emigrants from the United States, some observers turned their attention to already existing groups of ethnic Germans living in diasporic "colonies." Between 1849 and 1871 the absence of a centralized state authority with a claim to represent the entire German nation complicated the relationship between Germans at home and their fellow countrymen and women in the diaspora. Fears that ethnic Germans living abroad would gradually lose contact with their former homelands (and thus be lost to any future, united German state) intensified due to the unwillingness of the German Federation's member states to recognize the citizenship of emigrants who failed to report to consular officials every ten years or whose male children had not performed military service.[20] Since claims to citizenship and identity were typically based on one's birthplace or one's standing in the local community, it was difficult to reconcile increased social mobility and the global expansion of European power with the way in which Germanness could be defined, bestowed, and sustained outside central Europe.

In the postrevolutionary decades, the term *Auslandsdeutsche* increasingly replaced the older term *Auswanderer*. *Auslandsdeutsche* had distinct semiotic advantages over its predecessor. Denoting the foreign and the familiar in equal parts, it reflected the ambiguous, threshold status of those individuals living beyond the fatherland whom Germans at home wanted to include in their imagined community. The *Auslandsdeutsche* was a quintessential example of what Terence Ranger and Eric Hobsbawm termed the "invented traditions" that accompanied the modernization of European industrial society and the rise of popular nationalism.[21] Unlike the term *Auswanderer* (one who "wanders out"), which implied movement, mobility, and national dispersal, the connotations attached to the newer image of the *Auslandsdeutsche* imparted a sense of timelessness and enduring self. As a word not exclusively associated with trans-Atlantic migration, the *Auslandsdeutsche* was spatially and temporally more expansive than the *Auswanderer*. It was broad enough to include German speakers who had settled generations or even centuries earlier in southeastern Europe or central Asia, for example. The idea of an *Auslandsdeutschtum* evoked memories of the rupture, discontinuity, and separation between *Heimat* and abroad, even while endorsing a general incorruptibility and spiritual unity of the German people as an ethnically homogenous population.

Although the *Auswanderer* never disappeared from the German cultural lexicon, the phrases *Auslandsdeutsche* and *die Deutschen im Ausland* gradually emerged in the middle-class periodical literature of the 1850s and '60s as competing terms. Stories of German emigrants bound for America remained popular.[22] Yet the intensity of debates in the 1840s gave way to more colorful, ethnographic depictions of Germans living abroad in a wide variety of geographic settings. Their tone shifted from one of protest against government negligence to one of restrained, *Biedermeier* curiosity and paternalistic concern for their "kinfolk" abroad. In illustrated magazines such as *Die Gartenlaube*, travelers and journalists described the lives of ethnic German communities abroad in much the same terms as those used in contemporary, idealized accounts of German peasant life.[23] These popular reports combined elements of travel and adventure literature with folklore (Volkskunde), and they educated readers about the international sites where a German presence was noticeable. The most important source of information about the Auslandsdeutsche was the popular scientific illustrated magazine, Globus: Illustrierte Zeitschrift für Länder- und Völkerkunde, which its first editor, Karl Andree, modeled on a similar French publication, Le Tour du Monde: Nouveau Journal des Voyages.[24] First published in 1862, Globus later absorbed two competing publications devoted to overseas affairs, Das Ausland and Aus allen Weltteilen. The stories and illustrations in Globus were truly global in scope. One might read the latest report from a German geographic expedition in Asia, Africa, or the Arctic; learn about advances in telegraph communications and overseas travel; read an account of the California gold rush; find out about a meeting of the Berlin Anthropological Society; browse excerpts of scholarly works on "racial extermination" overseas; read about Germans in Naples, Australia, Hungary, or Tiflis; or learn about the character traits of the "three races" of Europe: Germanic, Slavic, and Latin-Romanic.[25] Middle-class print culture thus evoked German colonists without colonialism, who erected the signposts of Heimat and bourgeois sociability everywhere they went, from the remotest of locations on the imperial periphery to the heart of urban life in America and western Europe.

The German writers who sent such images back to readers at home performed a double role: as dispassionate ethnographic observers and as sympathetic conationals. To write about the language, customs, achievements, and physical characteristics of the Auslandsdeutschen was to investigate the familiar contours of the national Self, while exploring the strange but alluring landscape of the foreign Other. The tension between familiarity and difference – between identifying what all Germans had in common and acknowledging cultural differences within the German diaspora – produced a conflicted national identity that was defined in colonial terms. The "German abroad" was a repository of the liberal "spirit of 1848" – one who preserved regional values and exemplified the strength of the German Volk. The Auslandsdeutsche was also the ultimate cultural colonizer, bringing the values of hard work, spiritual vitality, classical education, and love of order to culturally underdeveloped lands in eastern Europe, Asia, Australia, Latin America, and the American West, just as he enhanced the cosmopolitan atmosphere of Europe's and America's most important cities. The "mixing" of the "German element" with the middle-class members of Anglo-Saxon origin in Britain and America, it was believed, would improve the moral and cultural fiber of the latter and militate against the "feminizing" impact of the French emigrants and stultifying influence of the Irish and other racially inferior populations. In this representation of German overseas identity, it is the mental dexterity, moral solidity, and masculine-coded vitality of the *Auslandsdeutsche* that reassured German readers at home that the intercultural encounters of their countrymen abroad were a reason to take pride in their overseas accomplishments.

For many middle-class Germans, the ongoing departure of thousands of families for new homelands overseas elicited feelings of both pride and protest. "Sie gehen nach Amerika" (They are going to America), an 1864 *Gartenlaube* report on an encounter between two German travelers and a group of emigrants bound for the United States, offers a case in point. The narrator, who writes of his "chance encounter" with the emigrants while on his own short journey up the Rhine, presents them as a microcosm of German domestic life. The group possessed everything necessary for the vitality and prosperity of a small community: "fresh-looking, strapping young boys, little children playing, mature and attractive little mothers, younger women and girls, and men ranging from adolescents with the first patches of facial hair to grey-haired fathers and grandfathers."[26] While expressing concern over their welfare and soberly noting that over six hundred thousand Germans had been lost to the fatherland between 1846 and 1851, the narrator does state approvingly that these emigrants seem well informed about conditions in the United States. They tell him that some of their forefathers had fled from the dictatorial policies of Louis XIV and the religious bigotry of the French Jesuits in the Palatinate to find refuge in Pennsylvania, and now they themselves were eager to flee the burdens of military conscription, unequal land distribution, and taxation that persisted in their German homeland. Aware that the Civil War in the United States was threatening their relatives' holdings in the Susquehanna Valley, they were seeking land in the more peaceful Great Lakes region. As the barge slowly makes its way along the waters of the Rhine, the emigrants recount how earlier German families had endured the hardships of colonial New York, going deep into the "heathen wild" to transform a parcel of land bought from "free Indian tribes" into a farming paradise. Those colonists' idyllic life of "peace and harmony" with the "brave Indians" had come to an abrupt end when the "greedy English governor of New York" robbed the German colonists of their land without paying compensation, forcing them to resettle in neighboring Pennsylvania. The group of emigrants also discussed the advantages of choosing a Bremen or Hamburg steamship for the Atlantic crossing rather than the cheaper English alternatives. The German ships, they explained, sailed directly to the east coast of America and were filled mainly with German passengers and crew who looked after emigrants. The English ships, in contrast, stopped in Britain to pick up Irish emigrants who "packed" the ship and "plundered" the possessions of the Germans on board.[27]

The account ends on a politically radical note. The narrator directly addresses emigrants living in America in the hope that they will publish their own tales and pictures in the *Gartenlaube*, despite the censorship of pro-1848 journalism in many German states. The appropriation of the *Auslandsdeutsche* as a symbol of the "spirit of 1848" was not uncommon in liberal publications like *Gartenlaube*. However, the article's focus on describing what the emigrants themselves said and knew about emigration was unusual. "Sie gehen nach Amerika" depicts the German emigrant families as active participants in the process of transnational migration. One of the male emigrants himself assumes the role of authoritative narrator, conveying the history of eighteenth-century German American life as well as the contemporary dangers of overseas travel. Thus the article's author positions himself as one who merely records the emigrants' voices. At the conclusion of the article, however, the author assumes the role of narrator again in order to admonish German readers to work to change the conditions in central Europe that induce their countrymen to leave in the first place.

The many stories nested within this article illustrate the "triangulation" that Zantop identified in German fantasies about South America and colonial Africa.[28] The emigrant-narrator recounts how the German settlers interacted in "peace and harmony" with Native Americans until a third party, the "greedy English governor," intervened. The German American settlers displace their own feelings of complicity in the destruction of the Indians by positioning themselves as equal victims of English colonial aggression. Unlike the Native Americans, however, the German "victims" are saved from eradication by their natural talents of survival, industriousness, and toughness as well as by the benevolence of the English Quaker William Penn. Penn's role as religious savior of the Palatinate Germans who had fled their homes to escape religious persecution opens up a second triangular relationship, linking German Protestants to English religious radicals who rebelled against the authoritarianism of Roman Catholic priests and French Bourbon kings. The tension between these two triangles – the one uniting Germans with "noble savages" against English colonial aggression, the other aligning German Protestants with English religious dissenters against French and Jesuit despotism – offers a sense of how complicated the Anglo-German relationship actually was during the nineteenth century.[29]

The structural similarities between colonial fantasies set in South America, as described by Zantop, and the tales of pioneering settlers in North America in *Gartenlaube* and *Globus* suggest that the cultural meaning of colonialism in precolonial Germany was broad enough to encompass both "civilized" and "uncivilized" lands. In an 1865 *Globus* article, a visitor to Cincinnati noted that an area bordering a major river canal had been named "Little Germany" or "Over the Rhine." "They are in fact very apt names," he wrote, "because one really believes that one has been transported into a German city as soon as one crosses the 'Rhine.' One hears hardly anything but German being spoken, the shops are adorned with German signs, and . . . the fact that every third house is a beer or wine pub would convince even an ethnographer that he was dealing with members and descendents of the Teutonic race."[30] Similar reports of German singing and shooting festivals in Chicago and New York also noted the positive impression that the immigrants made on the "Anglo Americans" with their vitality and organizational skills, which led some to speculate that the "German element" would rise to an equal level of social prestige and cultural respectability, while the "Irish influence" on American culture would remain modest. Other articles by foreign correspondents praised the work of "German pioneers in the West" who helped transform the "wilderness" on the frontier into fertile, productive farmland, an idealized German rural paradise that could never be attained in the cramped conditions of their former *Heimat*.[31] Many accounts focused on how Germans' love of music, conviviality, festivities, and beer drinking had helped to "liven up" the dreary work routines of Anglo Americans and had taught them "sensible ideas of relaxation and sociability" and "an appreciation for fine music."[32]

Articles in the *Gartenlaube* also suggested that German national spirit in the United States would encourage readers in the German states to persevere at the project of national unification. For instance, the accomplishments of the German American community in Baltimore, embodied by the architecture of the 1866 Concordia House, were the subject of laudatory *Gartenlaube* articles that aimed to demonstrate that Germans abroad could achieve a great deal by pooling their collective resources and overcoming regional loyalties.[33] German American life was presented as diligent and full of integrity, yet playful too. It served as a model for an idealized national identity that existed independent of the state, challenging the status of the military, bureaucracy, and dynastic state as the primary repositories of German character, values, and traditions. In foreign lands, free from the strains of regional strife and petty aristocratic prerogatives, the German national body could become a united whole: "[I]n these distant places," an observer of ethnic German communities in Australia wrote, "the German stands up for that which he is, as a German, and recognizes only one legitimate flag, that of the *schwarz-rot-gold*. This symbol, and this one alone, flies in Australia, along the waterfalls of the Mississippi, in Chile, or wherever else it may be. . . . Foreign governments may ban our flag, but the nation tightly holds onto it. The nation has its own banner."[34]

The prominence of nationalist symbols like the flag and resentment against the dynastic states in these accounts reflected the role played by exiled revolutionaries and other German expatriates in transnational literary networks of central Europe, the Americas, and the capital cities of western Europe.[35] Although they made up only a small number of the thousands of immigrants, these politically active exiles became the representatives of Germans who lived overseas. In the years between 1848 and 1871, they helped sustain in the minds of readers at home the idea of a unified, self-conscious global network of Germans overseas who preserved the ideals of 1848.[36]

The antigovernment sentiment of the early 1860s subsided, however, as many liberals at home and abroad saw a renewed chance for national unification in the rise of Otto von Bismarck. Germans living abroad also felt they gained prestige from the forceful manner in which Prussia had triumphed over its continental rivals. After the victories against Denmark, Austria, and France, a new and more masculine image of German power emerged in the cultural vocabulary of the *Auslandsdeutsche*. Those whom Anglo Americans had once described as quaint and homey and had mistakenly called the "Dutchmen" of their country (that is, the Pennsylvania Deutsch/Dutch) were now claimed as "Germanics," members of a "great power" of equal standing with the United States. "Only the Germanic element can rescue the Republic from the overgrown mass of Irish Celticdom that threatens it," a *Globus* reporter in New York explained in 1871. "Anglo-Americans," he suggested, were "starting to look a little more closely at the six million Germans here, only to discover that they are quite splendid and superb people."[37]

Not all observers of German cultural pioneers overseas believed, however, that such achievements would bring about much-needed social changes in central Europe. For some, the transfer of Germany's best scientists, scholars, and entrepreneurs to America and England meant that the German lands would remain politically and economically impoverished while the rest of the industrialized world profited from homegrown German talent. "This is a pattern that characterizes the lives of a great many German inventors and progressive-minded men in science. The entire civilized world is already more or less populated with German refugees, pioneers, and priests." The author continued on a more hopeful note: "they are the harbingers of world conquest." [38] In addition to their work as skilled craftsmen in Paris, London, or Moscow, he continued, Germans abroad were also important for the British Empire in the fields of science, technology, and telecommunications. The German founder of the Reuters telegraph wire service, despite early rejections from British newspapers, had erected a global network of information that fueled the expansion of the press, just as a German newspaperman had once helped establish the renowned London *Times*. The intellectual talents of the German linguist Max Müller not only contributed to the first translation of Sanskrit texts but also helped develop the tools that enabled the British East India Company to expand its cultural knowledge and political control of the Indian colony. [39] Fears of a German "brain drain" exacerbated the latent sense of cultural anxiety in even the most optimistic portrayals of German life overseas.

In the 1860s such fears represented part of a larger set of concerns among German readers at home about how global changes beyond their control might endanger the growth of a future, unified German nation. Counterposed to the laudatory accounts of cultural pioneers were disturbing tales of national decline, danger, and racial dissolution on the peripheries of the "civilized" world in Latin America, southeastern Europe, and central Asia. Here, isolated pockets of emigrants from a much earlier era were subjected to cultural assimilation and racial submersion into larger indigenous populations. These emigrants were not cultural pioneers who colonized foreign space, but cultural "fertilizer" (*Völkerdünger*) who themselves "went native" and thus disappeared from the German national body. [40] Images of the *Auslandsdeutsche* as a source of organic material for enriching the development of inferior cultures and uncivilized peoples articulated deep-seated anxieties about the precariousness of maintaining German national identity abroad. [41]

The anxieties surrounding the public discussions of German national decline and dissolution abroad were not limited to communities residing in North or South America. Travelers to southern Europe, Hungary, Romania, and Russia also returned with unsettling tales of a disappearing German diaspora that had considerably longer histories than those of the more recent trans-American emigrants. Unlike the more optimistic accounts of German cultural success in London, Cincinnati, New York, Baltimore, or Melbourne, the stories of ethnic Germans in southern and eastern Europe emphasized the gaping disparity between the German observer and the *Auslandsdeutsche*. Such reports took on a tone of distanced anthropological observation. For example, a Prussian officer who participated in the Spanish military campaigns in Morocco during the 1860s recounted his tale of meeting *Auslandsdeutsche* with dismay. While traveling through a remote, mountainous region in southern Spain, the officer came upon the remnants of a German settlement from the eighteenth century. The "colony" had become entirely assimilated into the local community, retaining only vestiges of their northern European ancestry: "Only the blue eyes of the inhabitants and lighter hair were proof of their German origin, especially the blond, rosy children's heads and faces that one saw peeking through doorways from time to time. Otherwise, they have become Spaniards in language and morals; there is no one left in the colony who can understand German." [42] Other articles on ethnic Germans in Hungary displayed a similar pessimism. Although a number of observers noted with pride the social prestige of select German communities in Transylvanian cities, the reports of smaller groups of ethnic Germans in rural areas that were overwhelmingly populated by Hungarians, Slovakians, and Ruthenians (Ukrainians) were filled with concern over their loss of national identity. The unavoidable "denationalization of our tribal brothers [*Stammesbrüder*]," one commentator concluded, would lead to the demise of the German "cultural element" in much of Hungary. While cultural assimilation would undoubtedly be dispiriting to many readers at home, he continued, one could take solace in the thought that the Germans settlers had proven to be a "superb cultural fertilizer," spreading superior moral values and personal behaviors to the surrounding populations and thus fulfilling in a sacrificial sense a "civilizing mission." [43]

The notion that Germans in the diaspora were used to enrich the racial and cultural makeup of local populations on the peripheries of the "civilized" world was the ultimate anticolonial fantasy. Rather than serving as the morally upright, physically powerful, and racially pure national pioneer who actively transformed arid, virginal lands, the *Auslandsdeutsche* was an organic resource for cultural cultivation in the service of others. The idea that emigration resulted in the dissolution and absorption of the German national body into the numerically superior local populations was a nightmarish scenario for many middle-class readers at home, for it suggested that German national identity abroad was particularly susceptible to decline. An 1869 *Globus* arti-

cle titled "Die Deutschenfresser in Russland" (The German eaters in Russia) exemplifies how, in response to such scenarios, the liberal sentiments
of the 1850s and '60s gave way to a more bellicose, nationalistic rhetoric in
debates over *Auslandsdeutsche*. [44] It warned that German communities long established in the Baltic provinces had recently become the target of pan-Slavic
hatred, which, the reporter surmised, derived from the unwillingness of emigrants to give up their "German" habits and integrate more completely into
the local population. "They have their own education, court system, and their
own historical development. They are in general moral and honorable people
– that is, they are typically German. And all of them speak German, go to
church, and have German wives who care for the kitchen, the laundry, and the
cleanliness of their children. The German children attend German schools,
learn with German books, and they themselves will become Germans just like
their fathers and mothers." [45] The pan-Slavic "German eaters," he continued,
wanted no less than the eradication and uprooting of their German-speaking
neighbors by severing all cultural ties to their original fatherland. "What do
they want? . . . That they forsake their language, convert in fear to Orthodoxy,
fight against their national brothers, spit on their pasts, and give up their
rights, in order to live in peace." [46] In the decade following national unification, the ethnic German communities in eastern Europe became the primary
focus for the right-wing elements of German middle-class nationalism, who
established local organizations to defend the interests of their "countrymen"
abroad and to lobby for a stronger diplomatic stance against "Magyarization"
and "Russification" initiatives in eastern Europe. [47] The right-wing version of
*Auslandsdeutsche* rhetoric imagined German communities abroad as "islands"
and "rocks" of national and racial solidity that were threatened by the rising
floodwaters of pan-Slavism and eastern European nationalisms. [48] The ideas
of Anglo-German brotherhood and cultural mixing once advocated by liberal
political exiles were now questioned by a generation of German nationalists
that was more race conscious and Darwinian in its thinking. In the political
climate of the 1890s, Anglophobia, skepticism about the national allegiances
of German Americans, and the end of the last major wave of trans-Atlantic
emigration all eroded the emigrant's importance as a positive symbol of overseas national identity. [49] The image of the *Auslandsdeutsche* and the quest for new
colonies in Africa as well as in German-controlled *Mitteleuropa* became fixtures
in the nationalist and racial imaginary of the German right. They acquired
an even greater sense of danger and impending national decline in the early
twentieth century.

## The Politics of Inclusion? German Identity beyond the Fatherland

How can recounting the rise of the *Auslandsdeutsche* as part of a history of colonial fantasy, emigration, and national identity benefit scholars of German cultural studies? Much recent scholarship in this field has examined the ways in
which Germans excluded specific kinds of individuals from the ranks of full
national membership, even while engaging in colonial and economic activity
that led to repeated encounters between themselves and representatives of
foreign cultures. From a postcolonial perspective it was this desire to keep
people and ideas segregated from and within local and national communities
that encouraged race-based notions of cultural identity, displaced domestic
fears onto the bodies of alien Others, and legitimized legalized forms of social
inequality and discrimination. Based on an examination of Germany's precolonial history, one can also argue that the reliance on ethnic, linguistic, and
racial signifiers as the prerequisites for German identity reflected an ongoing
effort to keep certain individuals inside the nationalist imaginary.

Colonialism, for many nineteenth-century Germans, meant not only the
departure of their fellow citizens to settle foreign lands and subjugate indigenous populations, but also the sustained effort to link "islands" of German
colonists in the periphery to a new and revitalized national center. German
claims of global influence were not always articulated in terms of imperial
supremacy nor universal, "civilizational" values. Sometimes they appeared as
calls for the worldwide unification of the German cultural diaspora, the *Auslandsdeutschtum*. Protecting these overseas communities from cultural assimilation and foreign domination was a continuing, liberal project of national
unification to extend the political power, economic influence, and cultural
prestige of the modern German state beyond the borders of central Europe,
thereby gaining a measure of international respect and geopolitical parity with
its western neighbors. Such sentiments emerged in German culture before the
rise of Wilhelmine imperialism and *völkisch* nationalism, at a time when neither a colonial empire nor a strong, modernizing nation-state had yet become
reality. Examining both the inclusionary and exclusionary roots of the German
overseas imagination helps us resist the temptation to draw overly simplis-
tic genealogical relationships between nineteenth-century colonial fantasies
and twentieth-century Fascist illusions of a racially pure *Volksgemeinschaft* and
a global will to power. At the same time, the historical specificity of German
colonial fantasies and constructions of national identity should not dissuade

us from exploring connections among the precolonial, colonial, and postcolonial periods of German history.

NOTES

1. Susanne Zantop, *Colonial Fantasies: Conquest, Family, and Nation in Precolonial Germany, 1770–1870* (Durham: Duke University Press, 1997).

2. Sara Friedrichsmeyer, Sarah Lennox, and Susanne Zantop, eds., *The Imperialist Imagination: German Colonialism and Its Legacy* (Ann Arbor: University of Michigan Press, 1998).

3. Willi Goetschel, "Epilogue: 'Land of Truth – Enchanting Name!': Kant's Journey at Home," in Friedrichsmeyer, Lennox, and Zantop, *Imperialist Imagination*, 321–36.

4. Zantop, *Colonial Fantasies*, 16, 202–3; Friedrichsmeyer, Lennox, and Zantop, "Introduction," in Friedrichsmeyer, Lennox, and Zantop, *Imperialist Imagination*, 18–25, 28–29; Marcia Klotz, "Global Visions: From the Colonial to the National Socialist World," *European Studies Journal* 16, no. 2 (1999): 37–68; Lora Wildenthal, "The Places of Colonialism in the Writing and Teaching of Modern German History," in *European Studies Journal* 16, no. 2, 9–23; Horst Gründer, ed., " . . . da und dort ein junges Deutschland gründen": Rassismus, Kolonien und kolonialer Gedanke vom 16. bis zum 20. Jahrhundert* (Munich: DTV, 1999); Pascal Grosse, *Kolonialismus, Eugenik und bürgerliche Gesellschaft in Deutschland 1850–1918* (Frankfurt: Campus, 2000), 10–17, 244–46; Andrew Zimmerman, *Anthropology and Antihumanism in Imperial Germany* (Chicago: University of Chicago Press, 2001), 239–47.

5. On the need for an analysis of German "colonial knowledge" embedded in popular culture, intellectual traditions, and mainstream social practice, see Geoff Eley, "German History and the Contradictions of Modernity," in *Society, Culture, and the State in Germany, 1870–1930*, ed. Geoff Eley (Ann Arbor: University of Michigan Press, 1996), 99–100, and Geoff Eley, "Problems with Culture: German History after the Linguistic Turn," *Central European History* 31, no. 3 (1998): 223–24.

6. Susanne Zantop, "Colonial Legends, Postcolonial Legacies," in *A User's Guide to German Cultural Studies*, ed. S. Denham, I. Kacandes, and J. Petropoulos (Ann Arbor: University of Michigan Press, 1997), 189–205.

7. Sebastian Conrad, "Doppelte Marginalisierung: Plädoyer für eine transnationale Perspektive auf die deutsche Geschichte," *Geschichte und Gesellschaft* 28 (2002): 146–69.

8. Woodruff D. Smith, *The Ideological Origins of Nazi Imperialism* (New York: Oxford University Press, 1986).

9. Klaus Bade, *Friedrich Fabri und der Imperialismus in der Bismarckzeit: Revolution – Depression – Expansion* (Freiburg: Atlantis, 1975); Klaus Bade, "Das Kaiserreich als Kolonialmacht: Ideologische Projektionen und historische Erfahrungen," in *Die deutsche*

Frage im 19. und 20. Jahrhundert, ed. Josef Becker and Andreas Hillgruber (Munich: E. Vögel, 1983), 91–108; Klaus Bade, ed., *Imperialismus und Kolonialmission: Kaiserliches Deutschland und koloniales Imperium*, 2nd ed. (Wiesbaden: Steiner, 1984); and Klaus Bade, "Die 'zweite Reichsgründung' in Übersee: Imperiale Visionen, Kolonialbewegung und Kolonialpolitik in der Bismarckzeit," in *Die Herausforderung des europäischen Staatensystems: Nationale Ideologie und staatliches Interesse zwischen Restauration und Imperialismus*, ed. Adolf M. Birke and Günther Heydemann (Göttingen: Vandenhoeck & Ruprecht, 1989), 183–215.

10. See especially Klaus Bade, *Homo Migrans: Wanderungen aus und nach Deutschland: Erfahrungen und Fragen* (Essen: Klartext, 1993); Klaus Bade, *Vom Auswanderungsland zum Einwanderungsland? Deutschland 1880–1980* (Berlin: Colloquium, 1983); and Klaus Bade, *Europa in Bewegung: Migration vom späten 18. Jahrhundert bis zur Gegenwart* (Munich: C. H. Beck, 2000).

11. Zantop, "Colonial Legends," 190–93, 199–202.

12. Hans Fenske, "Ungeduldige Zuschauer: die Deutschen und die europäische Expansion 1815–1880," in Wolfgang Reinhardt, ed., *Imperialistische Kontinuität und nationale Ungeduld im 19. Jahrhundert* (Frankfurt: Fischer, 1991), 87–123; Hans Fenske, "Imperialistische Tendenzen in Deutschland vor 1866: Auswanderung, überseeische Bestrebungen, Weltmachtträume," *Historisches Jahrbuch*, no. 97–98 (1978): 336–83; and Hans Fenske, "Die deutsche Auswanderung in der Mitte des 19. Jahrhunderts: Öffentliche Meinung und amtliche Politik," *Geschichte in Wissenschaft und Unterricht* 24, no. 3 (1973): 221–36.

13. Mack Walker, *Germany and the Emigration, 1816–1885* (Cambridge: Harvard University Press, 1964).

14. Walker, *Germany and the Emigration,* 195–246.

15. On nationalism, regionalism, cosmopolitanism, and ethnicity in Germany before 1871, see Abigail Green, *Fatherlands: State-Building and Nationhood in Nineteenth-Century Germany* (Cambridge: Cambridge University Press, 2001) and Brian E. Vick, *Defining Germany: The 1848 Frankfurt Parliamentarians and National Identity* (Cambridge: Harvard University Press, 2002).

16. See, for example, Franz Wigard, ed., *Stenographischer Bericht über die Verhandlungen der deutschen constituirenden Nationalversammlung zu Frankfurt am Main,* 9 vols. (Frankfurt: Breitkopf & Härtel, 1848), 8:5721–33. On the long-standing German interest in cultural and economic expansion into central and eastern Europe, see Henry Cord Meyer, *Mitteleuropa in German Thought and Action, 1815–1945* (The Hague: Nijhoff, 1955), 1–29.

17. Walker, *Germany and the Emigration,* 103–33; Frank Lorenz Müller, "Imperialist Ambitions in Vormärz and Revolutionary Germany: The Agitation for German Settlement Colonies Overseas, 1840–1849," *German History* 17, no. 3 (1999): 346–68.

18. Wigard, *Stenographischer Bericht,* 2:1055–62, 8:5709–30; Michael Kuckhoff, "Die

Auswanderungsdiskussion während der Revolution von 1848/49," in *Deutsche Amerikaauswanderung im 19. Jahrhundert: Sozialgeschichtliche Beiträge*, ed. Günter Moltmann (Stuttgart: Metzler, 1976), 101–45.

19. On German nationalist agendas in the Revolution of 1848–49, see Günther Wollstein, *Das "Grossdeutschland" der Paulskirche: Nationale Ziele in der bürgerlichen Revolution 1848/49* (Düsseldorf: Droste, 1977).

20. Axel von der Straten, *Die Rechtsordnung des Zweiten Kaiserreiches und die deutsche Auswanderung nach Übersee 1871–1914* (Baden-Baden: Nomos, 1997); Eli Nathans, *The Politics of Citizenship in Germany: Ethnicity, Utility, and Nationalism* (New York: Berg, 2004); and Dieter Gosewinkel, *Einbürgern und Ausschliessen: Die Nationalisierung der Staatsangehörigkeit vom Deutschen Bund bis zur Bundesrepublik Deutschland* (Göttingen: Vandenhoeck & Ruprecht, 2001). For comparative perspectives on German citizenship and national identity, see Rogers Brubaker, *Citizenship and Nationhood in France and Germany* (Cambridge: Harvard University Press, 1992) and Andreas Fahrmeir, *Citizens and Aliens: Foreigners and the Law in Britain and the German States 1789–1870* (New York: Berghahn Books, 2000).

21. Eric Hobsbawm and Terence Ranger, eds., *The Invention of Tradition* (Cambridge: Cambridge University Press, 1983).

22. Juliane Mikoletzky, *Die deutsche Amerika-Auswanderung des 19. Jahrhunderts in der zeitgenössischen Literatur* (Tübingen: Max Niemeyer, 1988).

23. See also Kirstin Belgum, *Popularizing the Nation: Audience, Representation, and the Production of Identity in Die Gartenlaube, 1853–1900* (Lincoln: University of Nebraska Press, 1998), 46–54.

24. On Andree and the links between liberalism, journalism, and popular geography, see Woodruff D. Smith, *Politics and the Sciences of Culture in Germany 1840–1920* (New York: Oxford University Press, 1991), esp. 45–46.

25. "Charakterbilder aus den kalifornischen Goldgegenden," *Globus* (1863): 54–56; "Anthropologische Beiträge I: Die Ausrottung wilder Völker durch die civilisierten Leute," *Globus* 10 (1866): 57–59; "Anthropologische Beiträge II: Fernere Betrachtungen über die Ausrottung uncivilisierter Völker," *Globus* 10 (1866): 141–43; "Dampferfahrten rund um den Erdball," *Globus* 11 (1867): 10–13; Karl Andree, "Die drei grossen Völkergruppen in Europa," *Globus* 12 (1867): 73–77; "Die deutsche Gesellschaft für Anthropologie, Ethnologie und Urgeschichte," *Globus* 17 (1870): 158; Friedrich Ratzel, "Die anthropologischen Gesellschaften," *Globus* 17 (1870): 204; "Die Deutschen und Schweizer in Neapel," *Globus* 3 (1863): 50–52; "Die Deutschen in Ungarn und Siebenbürgen," *Globus* 3 (1863): 224; "Ein deutsches Turn- und Gesangfest in Australien," *Globus* 4 (1863): 337–39; "Ueber die deutschen Kolonien bei Tiflis," *Globus* 5 (1864): 32.

26. "Sie gehen nach Amerika," *Gartenlaube* 6 (1864): 84–87; quotes on 86.

27. "Sie gehen nach Amerika," 87.

28. Zantop, "Colonial Legends," 189–205. On the issue of "triangulation," see also Katrin Sieg, "Ethnic Drag and National Identity: Multicultural Crises, Crossings, and Interventions," in Friedrichsmeyer, Lennox, and Zantop, *Imperialist Imagination*, 295–319.

29. Panikos Panayi, ed., *Germans in Britain since 1500* (London: Hambledon Press, 1996); Panikos Panayi, *German Immigrants in Britain during the 19th Century, 1815–1914* (Oxford: Berg, 1995).

30. "Die Deutschen in Cincinnati," *Globus* 8 (1865): 382.

31. "Pioniere des Deutschtums in fernen Westen," *Gartenlaube* 38 (1866): 597; "Die Deutschen in den Vereinigten Staaten," *Globus* 14 (1868): 123.

32. "Deutsche Volksfeste in Nordamerika," *Globus* 18 (1870): 62–63; "Wachstum und Bedeutung des deutschen Elements in Nordamerika," *Globus* 16 (1869): 286.

33. "Tabakfabrik von Gail und Ar in Baltimore," *Gartenlaube* 25 (1864): 389; "Ein Denkmal deutscher Eintracht in der Fremde," *Gartenlaube* 5 (1866): 76–78.

34. "Die Deutschen in Australien," *Globus* 2 (1862): 87.

35. Donald McLaughlin, "Written in Britain: Publications by German-Speaking Literary Exiles in the Nineteenth and Twentieth Centuries," in Panayi, *Germans in Britain*, 95–112; Hans-Ulrich Thamer, "Flucht und Exil: 'Demagogen' und Revolutionäre," in *Deutsche im Ausland, Fremde im Deutschland: Migration in Geschichte und Gegenwart*, ed. Klaus Bade (Munich: Beck, 1992), 242–48.

36. Ulrike Kirchberger, "The German National League in Britain and the Ideas of a German Overseas Empire, 1859–67," *European History Quarterly* 29, no. 4 (1999): 451–83; Ulrike Kirchberger, *Aspekte deutsch-britischer Expansion: Die Überseeinteressen der deutschen Migranten in Grossbrittanien in der Mitte des 19. Jahrhunderts* (Stuttgart: Steiner, 1999).

37. "Der deutsche Broadway in Newyork," *Globus* 20 (1871): 15.

38. "Deutsche Wissenschaft in England," *Gartenlaube* 9 (1865): 141; "Verdienstvolle Deutsche in Amerika," *Gartenlaube* 10 (1866): 159–60.

39. "Deutsche Wissenschaft in England," 141–43. On the relationship between German Oriental-language scholars and British colonialism in India, see Kirchberger, *Aspekte*, 277–307.

40. On this point see Walker, *Germany and the Emigration*, 132.

41. Walker, *Germany and the Emigration*, 80–87; Fenske, "Imperialistische Tendezen," 370–72; Georg Smolka, *Die Auswanderung als Politisches Problem in der Ära des Deutschen Bundes 1815–1866* (Speyer: Forschungsinstitut für Öffentliche Verwaltung bei der Hochschule für Verwaltungswissenschaften, 1993), 104–48; Bade, *Friedrich Fabri*, 64–66; and Walther L. Bernecker and Thomas Fischer, "Deutsche in Lateinamerika," in *Deutsche im Ausland*, 197–214.

42. "Die deutschen Kolonien in Spanien," *Globus* 5 (1864): 318.

43. "Das deutsche Element in Ungarn," *Globus* 8 (1865): 250–53.

44. "Die Deutschenfresser in Russland," *Globus* 16 (1869): 138–40.

45. "Die Deutschenfresser in Russland," 139.

46. "Die Deutschenfresser in Russland," 140.

47. For overviews of ethnic German communities in eastern Europe and Russia, see Heinz Ingenhorst, *Die Russlanddeutschen: Aussiedler zwischen Tradition und Moderne* (Frankfurt: Campus, 1997); Detlef Brandes, "Die Deutschen in Russland und der Sowjetunion," in *Deutsche im Ausland*, 85–134; Detlef Brandes, "Die Ansiedlung von Ausländern im Zarenreich unter Katharina II., Paul I. und Alexander I.," *Jahrbücher für die Geschichte Osteuropas* 34 (1986): 161–87; Günter Schödl, "Die Deutschen in Ungarn," in *Deutsche im Ausland*, 70–84.

48. Gerhard Weidenfeller, VDA – *Verein für das Deutschtum im Ausland – Allgemeiner Deutscher Schulverein (1881–1918): Ein Beitrag zur Geschichte des deutschen Nationalismus und Imperialismus im Kaiserreich* (Frankfurt: Peter Lang, 1976); Roger Chickering, *We Men Who Feel Most German: A Cultural Study of the Pan-German League, 1886–1914* (Boston: Allen and Unwin, 1984); Günter Schödl, *Alldeutscher Verband und deutsche Minderheitenpolitik in Ungarn 1890–1914: Zur Geschichte des deutschen 'Extremen Nationalismus'* (Frankfurt: Peter Lang, 1978).

49. Michael Ermarth, "Hyphenation and Hyper-Americanization: Germans of the Wilhelmine Reich View German-Americans, 1890–1914," *Journal of American Ethnic History* 21, no. 2 (2002): 33–58.

VANESSA AGNEW

# The Colonialist Beginnings of
# Comparative Musicology

In 1895 the Pacific enthusiast Arthur Baessler lamented that Samoan song and dance were already overly influenced by Germans whom the islanders had "too often heard singing." He would rather watch the old *sivas* than the latest popular dances that were performed to the constant accompaniment of *jupheidi-jupheida* (yo-ho-ho).[1] Comparative musicologists, articulating the parameters of the new discipline, shared his view. Music was a direct expression of a "people's character" (*Volkscharakter*) and hence only "authentic" examples of indigenous music could give rise to genuine scientific insights. Colonial contact, on the other hand, threatened to eradicate traditional musical forms, just as it threatened the very existence of "natural peoples" (*Naturvölker*). Only if researchers mounted research expeditions and used modern recording technology – the phonograph and the cinematograph – could they preserve "native" music in its unadulterated state and thereby contribute to a broader understanding of "natural peoples" in relation to "cultural" ones (*Kulturvölker*).[2]

Adopting anthropology's methodology, comparative musicologists Otto Abraham and Erich M. von Hornbostel further argued that culture had always been used inductively to draw conclusions about race. However, since "racial and tribal types" conformed to a country's "life ways and musical-artistic forms," "exotic" music could also shed light on a "people's temperament," their "economic conditions," and their "level of cultural development."[3] In claiming a new role for music as a determinant of human particularity, they allowed for some differentiation in the natural-cultural dichotomy that had come to dominate anthropological and musicological thought by the turn of the century.[4] Provided it was "authentic," music could demonstrate degrees of development even among "natural peoples." The German Pacific, with its complex of similar but different somatic and cultural types, would provide an ideal testing ground for just such theories about racial-cultural ordering and the effects of contact within a colonial context.

Indeed, scholarly interest in the Pacific, as well as Germany's other colonies, propelled the development of German anthropology and its intellectual cousin, comparative musicology (*vergleichende Musikwissenschaft*). The Wilhelmine period saw the first nationally sponsored ethnographic expeditions; it also witnessed the professionalization of anthropology and its subfields through the founding of academic chairs, professional societies, journals, museums, and other institutes devoted to the collection, conservation, and dissemination of knowledge about the imperial realm. [5] While it has long been argued that anthropology emerged in conjunction with colonialism, an acknowledgement that has resulted in an ongoing reexamination of the discipline, similar arguments have not been made about comparative musicology. [6] More than three decades after anthropology began to examine its disciplinary roots, the German precursor to ethnomusicology has yet to systematically interrogate its own imbrication in broader political, social, and cultural movements.

Thus, the standard musicological reference work in German, *Die Musik in Geschichte und Gegenwart* (henceforth MGG, 2000), prioritizes the work of Guido Adler, Alexander J. Ellis, and members of the so-called Berlin School – Carl Stumpf, Abraham, and Hornbostel. It emphasizes the emergence of urban institutions (for example, sound archives), empirical methods (phonography and tonometry), and theoretical frameworks (whether evolutionary, cultural-historical, ethnographic, philological, or psychological) as formative elements of the discipline. [7] While the MGG includes entries on musical exoticism as well as on music and dance in the former German colonies, it does not deal with colonialism as a historical phenomenon. By virtue of its absence, a key context of comparative musicology – German colonialism – is rendered doubly peripheral. Indeed, colonialism has been regarded neither as a category that organizes musical production nor as an issue that concerns musical analysis. The same cannot be said of the MGG's English-language corollary, *The New Grove Dictionary of Music and Musicians* (2001), a work that incorporates some of the theoretical insights produced by postcolonial and cultural studies during the past two decades. The *New Grove Dictionary* not only devotes an article to the subject of colonialism, it also treats colonialism within the respective entries on music in the former German colonies, musical exoticism, and the history of ethnomusicology. Bruno Nettl's crucial argument that colonialism has profoundly shaped musical cultures – that it represents "one of the most important influences on the history of world musics" – has thus far gained little currency in German musicological history and criticism. [8]

That colonialism goes unacknowledged in the MGG implicitly endorses the notion that comparative musicology was primarily a domestic phenomenon.

Early comparative musicology thus appears as an "armchair" discipline whose practitioners collected source material from ethnographic museums, world fairs, and traveling performers and then analyzed those sources under laboratory-type conditions.[9] The omission of colonialism elides the discipline's tacit origins beyond the urban center – that is, in travelogues, ethnographies, missionary reports, colonial documents, and sound recordings from the German colonies, and in the cross-cultural exchanges that gave rise to these sources. It eschews the complex interplay between metropolis and periphery, between musicologists in the imperial capital and ethnographers in the colonies. Implicitly, such elisions raise questions about the national, as well as international, parameters of German comparative musicology from its beginnings in 1885 to its heyday in the Weimar Republic.

Articulating the relationship between colonialism and music enables us not only to fill in some of the desiderata of German colonial history and its impact on Pacific cultures; it forces us to rethink some of our analytic tools. Applied to the question of music, colonial discourse emerges as a broader interpretive category than is often understood by contemporary postcolonial scholars. Rather than simply identifying a set of colonial tropes – expressions of colonial aggression, defensiveness, German superiority and native inferiority, for example – we might take a more contextual approach. In so doing, musical practices, institutions, interdisciplinary cooperation, and the reception of ethnomusicological works all become potential sources for analysis.

There are three fundamental ways in which colonialism came to bear on music: colonialism effected the development and change of musical style, sound, behavior, and conceptualization; it impacted the interpretation, appropriation, and instrumentalization of music within the colonial context; and it played a role in the development of ethnomusicology.[10] For the purposes of this analysis, I limit the focus to questions of disciplinary history and the interpretation of indigenous music by colonial scholars. Broaching the question of indigenous "music" raises certain methodological problems, not the least of which is a definitional one. Traditionally, the Pacific Islands have no abstract word comparable to "music," since music is often inextricable from dance and the ceremonies or feasts of which it is a part.[11] However, since early comparative musicologists often excluded dance from their study, this analysis necessarily brackets the indigenous context in which Pacific music may have occurred and deals instead with the broader cross-cultural framework. Definitional questions also extend to the "colonial." Favoring a culturalist over a materialist approach, I take colonial discourse to mean the set of arguments and practices that promoted and legitimized the territorial control and exploitation of a group of people by a state apparatus. A colonial discourse of music could thus be defined as the treatment and practice of music in a manner that instituted or justified colonial relations of power. Such a discourse included the use of music as a criterion of race, the introduction of Western musical practices and styles (for example, choral singing or military bands), and the prohibition of indigenous genres (for example, the Samoan pōula or "night dance," which included naked dancing and sexual innuendo). [12] The discourse stressed the superiority of Western music over indigenous Pacific music and subordinated some forms of indigenous music to others, thereby reinforcing the hierarchy among Pacific peoples. Focusing on the German Pacific, this essay traces the emergence of comparative musicology through the context of colonialism. It argues that comparative musicology, in close alliance with anthropology, contributed to a racial discourse that both justified German colonialism and implicitly sought to facilitate its enactment. By the same token, it shows that Pacific music frustrated comparative musicologists' analytic categories and called into question some of the fundamental assumptions of the discipline.

## A Superior Colonial Subject

German Samoa and German New Guinea may not have been of great economic significance to Germany, but the Pacific colonies, and the Samoan islands in particular, were of enormous cultural interest to German researchers. Early ethnographies and travelogues all make some reference to Pacific music, while the more scholarly ethnographies such as Augustin Krämer's *Die Samoa-Inseln* (1902–3), published in English as *The Samoan Islands* (1930), offers an in-depth study of Samoan music and dance, as well as the first significant notation of indigenous songs. [13] Given such scholarly interest, it is unsurprising that Pacific music held an important place within the developing field of comparative musicology. Indeed, the Berlin Phonogram Archive – the institutional home of early comparative musicology – held a large number of Pacific sound recordings collected by German researchers prior to the First World War. The Melanesian collection alone amounted to some 651 recordings made between 1904 and 1907 by anthropologists such as Richard Thurnwald and Emil Stephan. This Pacific material constituted a disproportionately large number of recordings compared with the Phonogram Archive's holdings of other non-European sources. [14] Recordings were made at the behest of ethnographers, colonial officials, travelers, exhibition impresarios, and representatives of the Phonogram Archive itself.[15] The earliest research on Pacific music was thus conducted under the auspices of the Berlin School and demonstrates an interdependence of metropolitan and colonial agents in the scientific study of Pacific peoples. Important examples of this early Pacific research include Hornbostel's transcription and analysis of recordings from the Solomon Islands and New Ireland (then New Mecklenburg, 1912, 1914, 1922); Mieczyslaw Kolinski's comparison of Malayan and Samoan songs collected from a 1910 visiting troupe in Berlin (1930); Georg Herzog's contribution to the 1910–12 South Seas Expedition and his transcription and analysis of music from the Truk and Caroline islands (1932, 1936); and Herbert Hübner's study of music from the Bismarck Archipelago (1938).[16]

The broad aims of this early musicological work were threefold: researchers attempted to preserve indigenous music for posterity and to make inferences about musical origins and about progress within an international context. Peculiar to the Pacific, however, was also the question of musical affinities among the Pacific's constituent parts. Underscoring this was a racial-geographic logic that sought to disambiguate what Johann Gottfried von Herder had referred to as the Pacific's "colorful painting" (buntes Gemälde) of human types.[17] Researchers categorized Pacific Islanders according to three major groups – Polynesians, Melanesians, and Micronesians – using a typology first proposed in the 1770s by the German naturalist, Johann Reinhold Forster.[18] By the early twentieth century this tripartite system denoted a hierarchical ordering of Pacific peoples and had become entrenched in linguistic and anthropological thought (see fig. 1).[19] However, Melanesia was regarded as posing a particular anthropological challenge since the somatic, linguistic, and cultural diversity of its inhabitants defied their ready categorization as a single "race."[20] In their various attempts to explain this diversity, ethnologists and comparative musicologists frequently argued that musical difference corresponded to physical difference. Scholars such as Hübner asked whether there was a direct correlation between somatic characteristics and musical ones, while Hornbostel, Kolinski, and Fritz Graebner all speculated whether the ancient dispersion of Pacific peoples could be reconstructed using evidence provided by latter-day Pacific musical cultures.[21]

Yet the challenge of Melanesia was, in fact, not unique, for the geographical-racial construct was generally inadequate to the task of describing the Pacific's somatic and cultural diversity. The simple schema posed the problem of reconciling three terms – culture, geography, and phenotype – that sometimes seemed mutually exclusive; either the same music was played by different-

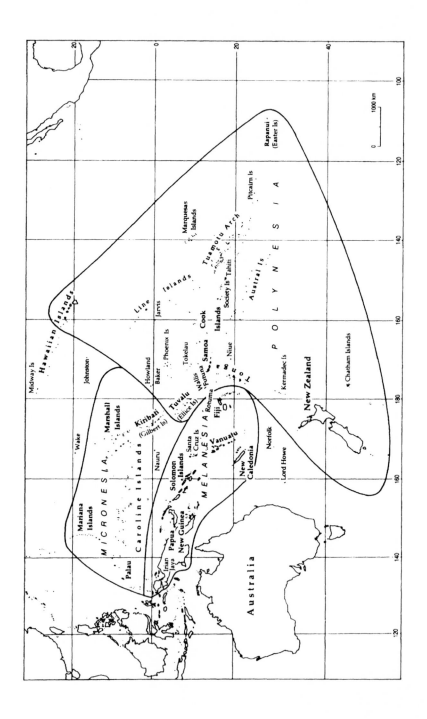

looking people, or the music was not in the "right" geographical location, or the "wrong" people seemed to play it. Rather than abandoning the Polynesian-Micronesian-Melanesian hierarchy, however, researchers vigorously attempted to negotiate the wealth of new data that came from the colonies, while reconciling firsthand observations with preexisting conceptions about Pacific peoples. The disjunctions reveal what was at stake for both colonial officials and researchers: a set of discursive preferences that configured Germany's Pacific empire as somatically and culturally Polynesian, or of Polynesian origin, in order to justify Germany's interest in "less desirable" parts of the Pacific. As the governor of German New Guinea, Rudolf von Bennigsen, made clear in his 1902 appeal for funding before a Reichstag assembly, it was the "proud, yet peace-loving and beautiful Polynesian" who provided Germany with a "very high idealistic purpose"; it was expressly this "beautiful tribe" that was "worthy of culture" and of German custodianship. With its claim to German superiority rooted in the notion of the superior colonial subject, Bennigsen's argumentation appealed to a sense of high-minded paternalism. Moved by such sentiments, the Reichstag parliamentarians ratified the colonial budget by "giving a lively cheer."[22] The fact that Bennigsen had been referring not to Polynesia but to the Mariana, Caroline, Palau, Gilbert, and Marshall islands – archipelagos thousands of miles to the northwest – suggests that there was little international prestige in being the colonial overlords of Melanesia and Micronesia, regions that made up the vast majority of Germany's Pacific empire. Drawing on Polynesian "capital" was then a means of recasting Melanesia and Micronesia in a more favorable light and inscribing Germany into a grander imperial narrative.

Krämer's ethnographic work is in keeping with this imperial narrative, for his Samoan researches were conceived in terms of a national-colonial enterprise.[23] The Imperial Navy supported his research, and the Colonial Office subsidized the publication of his ethnography. More significantly, perhaps, his study was represented – and seen – as contributing to the colonial good. As Felix von Luschan, director of the Berlin Museum of Ethnology, noted in a review of Krämer's book, the government had a responsibility to support such a project. A colonial enterprise could only avoid vast financial and human losses, he argued, if its organizers were adequately informed about ethnographic con-

Opposite: Fig. 1. "Polynesia, Micronesia and Melanesia," The Cambridge History of the Pacific Islands, ed. Donald Denoon et al. (Cambridge: Cambridge University Press, 1997), 7. Reprinted with the permission of Cambridge University Press.

ditions abroad. State support of ethnography was therefore justified in terms of both its utility and its economic value for future colonial ventures. Moreover, the cost of funding such research would be minimal compared with the vast sums that had already been squandered on the colonies. [24]

Music also figured in the construction of a superior colonial subject and a higher colonial purpose. Like generations of travel writers before him, Krämer praised Polynesian dances for their elegance, gracefulness, and, sometimes, overt sexuality. [25] Describing his arrival in a village on Upolu or Savai'i, he claimed that simply uttering "a few siva [dance] words would miraculously produce joyful dances, not official ceremonial dances, or fatiguing orgies, but innocent blossoms tossed [impulsively] into my lap." [26] Krämer's monograph illustrates such descriptions of spontaneous native hospitality with photographs of flower-clad young women, festive dances, and kava preparation. The photographic subjects are arranged in studio-like tableaux in order to substantiate a wide variety of anthropological claims about "native" customs and somatic characteristics. Numerous photographs show suggestively posed women and couch the erotic in a guise of learned respectability. [27] In keeping with the aestheticization of ethnographic material, many of the photographs use tapa (bark-cloth) mats and scrims painted with tropical scenery as backdrops so as to evoke the South Seas. By the same token the sheer decorativeness of the arrangement functions metaphorically, suggesting any island locus amoenus. In the photograph of a Samoan sitting dance, for example, the effect is both natural – the women assume a posture characteristic of the dance – and artful – the women are posed symmetrically and ornamentally against a painted scrim (fig. 2).

The image suggests not a prelapsarian island paradise – some of the women do, after all, look archly at the viewer – but sexual availability and visual gratification. As hospitable and pleasing purveyors of music and dance, Samoans served as the aesthetic yardstick against which other Pacific Islanders were measured. [28] In other words they constituted the "beautiful and culture-worthy tribe" whose members represented Germany's superior colonial subjects.

## Music and Race

In reflecting on the nature and order of human difference, early twentieth-century comparative musicologists followed in a long tradition of using music as a criterion of racial classification. During the late eighteenth century,

Fig. 2. "Samoan seated dance, by girls." Augustin Krämer, *The Samoa Islands*, trans. Theodore Verhaaren (Auckland: Polynesian Press 1995), 2:366.

South Sea voyagers such as Georg Forster and James Burney, son of the music historian Charles Burney, had observed Pacific musical cultures firsthand. According to Forster and Burney, indigenous music complicated, and sometimes even inverted, the racial hierarchies that were constructed on the basis of biological, environmental, moral, and sociopolitical criteria. [29] Such observations gave rise to a tentative, contingent coupling of music and race. In contrast, François Fétis would later attempt to systematically classify human beings on the basis of the musical scale, a system that was given credence even by the craniologist and rigorous empiricist Paul Broca. [30] Commenting on the work of Fétis and Broca, the Austrian musicologist Richard Wallaschek would also pose the question of race in relation to music but would frame it in oppositional terms: race was determined by physiognomy, not culture. By the late nineteenth century, skull measurements and gradations of skin and hair color had become more consistent indicators of race than musical characteristics. Wallaschek's own attempt to "establish a conformity between certain races and musical talent had been completely unsuccessful," but he conceded that it was an undertaking better suited to minds "more speculative" than his own. [31] Abraham and Hornbostel, on the other hand, argued that just as the names Bizet, Grieg, or Macagni were synonymous with French, Scandinavian,

49

or Italian music, so non-European music could reliably suggest cultural and psychological racial characteristics. [32]

The speculative enterprises that coupled music and race did not arise in the absence of empirical knowledge about non-Europeans. To the contrary, theorization about race increased in conjunction with colonial encounters and indeed went hand-in-hand with the scholarly study of subject peoples. It has thus become axiomatic that modern colonialism was contingent upon a belief in the inferiority of the subject population. While this assumption informed various assertions of cultural, social, economic, or political inferiority, it rested upon a biological notion of "race" that linked physical differences to innate moral attributes. Music had an illustrative (if not constitutive) function in the emerging concept of race: the existence of certain instruments or musical styles evidenced a particular geographical-racial grouping (Tahiti in the case of nose flutes, for example, and Tonga in the case of part-singing). However, using music as an arbiter of racial categorization would prove especially awkward in cases were somatic, cultural, or social characteristics seemed mutually exclusive.

## Colonial Comparative Musicology

If Krämer's anthropological research was indicative of the prevailing colonial view of Pacific music, comparative musicologists, working in close collaboration with colonial officials and anthropologists, can be shown to have shared many of their outlooks and aims. Hornbostel, for example, collaborated with Stephan and Graebner on their New Mecklenburg ethnography, publishing a "Notiz über die Musik" (Note about the music) as part of the expeditionary findings. Far from being a disinterested scientific enterprise, the 1904 expedition to New Mecklenburg in the Bismarck Archipelago was conceived by the Colonial Office and sponsored by the navy and the Berlin Museum of Ethnology. Museum director Felix von Luschan's instructions to Stephan make clear that the ethnographic research was intended to serve a greater purpose in keeping with Colonial Secretary Bernhard Dernburg's new program of "scientific colonization." The expedition's aim, said Luschan, was to provide insights into the "character and customs of the natives, the population density, [and] the possibility of labor recruitment." [33] Stephan and Graebner were themselves mindful of the strategic significance of their undertaking and argued along typically colonialist lines that it was high time Germany took its rightful place alongside Britain in the imperial pantheon. [34]

This is not to suggest that fin-de-siècle ethnomusicological research was of the same order as colonial propaganda. Officials such as Wilhelm Solf, the first governor of Samoa, had a clear program for "improving" indigenous social and cultural practices. Even as Solf expressed doubts about the future success of such policies, he championed ethnography as crucial to understanding colonized people's "customs, habits, [and] their juridical structures."[35] To maintain colonial rule, he sought to comprehend their world "as it was reflected in the minds of the people."[36] Comparative musicologists and ethnographers had no such overt agenda for social or cultural change – indeed, they feared it. That is to say, they sought to preserve the music of peoples who were allegedly on the verge of extinction. For this reason, however, it becomes all the more interesting to explore the ways in which musical studies of various kinds were nevertheless commensurate with colonial interests.

In the attempt to insist on racial-cultural separation and purity, the question was how to reconcile, for example, the existence of "Polynesian-looking" people on the "Melanesian" island of Ontong Java.[37] Hornbostel would ask similar questions of music in the Solomon Islands, specifically, the German colonies of Bougainville and Buka. For instance, the panpipe was the most ubiquitous musical instrument on these islands, even though Bougainville and Buka were adjacent to New Guinea and hence belonged geographically to Melanesia.[38] How could these supposedly "inferior" Melanesians be the possessors of an instrument that was considered culturally "superior" because of its (comparatively) wide tonal range and association with the classical Greek panpipe? Such disjunctions are evident in an undated photograph entitled *Musizierende Männer von Buka* (Music-making men from Buka) from the picture archive of the German Colonial Society (fig. 3).[39] The men are arranged as a panpipe ensemble, apparently performing on their instruments, although it is clear from the men's embouchure, the casual manner in which some of them are holding their instruments, and the fact that they are huddled together, that they are posing rather than playing. Indeed, the group is staged according to the anthropological conventions of the day – some individuals are in profile, others frontal – in order to demonstrate phenotype.[40]

The choice of individual subjects reflects not somatic diversity so much as musical variation: the various sets of panpipes range in size from a few inches to several feet. This suggests that the instrument has been developed to its potential: the Buka panpipe is apparently an ensemble instrument, its music possibly polyphonic, and, judging by the number of bamboo pipes, relatively wide in tonal range. Such sophistication stands in contrast to then current assumptions about "natural peoples" (*Naturvölker*), specifically Melanesians –

Fig. 3. "Musizierende Männer von Buka" (*Deutsche Kolonialgesellschaft Bildarchiv*).

namely, that a narrow tonal range, lack of polyphony, and undeveloped form of instrumental music corresponded to a primitive, more "original" musical culture.[41] The apparent complexity of the Buka islanders' musical culture would seem to defy such assumptions; it might not elevate them above their status as "natural peoples," but at least the Buka islanders might share some musical attributes with "non-European cultural peoples" (*aussereuropäische Kulturvölker*).[42] At the same time the image conveyed by the squatting men in the foreground is at variance with the cultural claims made on behalf of their instruments. The men's simian posture and glowering look is at once malevolent and precultural. The group is regulated neither by its orderly arrangement nor by the innocuousness of its musical activity, and the overall impression is one of wildness barely contained. The photograph thus presents the viewer with a set of contradictions in which culture vies with physiognomy, and hence with nature, and sociability with savagery. The task for both comparative musicologists and ethnologists would be to resolve some of these discursive contradictions. How, they would ask, could indigenes have such complex music if they were Melanesians? Put another way, how could they be Melanesians if they had such complex music?

Hornbostel's "Notiz über die Musik" grappled with such questions while attempting to uphold current anthropological assumptions about the inhabitants of the Bismarck Archipelago. While the anthropological evidence prevaricated on the question of race – the New Mecklenburg islanders were an apparent "mix" of peoples – the musicological findings were unambiguous.[43] According to Hornbostel, their panpipes proved a historical connection between Java and the South Sea islands.[44] The ethnography would support this and, in the final analysis, the New Mecklenburgers were drawn into the Polynesian ambit. They were, argued Stephan and Graebner, part of a "broad conquest route along which the proto-Polynesians gradually . . . pressed forward from the south-east Asian archipelago to the islands of the South Seas."[45] In making such arguments Stephan and Graebner coupled German New Guinea in the western Pacific with German Samoa in the central Pacific. This not only established the anthropological, ethnographic, and cultural affinities between Melanesia and Polynesia; it also established a historical precedent for Germany's Pacific empire. In effect latter-day German colonists were simply following where ancient "colonists" (Kolonisten) had gone before.

Hornbostel's Die Musik auf den Nord-Westlichen Salomo-Inseln (The music on the North-West Solomon Islands, 1912), a supplement to Thurnwald's Pacific ethnography, Im Bismarckarchipel und auf den Salomoinseln (In the Bismarck Archipelago and on the Solomon Islands), offers another example of the cooperation between anthropology and comparative musicology. Thurnwald conducted his research on a 1906–9 expedition to the Bismarck Archipelago and the Solomon Islands – an enterprise that received financial aid from the Berlin Museum of Ethnology, technical assistance from the Phonogram Archive, and organizational support from colonial officials such as Albert Hahl, the governor of German New Guinea. The expedition collected a vast amount of ethnographica, including more than three thousand artifacts, two hundred skulls, and an equally impressive number of photographs and anthropological measurements. Thurnwald's contribution to ethnomusicological research was no less remarkable, encompassing as it did a large number of phonograph recordings as well as music transcriptions from various island groups.[46]

For Thurnwald indigenous cultural achievements offered an index of the islanders' "cultural level" (Kulturstufe), which was in turn correlated to their physical appearance or "external nature" (äussere Natur). [47] Such arguments were wholly in keeping with a deterministic and hierarchical racial discourse that subordinated Melanesians to Polynesians. The musical examples collected and described by Thurnwald raised a related set of problems for Hornbostel. The music of the Bougainville Solomon Islanders, in particular their polyphonic "yodeling songs," struck him as unexpectedly complex and, in comparison with the music of neighboring Melanesian islanders, "pleasing to the ear of the European" (dem Ohr des Europäers angenehm). [48] The sophistication of the panpipe, the existence of "orchestral" playing, and the combination of instrumental and vocal music were all highly unusual among so-called natural peoples. [49] Polyphony could not be attributed to European influence, Hornbostel reasoned, for Western missionaries had newly arrived, and the latest indigenous songs made no attempt to imitate Christian hymns or European melodies. Could it corroborate an idea first espoused by James Cook more than a century earlier that the Solomon Islanders had invented polyphony on their own? If so, this "semi-barbarian people" (halbbarbarisches Volk) would have reached a level of musical complexity that had eluded even the Greeks, Romans, and Chinese. Hornbostel could not answer in the affirmative. Reinforcing the Polynesian-Melanesian hierarchy, he reasoned that polyphony was not an autochthonous Melanesian invention after all. Rather, as with the panpipe, polyphony's "tool and perhaps its source" (ihr Werkzeug und vielleicht . . . ihre Quelle), it was a Polynesian import that had penetrated the Melanesian area. [50]

The collaboration between comparative musicology and anthropology suggests not simply that the disciplines shared a common research agenda. It shows that Berlin comparative musicology depended upon the ethnomusicological work produced in the colonial margins. More importantly, comparative musicological findings were used to bolster racial anthropology that was produced with the aim of expediently governing the colonies and of justifying the empire to a domestic public that more readily identified with Polynesians than Micronesians or Melanesians. Hornbostel's work, like that of other comparative musicologists, was used as supporting evidence. If "natural peoples" were capable of some independent musical innovation and progress, their creative abilities were nonetheless constrained by their racial type; more "complex" musical phenomena could only be the product of correspondingly "superior" peoples who had colonized the surrounding regions.

Comparative musicologists wanted to save indigenous music and indigenous peoples with it. Such sentiments have often been termed antiracist or anticolonialist because of their perceived relativism, lack of Eurocentrism, and critique of imperial influence. [51] However, comparative musicology's salvage mission hinged on assumptions about indigenous authenticity and static culture that were patently false. As comparative musicologists' findings actually showed, Pacific musical cultures underwent ongoing change: musical instruments, styles, and practices did not exist in hermetic isolation any more than the people who performed them. Cross-cultural musical exchange was messy, generating new forms of acculturated music that sometimes even returned to the metropolis from the periphery. Krämer's own attempt to introduce the German song "Gigerl sein, das ist fein" (Being a joker, that's fun) to Apia in 1894 offers a case in point, for the song would soon travel back to Germany with a troupe of visiting islanders. "In 1896," he recalled, "the Samoan group sang it daily in Berlin to one of their dances, but no one will have detected anything nearly resembling the original melody." [52] We are left with a tantalizing image of a comparative musicologist like Hornbostel recording this example of "authentic" Samoan music for the Phonogram Archive in Berlin.

That the song traveled back in an altered form gives some indication, however, that Pacific Islanders defied ready categorization. As Hornbostel had to concede in his article "Musik der Eingeborenen" (Music of the indigenes) in the *Deutsches Kolonial-Lexikon* (German colonial encyclopedia), in musicological terms, the line demarcating "natural" and "cultural peoples" was blurry. [53] The Polynesian-Micronesian-Melanesian construct also proved inadequate to the task of describing Pacific peoples. Perhaps the most fundamental challenge to comparative musicology, however, was the notion that cross-cultural musical contact ought to be avoided. It had after all given rise to musical phenomena – the panpipe and polyphony – whose European antecedents were themselves the subject of considerable speculation. While these correctives to the discipline did not take immediate hold, they did give rise to a welter of research questions that would occupy comparative musicologists from the founding of the discipline to the present day.

### NOTES

I am indebted to Kader Konuk, Celia Applegate, and the editors of this volume for their feedback and to Adam Brown for his research assistance. Research for this essay was supported by a Franklin Research grant from the American Philosophical Society and by the University of Michigan.

1. Arthur Baessler, *Südsee-Bilder* (Berlin: Georg Reimer, 1895), 38.

2. Otto Abraham and Erich M. von Hornbostel, "Über die Bedeutung des Phono-
graphen für vergleichende Musikwissenschaft," *Zeitschrift für Ethnologie* (1904): 222–
23. See also Carl Stumpf and E. M. von Hornbostel, "Zur Einführung," in *Sam-
melbände für Vergleichende Musikwissenschaft* (Munich: Drei Masken, 1922), 347.

3. Abraham and Hornbostel, "Über die Bedeutung," 222–23.

4. On the nature-culture dichotomy, see Alfred Vierkandt, *Naturvölker und Kulturvölker* (Leipzig: Duncker and Humblot, 1896).

5. See Dieter Christensen, "Erich M. von Hornbostel, Carl Stumpf, and the Institutionalization of Comparative Musicology," in *Comparative Musicology and Anthropology of Music: Essays on the History of Ethnomusicology*, ed. Bruno Nettl and Philip V.
Bohlman (Chicago: University of Chicago Press, 1991), 203–5. For an account of the
limitations of this process of professionalization, see Benoit Massin, "From Virchow
to Fischer: Physical Anthropology and 'Modern Race Theories' in Wilhelmine Germany," in *"Volksgeist" as Method and Ethic: Essays on Boasian Ethnography and the German
Anthropological Tradition*, ed. George W. Stocking Jr. History of Anthropology Series 8
(Madison: University of Wisconsin Press, 1996), 79-154.

6. See, for example, Andrew Zimmerman, *Anthropology and Antihumanism in Imperial Germany* (Chicago: University of Chicago Press, 2001); Talal Asad, ed., *Anthropology and the Colonial Encounter* (New York: Humanities, 1973). From at least the 1980s
onward Anglo American ethnomusicology has adopted a more reflexive, contextual approach to its history as a discipline. See, for example, Daniel M. Neuman,
"Epilogue: Paradigms and Stories," in *Ethnomusicology and Modern Music History*, ed.
Stephen Blum, Philip V. Bohlman, and Daniel M. Neuman (Urbana: University of
Illinois Press, 1991), 268-77.

7. Dieter Christensen, "Musikethnologie: Geschichte und Inhalt des Faches bis
1945," in *Die Musik in Geschichte und Gegenwart; Allgemeine Enzyklopädie der Musik: Begrün-
det von Friedrich Blume* (New York: Bärenreiter; Stuttgart: Metzler, 1994), 1259-60.

8. Bruno Nettl, "Colonialism," in *The New Grove Dictionary of Music and Musicians*, ed.
Stanley Sadie, 2nd ed. (London: Macmillan Reference; New York: Grove, 2001), 150.
Music is not alone in this regard. Only within the past decade have scholars begun
to analyze modern German culture generally in terms of postcolonial theory. See, for
example, Susanne Zantop, *Colonial Fantasies: Conquest, Family, and Nation in Precolonial
Germany, 1770–1870* (Durham: Duke University Press, 1997); see also Vanessa Agnew,
"Red Feathers, White Paper, Blueprint: Exchange and Informal Empire in Georg
Forster's 'Voyage round the World' (1772–1775)" (PhD diss., University of Wales,
1998); Sara Friedrichsmeyer, Sara Lennox, and Susanne Zantop, eds., *The Imperialist Imagination: German Colonialism and Its Legacy* (Ann Arbor: University of Michigan
Press, 1998).

9. For references to early comparative musicology as an "armchair" and predominantly metropolitan undertaking, see Christian Kaden, "Hornbostels Akustische

Kriterien für Kulturzusammenhänge," in "Vom tönenden Wirbel menschlichen Tuns": Erich M. von Hornbostel als Gestaltpsychologe, Archivar und Musikwissenschaftler: Studien und Dokumente, ed. Sebastian Klotz (Berlin and Milow: Schibri-Verlag, 1998), 89; Mervyn McLean, "Oceania," in Ethnomusicology: Historical and Regional Studies, ed. Helen Myers (New York and London: Norton, 1993), 393; Eric Ames, "The Sound of Evolution," in Modernism/Modernity 10, no. 2 (April 2003): 297–325; Christensen, "Musikethnologie," 1261.

10. While colonialism's effect on musical change in the Pacific cannot be dealt with here, such a treatment might examine colonial and missionary policies vis-à-vis indigenous musical life (for example, the introduction of military bands, hymns, and musical notation and the cultural or social effects of prohibiting some indigenous musical idioms and privileging others). Nettl, "Colonialism," 150. See also Music-Cultures in Contact: Convergences and Collisions, ed. Margaret J. Kartomi and Stephen Blum (Basel: Gordon and Breach, 1994).

11. Barbara B. Smith, "Pacific Islands: Introduction," in The New Grove Dictionary of Music and Musicians, ed. Stanley Sadie, 2nd ed. (London: Macmillan Reference; New York: Grove, 2001), 57.

12. In 1902 Krämer described the sa'ē, the final section of the night dance. Richard M. Moyle, Traditional Samoan Music (Auckland: Auckland University Press, 1988), 220–22.

13. Augustin Krämer, The Samoa Islands: An Outline of a Monograph with Particular Consideration of German Samoa, 2 vols., trans. Theodore Verhaaren (1903; repr., Auckland: Polynesian Press, 1995), 2: 47–48. Other examples of ethnographies and travelogues dealing with Samoan music can be found in Moyle, Traditional Samoan Music, 7.

14. Herbert Hübner, Die Musik im Bismarck-Archipel: Musikethnologische Studien zur Kulturkreislehre und Rassenforschung (Berlin: Bernhard Hahnefeld Verlag, 1938), 1.

15. For an account of the early Samoan recordings, see Moyle, Traditional Samoan Music, 7–8.

16. McLean, "Oceania," 392–93.

17. Johann Gottfried von Herder, Ideen zur Philosophie der Geschichte der Menschheit, ed. Martin Bollacher (1784; repr., Frankfurt am Main: Deutscher Klassiker Verlag, 1989), 237.

18. For a discussion of the tripartite paradigm and its racist overtones, see Jocelyn Linnekin, "Contending Approaches," in The Cambridge History of the Pacific Islands, ed. Donald Denoon et al. (Cambridge: Cambridge University Press, 1997), 7–9; and Nicholas Thomas, Out of Time. History and Evolution in Anthropological Discourse, 2nd ed. (Ann Arbor: University of Michigan Press, 1996), 31–32.

19. Forster's thesis concerning the Asian-Polynesian connection was elaborated upon by linguistic studies conducted by Wilhelm von Humboldt and Friedrich Müller, among others. Krämer, The Samoa Islands, 35.

20. Georg Thilenius, "Melanesien," in *Deutsches Kolonial-Lexikon*, ed. Heinrich Schnee (Leipzig: Verlag von Quelle und Meyer, 1920), 537.

21. Citing Erich M. von Hornbostel on the panpipe, Graebner argued that cultural commonalities between the Indo-Melanesians and Americans demonstrated a historical connection between the two. "Krückenruder," in *Baessler-Archiv: Beiträge zur Völkerkunde* (Leipzig and Berlin: B. G. Teubner, 1913), 202. Mieczyslaw Kolinski analyzed early Berlin Phonogram Archive recordings of Malayan and Samoan songs in order to compare "racial" similarities. On the basis of his findings, Kolinski argued that Samoa had originally been colonized by Malaya. "Die Musik der Primitivstämme auf Malaka und ihre Beziehungen zur samoanischen Musik," *Anthropos* 25 (1930): 585–648.

22. " . . . so glaube ich doch, daß wir einen sehr hohen ideellen Zweck dort verfolgen können. Dieser Zweck besteht darin, die Polynesier zu erhalten . . . [Der Polynesier] ist ein stolzer, aber doch friedliebender Mensch und ein schöner Mensch, und Deutschland sollte sich eine Ehre daraus machen, die Polynesier in ihrem Bestande zu erhalten und allmählich zur Kultur zu erziehen. Um so mehr sollte Deutschland daran festhalten, daß dieser Zweck allein genügt, um diese Inseln sich zu erhalten und ihre Verwaltung auzugestalten . . . Die Inseln sind es werth, in politischer, auch in wirtschaftlicher Beziehung und vor allen Dingen aus dem Grunde, daß es sich bei ihren Bewohnern um einen schönen der Kultur werthen Menschenstamm handelt, dem Deutschen Reich erhalten zu bleiben und vom Deutschen Reich so verwaltet zu werden, wie sie es müssen." Reichstag Proceedings, 10th Legislative period, 159th Session, March 6, 1902, vol. 5, Berlin 1902, p. 4637, quoted in Hermann Joseph Hiery, *Das Deutsche Reich in der Südsee (1900–1921): Eine Annäherung an die Erfahrungen verschiedener Kulturen* (Göttingen and Zurich: Vandenhoeck and Ruprecht, 1995), 28–29.

23. See Harry Liebersohn, "Coming of Age in the Pacific: German Ethnography from Chamisso to Krämer," in *Worldly Provincialism: German Anthropology in the Age of Empire*, ed. H. Glenn Penny and Matti Bunzl (Ann Arbor: University of Michigan Press, 2003). For a discussion of Krämer within the colonial context, see also George Steinmetz, "The Uncontrollable Afterlives of Ethnography: Lessons from 'Salvage Colonialism' in the German Overseas Empire," in *Ethnography* 5, no. 3 (2004): 251–88.

24. Felix von Luschan, "Krämer, Dr. Augustin, Die Samoa-Inseln: Entwurf einer Monographie mit besonderer Berücksichtigung Deutsch-Samoas," *Zeitschrift für Ethnologie* (1903): 1037.

25. See, for example, George Turner, *Samoa: A Hundred Years Ago and Long Before* (London: Macmillan, 1884), 125.

26. Krämer, *The Samoa Islands*, 2:374. The *siva* was a standing dance performed by one or more women with choral accompaniment. The genre became more popular

58

with missionary attempts to stamp out the pōula. Moyle, *Traditional Samoan Music*, 231–32.

27. Such "scientific pornography" suggests a familiar nexus of consumer culture and popular ethnography that was also evident in, for example, the colonial tin-figure toys and postcards that titillated the mass market.

28. See George Steinmetz, " 'The Devil's Handwriting': Precolonial Discourse, Ethnographic Acuity, and Cross-Identification in German Colonialism," *Comparative Study of Society and History* (2003): 60–66.

29. Vanessa Agnew, " 'Scots Orpheus' in the South Seas, Or, the Use of Music on Cook's Second Voyage," *Journal for Maritime Research* (May 2001): 1–25, access at www.jmr.nmm.ac.uk/jmr.

30. See François Joseph Fétis, "Sur un nouveau mode de classification des races humaines d'apres leurs systémes musicaux," *Bulletins de la Soc. D' Anthrop.*, t. ii., Séri ii. (Paris, 1867): 134, cited in Richard Wallaschek, *Primitive Music: An Inquiry into the Origin and Development of Music, Songs, Instruments, Dances, and Pantomimes of Savage Races* (London: Longmans, Green, and Co., 1893), 65.

31. Wallaschek, *Primitive Music*. See also Stephen Jay Gould, "Measuring Heads: Paul Broca and the Heyday of Craniology," *The Mismeasure of Man* (New York: Norton, 1981).

32. Abraham and Hornbostel, "Über die Bedeutung," 222.

33. Felix von Luschan to Emil Stephan, June 6, 1907, Archiv des Museums für Völkerkunde, 1B71, vol. I, 1093/07, cited in Zimmerman, *Anthropology and Antihumanism*, 221.

34. Emil Stephan and Felix Graebner caviled about the renaming of the new German possessions. Germany could only take its place alongside the "maritime queen Albion," they argued, if it could be seen to have triumphed over Britain, for possessing "Neu-Pommern" and "Neu-Mecklenburg" conferred no honor, whereas possessing "Neu-Britannien" and "Neu-Irland" (the same islands under their old names) would have done so. *Neu-Mecklenburg (Bismarck-Archipel)* (Berlin: Dietrich Reimer, 1907), 11.

35. Wilhelm Solf, *Kolonialpolitik: Mein politisches Vermächtnis* (Berlin: Reimar Hobbing Verlag, 1919), 33.

36. Solf, *Kolonialpolitik*, 42.

37. The categories still trouble contemporary ethnomusicology. See Smith, "Pacific Islands," 62–63.

38. Erich M. von Hornbostel, "Die Musik auf den nord-westlichen Salomo-Inseln," in Richard Thurnwald, *Forschungen auf den Salomo-Inseln und dem Bismarck-Archipel* (Berlin: D. Reimer, 1912), 463, 494.

39. *Deutsche Kolonialgesellschaft Bildarchiv*, access at www.stub.bildarchiv-dkg.uni-frankfurt.de/CD/7101/3162/3896/imgooo4.jpg.

40. See, for example, the frontal/profile anthropological photographs assembled in the "human atlas," in Richard Neuhauss, *Deutsch Neu-Guinea: Völker-Atlas*, ed. Rudolf Virchow Association (Dietrich Reimer [Ernst Vohsen]: Berlin, 1911).

41. See Erich M. von Hornbostel, "Musik der Eingeborenen," in *Deutsches Kolonial-Lexikon*, ed. Heinrich Schnee (Leipzig: Verlag von Quelle und Meyer, 1920), 603.

42. Hornbostel, "Eingeborenen," 602.

43. Hornbostel, "Notiz über die Musik," in Stephan and Graebner, *Neu-Mecklenburg*, 18.

44. Hornbostel, "Notiz über die Musik," 134.

45. Hornbostel, "Notiz über die Musik," 192.

46. Richard Thurnwald, "Im Bismarckarchipel und auf den Salomoinseln, 1906–09," *Zeitschrift für Ethnologie* 42 (1910): 99.

47. Thurnwald, "Im Bismarckarchipel," 142–43.

48. Hornbostel, "Salomo-Inseln," 493.

49. Hornbostel, "Salomo-Inseln," 492.

50. Hornbostel, "Salomo-Inseln," 494.

51. See, for example, H. Glenn Penny, *Objects of Culture: Ethnology and Ethnographic Museums in Imperial Germany* (Chapel Hill: University of North Carolina Press, 2001), 3.

52. Krämer, *The Samoa Islands*, 2:424–32.

53. Hornbostel, "Eingeborenen," 602.

# PART 2

# Orders of Colonial Regulation

## Sex and Violence

SARA LENNOX

# Race, Gender, and Sexuality in German Southwest Africa

## Hans Grimm's *Südafrikanische Novellen*

In the introduction to *Das Deutsche Südwester Buch* (The German Southwest African book), Hans Grimm constructed his own narrative of German Southwest Africa's history from the days of its earliest German settlement to the time of the book's publication in 1929.[1] Bitter about the loss of the German colonies and the hardships endured since 1914 by Germans remaining there, Grimm recalls the period before 1914 as something of a colonial golden age: "In few new countries, in perhaps not a single other one, was so much productive work carried out in six short years – work that gives rather than takes, work that creates possibilities – as was the case in German Southwest from 1908 to 1914" (28). To Grimm, as to many other colonial enthusiasts, German Southwest Africa provided Germans inhibited by the strictures of their European homeland a new locale where they could realize their German potential, for it was to such energetic, not enervated, Germans that the colony appealed: "It attracted people who left their cramped conditions to seek a new German land and who were prepared to work hard, not for a peaceful old age in the old homeland, but so that their children could get ahead in a new German world" (10). Portraying the colony as a settlement area where, in Woodruff Smith's words, "the traditional virtues of German culture could flourish in a setting of small-unit agriculture," Grimm eulogizes the prosperous, solid, and aesthetically pleasing German homes of hardworking German families that filled the colony in the years before the Great War: "From 1907 on, farmhouses sprang up everywhere, not as elsewhere built out of corrugated tin and wood, not mud huts built any which way, but wherever and as soon as it was possible, out of solid stone and with hard work and care and love, often with an astonishing sense of beauty, so that in that sunny distant place far away the man and his wife and the children they had or hoped for could own a real home that they could proudly love, and of course flowers and trees grew around the lonely farmyards" (29).[2] Looking back on that era, Grimm recalls something of an

63

agrarian land of milk and honey: "It was truly a wonderful time, it was a time in which everyone in that bright country could believe that the good fairy would surely stop by some happy morning, since she was journeying through the whole land" (30).

However, the texts that Grimm wrote about German Southwest Africa during that alleged heyday tell a different story, and it is the two texts from Grimm's *Südafrikanische Novellen* (South African novellas, 1913) addressing conditions in German Southwest Africa, "Dina" and "Wie Grete aufhörte, ein Kind zu sein" (How Grete stopped being a child), that I examine in this essay. [3] Marcia Klotz observes about Grimm's work in general: "[I]t is hard to find any textual support for [the] assertion that Grimm presents colonial life as utopian. Instead, the reader of his colonial oeuvre is confronted with a seemingly endless procession of hard-luck stories, often ending in the tragic, meaningless death of the protagonist, whose courage and hard work prove insufficient when confronted with the harsh challenges of the frontier."[4] Grimm scholars such as Klotz and Peter Horn have advanced more or less Freudian analyses of the dilemmas of those protagonists, torn between their longing for an absolute pre-Oedipal freedom beyond the law and their obligation to uphold European standards, a struggle that is played out through their sexual relations with black and white women. [5]

Though I find such arguments altogether convincing, in this essay I advance a somewhat different reading. My examination of the novellas is premised upon Ann Laura Stoler's Foucauldian postulation that hegemony in colonial – and probably all other – societies depends on the regulation of desire and sexuality. [6] Sexual relations in the colonies and in texts about the colonies, a matter of "unlimited interest" among "colonial observers and participants in the imperial enterprise," Stoler remarks, are thus not tropes or "stand-ins" for other sorts of relations but important sites of social control themselves (635). As Stoler puts it: "[W]ith a sustained European presence in colonized territories, sexual prescriptions by class, race and gender became increasingly central to the politics of rule and subject to new forms of scrutiny by colonial states" (635). Lora Wildenthal has recently explored the particular relevance of this general observation for the German colonies. She shows that two contradictory premises underlay attempts to regulate sexual relations. [7] On the one hand German men insisted upon their unlimited patriarchal prerogative to the sexual (and marital) partners of their choice, whatever their racial identification. On the other hand the peculiarities of German citizenship law meant that at least the legitimate progeny of mixed-race sexual unions would count as German, thus constituting a clear threat to the racial hierarchies on which German colonial control depended. In this essay I maintain that Grimm's two novellas comprise fictional attempts to reconcile these contradictory discourses of race and gender in German Southwest Africa as well as in the homeland. I thus argue that Grimm's texts situate him vis-à-vis existing discursive or ideological positions and also undertake the work of producing ideology themselves. Since, as Wildenthal has shown so convincingly, these contradictions could not easily be resolved in reality, Grimm necessarily falls short as well in his two quite different efforts to harmonize them imaginatively.

In "Dina," I propose, Grimm takes recourse to the earlier model of the heterosexual colonial romance that Susanne Zantop identified in *Colonial Fantasies*. [8] As Zantop describes it, such a framing of the colonial relationship became the "master fantasy" of the latter half of the eighteenth century, a "symbolic representation" that marks the transformation of colonial emphasis "from conquest and pillaging or trading to permanent colonial settlements and long-term economic exploitation." Within colonial discourse this new narrative of the European colonizer wooing the native woman is predicated upon "a shift to 'love' (rather than expediency, lust or violence) as that which unites the universal 'family.'" As Zantop emphasizes, it also "conveniently displaces the native man – not to mention the European woman, who is absent from the scene to begin with" (123). If Grimm is indeed drawing upon this earlier paradigm in "Dina," it is possible to argue that at the very moment when, as Wildenthal has shown, the debate over race mixing was raging in Germany and the colonies, in this novella Grimm is not primarily talking about interracial sex at all. Indeed, one might maintain that Grimm in some respects dodges the entire debate by frequently emphasizing that it is not sexual desire or lust that motivates the attraction of his protagonist, variously called *der Holsteiner* (the Holsteiner) or *der Wachtmeister* (the constable) but never explicitly named, to the native woman Dina. Even at the novella's conclusion the sergeant, who has often commented upon narrative developments, insists: "He didn't have anything to do with her and didn't want anything from her" (64). On the contrary, the constable's desire has been appropriately regulated, and he knows that European men properly desire only European women. When he discovers that the sergeant is having sex with Dina, he thinks to himself: "I should consider getting married in Germany. . . . You have to go and get a real white woman, otherwise you gradually start wanting the wrong kind of thing" (25). However, by emphasizing Dina's casual liaison with the sergeant, Grimm also fatally complicates his colonial romance, as the novella's conclusion will make evident, by portraying Dina not as a bashful and virginal Pocahontas or Yarico wishing to yield her charms only to her European master, but instead as seductive and sexually promiscuous, in accordance with later stereotypes projected onto native women.

However, Dina cannot be reduced to her sexual function alone. For the constable she stands in a metonymic relationship to the colony itself. At home in Germany he finds her image constantly in his thoughts: "Always just Dina. Is a human trace, or even a human creature, representative of the Namib, of the dead land itself? Oh, certainly not" (28). The denial, of course, only emphasizes the fact that Dina plays precisely this representative role. The novella's otherwise rather cryptic first sentences may suggest that the constable's fascination with the native woman has little to do with Dina herself, but instead derives from the German-specific fantasies he has projected onto her: "She wasn't named Dina at all, but to the constable from the police force who found her and asked her, her gibberish sounded something like that, and he was used to the name from his sister-in-law at home in Holstein. So he said, her name is Dina, and he wrote it down in his report, too, and so she was called Dina" (11). His fixation on Dina and her larger context clarifies to the constable, returning home to search for a bride, that he no longer belongs in Germany, and he only bores potential German sweethearts with his obsessive stories of Africa: "After these six confused weeks he recognized more and more clearly that he was a foreigner in his homeland" (27). As Wildenthal emphasizes, one of the questions that emerges from the colonial debates is whether it was a particular kind of German man who succeeded in spreading Germanness throughout the colony, or whether German masculinity was itself transformed by the colonial experience. Whatever may be the case here, in this respect Grimm's protagonist, identified only by his occupation and regional origin, is presented as a typical figure, for, as Klotz has noted: "Grimm is careful to keep [his] figures from developing into full characters – they always remain 'types,' reducible to their political function, either as promoters or as inhibitors of the colonial project" (123).

Only on the return voyage does the constable meet another typical colonial figure, the German woman who has chosen to combat the purported "surplus of women" in Germany by seeking a husband in German Southwest Africa: "She didn't want to turn into an old maid at home and had decided to travel to the colony in anger and hope" (29). But here Grimm also draws upon an earlier masculine colonialist discourse that, according to Wildenthal, represents "the colonies as a place of freedom from German women" (3). This typified German woman (who is named but once) realizes even on shipboard that she can be happy only in Germany: "But even before Southampton she recognized that she would never be able to put down roots away from home, no matter what happened. Her homesickness was as big and strong as the Holsteiner's accustomedness to faraway places" (29). This lack of compatibility is not represented as entirely the woman's failure; significantly, both Dina and the German woman are introduced with the same slightly unflattering term, *Person*. As in the case of the women he had unsuccessfully tried to woo in Germany, it never occurs to the clueless constable that he again might be projecting his own needs onto her, for "he considered it natural that she would share his interests" (29). Klotz is quite right to emphasize that it is not the German woman's excess prudery or frigidity that dooms their sexual union. Lying in bed on the ship, thinking of the constable's physical attributes as the soft sea breezes play over her body, the German woman is certainly endowed with her own independent desire; that she later lies naked on the seashore pondering why the relationship does not satisfy her – "Are you supposed to miss out on things your whole life long and regret it?" (53) – is certainly an indication that Grimm does not attribute the marriage's failure to an excess of German conventionality. Rather, it appears that the desire of the German constable and his German wife are utterly irreconcilable with regard to life in the colonies. The utopian partnership of German man and woman, which Grimm saw as enabling the creation of German homes in German Southwest Africa and which other colonialists saw as essential to the creation of new models of Germanness in the colonies, is here rendered impossible.

Nor is it at all the case that Grimm represents the constable as "going native," absent the support and companionship of a German woman. On the contrary, the constable is responsible for one of the police posts established to deter diamond theft, and Grimm praises the very German "net of orderliness" established by such posts (22). Indeed, a competition arises over which post can become most homelike: "And so it became a kind of contest to achieve the most propriety and comfort possible in each station and dwelling with those scanty means, and even, despite their completely miserable rations, to put something decent on the table when comrades in the service came to visit" (22). The constable's post wins the competition hands down. A visitor to the post attributes its German propriety to Dina's female presence: "Well, you can do things in style almost like mom at home if you've got a female there" (23). For Dina's German masters have taught her how to produce Germanness: "We just taught and showed her everything" (23). Ironically, however, the true white German wife produces only a widely discussed disorder, which Grimm attributes to her incapacity to establish an appropriate white female presence in the colony: "If the foreign woman had known what she was doing, to use the common expression, she could have had an effect like a noblewoman of old. . . . With mothers and sisters and sweethearts so far away, every white man in the dead land would have had to carry a little smile from her in his heart that would have kept him going. . . . But she didn't know what she was doing" (38–40).

As Klotz has observed about a discourse on the colonies that Frieda von Bülow helped to establish: "The colonies [had to] be pursued no matter what the cost, not because they made money, but because they made real men" (47). At home in Germany the constable recognizes that the colony has enabled him to become more masculine and phallic – bigger – than his German mother ever permitted: "Once he dreamed at night, he had slept in open fields his whole life long, and his limbs [Glieder] grew long because of all the space, and now his good dead mother gave him a beautiful bed, . . . but that was a problem, he was just too cramped because he wasn't used to it" (27). But the representation of Dina as a lascivious native woman allows his German wife to understand that phallic power literally and to attribute her own difficulties to an actual love affair between Dina and the constable: "It's like scales fell from my eyes. Now I know everything. I've figured out the whole pack of lies" (42). Eventually she responds by taunting him into breaking a wild horse, from which he falls, crushing his hand so badly that Dina must amputate it with an axe to save him from a gangrenous death. And with this symbolic castration, Dina decrees his symbolic love affair with her, the colony, to be finished, for a castrated man is of no more use to her: "Can Baas fight for me without hand? Can Baas shoot without hand? Can Baas feed me without hand? No, Baas can't do it" (61). Contrary to appearances, Grimm's novella is not about the race question, but about the woman question in the colonies, and he appears to argue, in some contrast to Das Deutsche Südwester Buch, that if the colonies make better German men, German women in the colonies nonetheless prevent those men from pursuing their colonial future.

The second novella of the collection Südafrikanische Novellen that addresses German Southwest Africa, "Wie Grete aufhörte, ein Kind zu Sein," is, however, very much concerned with questions of gender, race, and sexual relations in the colony, though it pays very little attention to the condition of Germanness. One might speculate that this novella, which Grimm situates at a very specific point in colonial history, 1903, may be intended to address a moment

68

of ideological transition in German Southwest Africa from an earlier period of "imperial patriarchy," as Wildenthal terms it, when German men had enjoyed a sexually and otherwise freewheeling way of life that would have been quite impossible in Germany, to a time dominated by concerns about race mixing, understood as "a social phenomenon with dire economic, cultural and biological consequences for all Germans" (93). The situation of the German farming couple that was so important for the idyll that Grimm invokes in *Das Deutsche Südwester Buch* is almost entirely absent in this novella. Indeed, Grimm is able to avoid the issues of economic survival, German women, and Germanness altogether through the configuration of his main characters. After the death of his wife, Mary Percy, a Scottish Highlander who didn't understand German, Karl von Troyna, a German aristocrat who receives regular payments from home and thus is not required to concern himself with the business of sustaining a colonial farm, can conclude "that he wasn't fit to be a farmer any more" (135). He sends his daughter, Grete, away to a convent school and distraughtly devotes himself to the gentleman's pursuits of riding, drinking, hunting, cards, and patrolling the borders with his friend, a lieutenant colonel of the Cape Police, who is eventually transferred for being "too sympathetic to Germans" (130). Grimm's text thus begins by stressing the solidarity of all whites in southern Africa and the irrelevance of national allegiances to colonial men's commitment to a particular way of life (a common racial affiliation that properly "trumps" more trivial national rivalries): "The friends had a fine international pact," the narrator observes, "which, to be sure, was not ratified in London and Berlin" (136).

Grimm's narrative then moves from a portrayal of the pleasures of imperial patriarchy to a dissection of the dangers that race mixing poses to racial and sexual authority. As the narrator comments with some sympathy, "There aren't very many white men at all who can endure a life deprived of every female influence, and in Troyna's case there was also the constant aching grief and longing" (135). In the absence of white female companionship, Troyna begins a sexual liaison with the mixed-race woman Ellen, whose white father he had inadvertently killed in a border skirmish. Ellen and her brother Alfred call themselves Hundasi, an ethnic group that the lieutenant characterizes as "the only good-looking bastards of the colony," "hot and beautiful and beautiful and hot and false as sin" (143). They purportedly challenge white authority on the Cape by regarding themselves as "equal to the whites" (142–43). To the lieutenant the mere fact of Troyna's liaison with Ellen is no basis for criticism: "It's his business alone" (145). In another context Wildenthal has observed:

"For imperial patriarchs, racial hierarchy did not require racial purity; sexual relationships with colonized women, far from damaging German authority, expressed that authority" (81), a statement that can be understood as a useful gloss on the lieutenant's attitude. However, a problem arises because Troyna is so sexually besotted by Ellen that he fails to uphold racial hierarchies: "But nights she was queen, and her power had become so great that the man, like many men who think that they're in control around women, had long since fallen under her domination and sank, sank, sank, the more hotly she loved him and he loved her in return" (147). As a consequence Troyna fails to maintain appropriate racial authority over the natives who work for him; as the lieutenant observes: "He's overstepped the limits with her, and that's a concern for us all" (145). Indeed, while Ellen, "who dressed like an English gentrywoman from a good family" (146), seeks racial parity, Troyna's friends refuse to visit. He increasingly loses his grasp on his own place in the racial hierarchy: "Without work, without stimulation, with limited intellectual needs, Troyna almost forgot that he was a white man, and the spell lasted a year, during which it came to pass that no one visited him any more except coloreds, and his *Bambusen* [servants] got just a little, by a hair's breadth, more insolent than a white man can allow" (148).

In the novella two events dramatically intervene to restore racial order and signal the ideological transition from colonists' easy tolerance of male sexual access to native women to a much firmer proscription against all cross-racial sexual connections: the arrival of the white woman and the beginnings of race war. Wildenthal notes: "Contemporaries and historians alike have observed that as more white women settled in colonies, racial separation and hierarchy became more marked" (79). Troyna's daughter, Grete, is a second-generation colonist, born in the colony – a member of the group to whom Grimm arguably addresses this narrative. She is at one point termed a "real daughter of the colony" (152). At another point she is called a "child of the master race" (158). She knows how to protect her racial prerogatives and puts natives in their place much more decisively than her father does. But Grete refuses to accede to gender hierarchies and act like a white woman. Instead, she insists on her access to male prerogatives – perhaps Grimm's jab at contemporary feminists – and, though at almost fifteen she is "really already a young lady" (155), she rides wildly about the country on a man's saddle in her outgrown and revealing Scottish kilt. This, as the British missionary's wife chides her, is "boys' dress, or maybe even in the Highlands men's dress" (187). Such a failure to honor gender hierarchies, to assume the white woman's role, can

– as Grimm shows – also destabilize racial hierarchies. Grete allows Ellen's brother, Alfred, to take his liberties with her because he supports her free-wheeling life-style: "He's a cheeky fellow, but he knows what I like and can show me everything, . . . but he's insolent, a very insolent fellow" (161). In her fondness for Alfred, Grete eventually almost forgets racial distinctions alto-gether, though they remain very real for the manipulative young man: "When she looked at the boy there was a soft glow in her eyes, and it slipped her mind for the first time that he belonged to another race than she did, and she also didn't notice that his eyes got small and hot and piercing in response to her gaze and that his hands dared hesitantly but greedily to grasp at her in play, because those hands didn't disturb her any more" (172). In a passage that must have been shocking to contemporary readers, a Boer hunting companion hints nastily at the potential of a sexual relationship between Grete and Alfred that would parallel that of her father and Ellen: "A pretty 'meisje' and a damned handsome fellow, the Hundasi, like his sister, just like his sister Ellen" (167). If, as Wildenthal has claimed, "white women could appear as the solution to race mixing or as the reason race mixing had to be stopped" (121), then Grete satisfies both criteria.

It might be argued that the threats to Grete's racial and sexual purity are a direct consequence of Troyna's dereliction of duty as farmer and father while he plays the role of imperial patriarch, leaving his young daughter at home to manage the farm alone while he desports himself freely about the countryside. She is thus forced to find her own solution not just to the particular danger that Alfred represents, but to the more general danger of native refusal to recognize white authority, represented most drastically in the form of a native uprising. As the Boer reports to her: "Miss von Troyna, in Warmbad the Bondels have rebelled against your Duitsers. All the Duitsers there have been shot dead" (175). Klotz identifies the rebellion as the Bondelswart uprising of December 1903 (154), but Grimm is clearly also invoking the next three years of war with the Herero and Nama, as he indicates on his novella's first page. Here the representation of the uprising conforms to the then-dominant interpretation of colonial war as race war: "Africans had inexplicably turned on German men and women using duplicitous, unconventional methods, and were never again to be trusted with any notable measure of liberty" (Wildenthal, 152). For Grete the general problem of race war in the colony intersects with racial insurrection in her own home. Ellen has agreed to supply the rebels with weapons secretly stored at the farm because the leader of the uprising promises her she will become mistress of the farm if she accedes: "They say I can live with the man here in the house, really right here in the house, and nobody will be allowed to do anything to him if I give them the weapons" (203). In the role of white woman, Grete is thus called upon to assume the task of saving white people in the colony altogether: "Only I can save Dad's property. Poor Dad! Only I can save you yourself. That's right, and all the other white people that live around here. For they belong to me and I to them" (205).

It's debatable when exactly Grete "stops being a child." Perhaps it's when she dreams that Alfred is drinking milk from her young breasts. She doesn't understand the dream, asking herself: "How can it be that a man is the child of a child and a Hundasi to boot?" (199). Peter Horn suggests it is at the moment when she recognizes that "being an adult means taking on the 'whiteman's burden,' responsibility for the 'childish races' of the world" (329). Or perhaps it is when she symbolically loses her virginity, overhearing a "lecherous and drunken" Ellen recount the graphic details of her relationship with Troyna "of the sort that no grown son should ever learn about, though he may have fallen out with himself and the world for months and years." Perhaps it is when she discovers that Ellen believes it is only the presence of Grete, "that arrogant dumb impertinent child," that has prevented her from being "the long-standing mistress at Stylplaats" (202) and that Ellen has for that reason allied herself with the Bondels. Physically ill at the thought that "she lay in my mother's bed" (204), Grete may become a woman at the moment when she guns down Ellen and Alfred with her father's Browning pistol. Certainly she has ceased to be a child when, after her father's belated arrival, she attires herself in her mother's adult white female clothes for the first time before she will leave the house, becoming her mother's veritable likeness. "Even her father gave a start and scarcely recognized his daughter in the beautiful, pale, budding young woman" (212). Superstitious natives fear "that the dead white lady of Stylplaats had been resurrected as a ghost" (213), which protects the farm from harm during the next three years of warfare. A 1912 statement Wildenthal cites from a German East African newspaper may be germane to Grimm's point here: "[T]he European woman alone can solve the problem [of race mixing]. Only she can accomplish something positive. All so-called disciplinary measures belong to the realm of prohibitive and negative decrees, in which no real value resides: nature cannot be driven out with a pitchfork" (120). In Grimm's text the white woman insists upon – and enforces – proscriptions against miscegenation, represented as the force that can prevent race mixing and, Grimm implies, the race war that may be its consequence, as he stresses in the novella's last sentence: "For the revenge of the white woman may last forever" (213).

Contemporary readers must have found Grimm's resolutions to pressing issues of colonial life ideologically and emotionally compelling. Yet it is also important to stress that these two powerful novellas ultimately fail to postulate real political solutions to two of the ideological dilemmas most urgent for the German colonies: race mixing and the role of the German woman. Given German men's continuing attraction to native women, perhaps Grimm was proposing that the only realistic response was that carried out by his heroic character, Grete: namely, to dispose of natives altogether. Indeed, genocide was the policy undertaken by General Lothar von Trotha in the war against the Herero and Nama that is announced indirectly at the conclusion of "Wie Grete aufhörte, ein Kind zu Sein." Interestingly, in the introduction to *Das Deutsche Südwester Buch* Grimm also delicately inquires whether getting rid of Africans altogether might in fact best facilitate German settlement: "It might be the case that a land whose climate is suited for white people and white labor might finally more easily become a land of white labor, though it would be a difficult step, if the colored inferior race were absent or were not very numerous" (25). At the time of the colonial wars in German Southwest Africa, however, genocidal policies were very unpopular with the German public at home. In the colony eradicating the African population altogether would have eliminated the source of cheap labor necessary to staff German farms and industries. Grimm illustrates this dependence on native labor with the example of the Troyna property.

Moreover, Grete's assumption of a form of womanhood mirroring that of her Scottish mother tells us nothing about German women and their relationship to Germanness. This national identity is especially significant in a text that increasingly stresses national differences. The British missionary's wife insists, for instance: "There are a lot of problems with the way the Germans do things. That is our opinion" (184). We know nothing about how Mary Percy adapted to colonial life except that she died there giving birth to her second child, and her ignorance of German suggests that she was especially unsuited for the German colonies. Grimm repeatedly emphasizes that Grete's female suitability for the colonies (including her fluency in German and English) derives from the fact she was born there.

In a promotional flier from 1908, the Women's League of the German Colonial Society maintained: "The German soldier has conquered the land with the sword, the German farmer and trader seek to develop its economic potential, but *the German woman alone is called upon and able to keep it German"* (Wildenthal, 144). In neither novella, however, does Grimm portray German women performing that task, and in "Dina" the German woman's incapacity to do so results in the emasculation of a German man. Thus, though colonial associations and colonists themselves conceived German women to be essential to German economic and cultural success, Grimm – at least in these novellas from the colonial period and despite his arguments to the contrary elsewhere – fails to show us that German women are able to carry out these functions in German Southwest Africa. Grimm's two texts are situated at a point of ideological transition within German colonialism, and he can neither decide between nor reconcile the two options he explores. On the one hand he seems loathe to relinquish the promise of sexual freedom that lured so many "manly men" to the colonies in the earlier era, which is why, in Grimm's texts, every man who tries to domesticate himself and settle down with a good white woman comes to naught. On the other hand Grimm cannot simply embrace the race mixing that earlier era implied, because he is convinced, like most of his contemporaries, that the German race is seriously imperiled by that temptation. These novellas hence turn obsessively around his inability to decide between those two sexual regimes and simultaneously reveal that attentiveness to the interplay of categories of gender, race, sexuality, and nation is crucial to an understanding of the complex reality of German colonialism. If Grimm's novellas are regarded as interventions into ideological debates taking place at a specific point in time, then Grimm's inability in 1913 to contrive an imaginative resolution to the debates that rent the colonial project is very significant indeed. Though he may regard German settlement colonialism as a panacea for the ills confronting the homeland, the irresolvable contradictions of German colonial reality mean that Grimm is also unable to produce a satisfying fictional narrative detailing what would be necessary for the German colonial project to succeed.

## NOTES

1. Hans Grimm, *Das Deutsche Südwester Buch* (Munich: Albert Langen, 1929).

2. Woodruff D. Smith, "The Colonial Novel as Political Propaganda: Hans Grimm's *Volk ohne Raum*," *German Studies Review* 6 (1983): 215–35 (quotation cited, 216).

3. Hans Grimm, *Südafrikanische Novellen* (Munich: Albert Langen, Georg Müller, 1933).

4. Marcia Klotz, "White Women and the Dark Continent: Gender and Sexuality in

German Colonial Discourse from the Sentimental Novel to the Fascist Film" (PhD diss., Stanford University, 1994), 125.

5. Peter Horn, "Die Versuchung durch die barbarische Schönheit: Zu Hans Grimms 'farbigen' Frauen," *Germanisch-Romanische Monatsschrift* 35, no. 3 (1985): 317–41.

6. Ann Laura Stoler, "Making Empire Respectable: The Politics of Race and Sexual Morality in 20th Century Colonial Cultures," *American Ethnologist* 16, no. 4 (November 1989): 634–60.

7. Lora Wildenthal, *German Women for Empire, 1884–1945* (Durham: Duke University Press, 2001).

8. Susanne Zantop, *Colonial Fantasies: Conquest, Family, and Nation in Precolonial Germany, 1770–1870* (Durham: Duke University Press, 1997).

KRISTIN KOPP

# Constructing Racial Difference
# in Colonial Poland

In Clara Viebig's 1904 novel *Das schlafende Heer* (The sleeping army), the protagonist Peter Bräuer has received a parcel of land in the Prussian province of Posen (Poznań) from Bismarck's Royal Prussian Colonization Commission. Standing in the scorching sun, he is surrounded by a seemingly endless ocean of bountiful wheat fields, while the strong wind casts undulating waves across the grassy expanse of the plain. It promises to be a good harvest.

Hanns-Martin Doleschal, a local German landowner and proponent of internal colonization, carefully studies Bräuer's features, attempting to size up this latest addition to his struggling German settlement. Despite the richness of the crops, Bräuer expresses disappointment with his colonial experience, which leads Doleschal to inquire after his new neighbor's motivations for relocating his entire family – his wife, four young daughters, and oldest son, Valentin – from their home in the Rhine Valley to this German colony in the eastern Posen outback. Doleschal would like to hear an affirmation of his own strongly held, nationalistic convictions: the German cultural mission to bring civilization to the primitive Slavic frontier, the importance of securing this territory as the site of German *Heimat*, and the importance of pressuring the region's Polish population into Russian migration by increasing German settlement. Bräuer's motivations, however, leave Doleschal disillusioned, for they prove to be of a far more individualistic nature than he had hoped:

> I have a good amount of savings, but in the Rhine Valley, it doesn't mean anything – there are a lot of people there who have money. But in Posen, it still counts for something because the Polacks are poor. And I thought: at any rate, I've got enough for a good start. When I talked to Valentin about it, he was immediately fired up. He had loved books about Indians when he was in school, and what about those Karl May stories? – Hey, that man can sure write a good book! I even liked to read them. And so we were really ready to go.[1]

Karl May's Old Shatterhand – in Posen? In Clara Viebig's best-selling novel, it is not national duty that has brought Peter Bräuer to the Prussian east, but a desire for the personal wealth and performative adventure marking positive masculine identity in contemporary popular fiction. With a fantasy image of cowboys charging through the untamed landscape and amassing quickly earned fortunes, Bräuer seems to have effortlessly mapped Karl May's American Wild West onto Germany's Polish eastern provinces. However, the set of expectations thereby evoked becomes the source of Bräuer's subsequent disappointments and failures, for the lack of Indians leaves the fantasy incomplete. In this scene Bräuer expresses frustration at the local laws restricting his free use of firearms, and he comes to wish he had emigrated to America instead, where he would be free from such limitations imposed by civilization, in a place "far far away, where there are still savages."[2]

In Bräuer's imagination the presence of the Indian – positioned as the savage, colonial Other – serves to secure freedom of agency for the white male colonizer in America. In the "Wild East" he seeks this same subject position, but it is not made available to him in the same way, because the otherness of the Polish natives functions differently. Bräuer seems to desire the semantic clarity of direct physical combat between the European conqueror and his native object. In the absence of such overt hostility, Bräuer has been left blind to the oppositional practices mobilized by the Poles, which are rendered much more insidious as a result. Viebig's novel shows that the threat to the German colonists posed by the Polish natives requires a different kind of defense than that offered by the gun Bräuer so strongly desires. His inability to identify and respond to this threat will be the cause of his demise.

*Das schlafende Heer* invites the reader to imagine a landscape of colonial conquest in the "Wild East" – a space in which western civilization meets eastern barbarism and German order seeks to discipline Polish chaos. The novel works to construct categories of otherness between German and Pole, and Bräuer's fantasy of Indians serves as a reminder that this opposition between colonizer and colonized in the east must necessarily look different than in encounters overseas. Of focused interest are the moments of slippage threatening the stability of the dichotomous conceptual model, where porous demarcations of difference encountered in the fluid borderlands give rise to a crisis of identification. Overseas, German colonial activity brought white Europeans into contact with natives who were held to be securely identifiable through the visible signs of racial difference. In the adjacent Polish regions, such classification practices proved unreliable. If, in colonial discourse, fundamental differences – of civilization versus barbarism, historical progress versus natural stasis, and human reason versus animal instinct – were mapped onto the categories of racial difference over spatial distance, then adjacently located, "white" Poles presented a formidable conceptual problem. In this essay I explore literature's relationship to the project of internal colonization – specifically, the strategies mobilized by Clara Viebig and others in an attempt to anchor and contain the identificatory mobility of the Poles within an imagined space of absolute otherness.

## Inner Colonization

In the events leading to the German unification of 1871, the Polish minority had resisted inclusion in Bismarck's new political state. Comprising approximately 6.3 percent of Germany's population, the Poles were largely concentrated in Prussia's easternmost territories, which had been annexed during the dismantling of Poland in the partitions of 1772–95.[3] In these regions the Poles comprised population majorities, presenting Bismarck with a thorn of difference lodged in the side of the ethnically defined nation. His *Kulturkampf* policies of the 1870s were largely an attempt to forcefully assimilate the Polish minority in order to preempt their resistance. However, the measures Bismarck introduced to create national homogeneity – weakening the Catholic Church and banishing the Polish language from the public sphere – instead elicited the mobilization of Polish ethnic-national opposition, resulting in increased antagonism between Germans and Poles.

The assimilationist plan had failed, and Bismarck therefore shifted his approach in the following decade, as attempts to absorb the Polish minority gave way to the goal of gradually eliminating it. This decade witnessed the massive eviction of thousands of Poles into Russia as well as the launching of Bismarck's internal colonization campaign. In 1886 the *Königlich Preussische Ansiedlungskommission* (Royal Prussian Colonization Commission) was founded; endowed with an initial fund of one hundred million marks, this government agency was commissioned to acquire large estates from the Polish gentry, to parcel this land, and to sell these plots at subsidized rates to German family farmers brought into the region from the west.

Although the project did not meet with any great success, conservative nationalists were outraged when these anti-Polish measures were relaxed under the subsequent Caprivi government. In an attempt to reroute German policy in the east, activists founded the *Verein zur Förderung des Deutschthums in den Ostmarken* (The Society for the Support of Germandom in the Eastern Marches) in 1894. After 1899 it was known as the *Ostmarkenverein* (The Eastern Marches

Society), but also as the "HKT." Its members were known – often pejoratively – as *die Hakatisten* (the Hakatists), a term created from the first letters of the last names of the group's founders: Ferdinand von Hansemann, Hermann Kennemann, and Heinrich von Tiedemann.

The *Ostmarkenverein* claimed that its agenda was not anti-Polish, but instead, merely pro-German and devoted to the cause of strengthening the economic and cultural position of the ethnic German population in the east. However, they justified the need for such support by insisting that the Poles presented an insidious threat to German national and cultural integrity in these regions. The organization's main propagandistic strategy involved a depiction of German-Polish relations in terms of a struggle to assimilate and subsume one group into the other: either the Poles would be successfully germanized, they argued, or else the region's Germans would be confronted with the constant menace of polonizing forces. In representing this conflict a strong equation was drawn between the language one spoke and the national loyalty and political convictions one maintained – to speak German was to be German – and involved an assumed adoption of German cultural values and an allegiance to the goals of the German nation.

In order for this assimilationist model to function, the reverse had to hold also: Germans who came to speak Polish *became Poles*. Somewhat paradoxically, the tendency of conversion was rendered much stronger in this direction. The rhetoric of the *Ostmarkenverein* warned that individual Germans were more likely to be drawn down into the "depths of eastern barbarism" than the Poles were to be lifted up to enjoy the achievements of European civilization. The *Ostmarkenverein* could thereby claim a degree of national urgency, and its agenda accordingly took on an aggressive edge: it called for Germans to boycott both Polish migrant labor as well as Polish businesses; for the increased elimination of the Polish language from the public sphere; as well as for an increase in measures forcing ethnic Poles out of Germany and into Russia.

It is interesting to note that the majority of the organization's members were neither large landowning Junkers nor small-farming German colonists – those whose interests the *Ostmarkenverein* professed to most directly represent. Instead, the society's membership was largely composed of Germans belonging to the institutional apparatus brought in to administer the east: state officials, schoolteachers, and Protestant pastors.[4] Economically, the Junkers benefited from the seasonal Polish labor coming in from Russia to harvest their crops and were not in favor of the *Ostmarkenverein*'s antimigrationist platform. The German colonists, meanwhile, realized that they would benefit from a cooperative relationship with their Polish neighbors, and the antagonistic practices of the "Hakatists" would only introduce obstructive hostilities.[5]

With limited local effect, the *Ostmarkenverein* functioned most prominently and effectively as a nationwide propaganda organ. Its journal, *Die Ostmark*, became a primary source of information for the coverage of the "Polish Question" in the German nationalist press. With its incendiary views, this organ played a dominant role in shaping national-conservative public opinion regarding Germany's eastern regions.[6] The *Ostmarkenverein* also fought its cultural battle by opening libraries in the eastern provinces and then financially supporting the literary production of the "carefully chosen reading material" with which their shelves were to be stocked.[7] The goal of the *Ostmarkenverein* was to foster the development of a literature supporting an aggressive German Polenpolitik.[8]

Their text of choice was the *Ostmarkenroman* (novel of the eastern marches), a genre originating in the early 1890s and developed over the course of the following two decades. This stylistic hybrid combined textual elements and strategies derived from both the *Heimat* movement as well as the colonial novel. The *Ostmarkenroman* is accordingly characterized on the one hand by intimate rural settings and trivial romance plots reaffirming traditional social values.[9] On the other hand these texts enact a relocation of the *Heimat* ideal onto foreign territory through depictions of German colonists civilizing the world's barbaric elements as a result of their cultural labor. These texts are not merely colonial on a thematic, narrative level in their depiction of German colonists in the Polish provinces but are also structured throughout by the racial and spatial tropes of a colonialist ideology. As I will examine below, the former involved strategies of identifying the Pole as belonging to a race distinct from that of the German. A German eastern-colonial discourse constructed this Slavic race as one inherently unable to progress or develop in the absence of western civilizational influence. However, the same primitivity that seemed to necessitate external intervention was also linked to threatening sinisterness legitimating aggressive German policy to either contain or eliminate it.

## The Threatening Pole

Clara Viebig's *Das schlafende Heer* is regarded as the most successful text originating out of the *Ostmarkenroman* genre, both in its developed literary style (many of its fellow texts are of strikingly poor quality) and in its popularity. *Das schlafende Heer* was a national bestseller in 1904 and 1905, not only in the

Prussian eastern provinces but also in the western regions of Germany. Due to its broad circulation, Viebig's novel contributed more to the popular imagination of the Prussian east than any other *Ostmarkenroman*.

In the text the conflict between Germans and Poles serves to unite several different narrative strands and character studies into a conceptual whole. A three-year time period is framed in the beginning by the arrival of the Bräuers in the colony and ends with their departure. During their stay the reader encounters a variety of typecast figures populating this eastern landscape: Doleschal, the "Hakatist" whose nationalistic provocations elicit much local conflict; the arrogant Polish aristocrat Garczynski and his highly temperamental wife, whose only desire is to sell their estate and join fashionable society in the city; the Polish shepherd Dudek, who imagines that a Polish army sleeps under the earth, waiting for the right moment to rise and force the Germans from the Polish homeland; and various Jewish traders, Polish servants, and village personalities who all try to negotiate favorable positions for themselves in this embattled landscape. As the narrative point of view shifts from character to character, from German to Pole, and from one set of convictions to its opposite, the reader's identificatory sympathies are intentionally rendered ephemeral. There is no central protagonist to guide the reader through the labyrinth of competing antagonisms, yet patterns nonetheless emerge that ultimately serve to affirm a sense of legitimacy and urgency for the support of Germany's project of eastern colonization.

This intervention is accomplished through employing a gendered master narrative of German colonial defeat frequently encountered in the *Ostmarkenroman* genre. Typically, a young German "greenhorn" travels from the pure and safe origins of his western *Heimat* into the distant Prussian-Polish frontier. Here, he becomes obsessed with a native Polish woman; he is never able to possess her fully but comes to pursue her at the cost of all else. In his infatuation he loses grounding in his German identity and allows himself to become "polonized." The result is a loss of autonomous agency and the control over the situation that he – as German colonizer – could have exercised. This fallen hero ultimately meets with some version of doom. This might take the form of complete financial and social ruin, as is met by the protagonist in Carl Busse's *Im polnischen Wind* (In the Polish wind, 1906); his suicide in humiliated demasculinization, as in Traugott Pilf's "Rauhreif" (Frost, 1908); or – as is the case with Valentin in Viebig's novel – his death under the power of a landscape that he has failed to master.[10]

In Bräuer's conversation with Doleschal, the warning signs of Valentin's immanent fall are apparent. Life as a colonist in the "Wild East" hasn't lived up to Bräuer's expectations, and as a result his initial enthusiasm has given way to a tired disappointment. He complains to Doleschal of his substandard housing, the threats to his crops, and his wife's inability to handle the harsh climate of the new landscape. Of greatest concern to Bräuer, however, is the behavior of his only son, Valentin, who has become lazy and irresponsible, neglecting the needs of the family farm. Valentin is infatuated with a local girl and may just be lovesick. However, the girl is Polish, and Bräuer thus fears his son's behavior indicates that he has fallen victim to her degenerate, polonizing influence.

In the imagination of the Ostmarkenroman authors, it is the marriage between a German man and a Polish woman that represents the greatest danger, for within the domestic parameters established by this relationship, the Polish woman is able to gain a powerfully assimilating agency. In Traugott Pilf's short story "Sehend geworden" (Gaining sight, 1908), the poor eyesight of the German Pastor Herzog metaphorically represents his blindness for what is taking place amongst his parishioners. Regaining his vision, he turns his attention to what the text understands to be the far-reaching sociopolitical implications of German-Polish marital unions: "The pastor now paid particular attention to the mixed marriages, which weren't rare. Indifference and carelessness, and most likely calculating intention brought the different confessions and races together. It wasn't often that a Polish man married a German woman; usually, it was the other way around. But in either case, one thing was certain – that the children would be Catholic and speak Polish. And the German man would be bent toward the water of the Polish language like a pliant and yielding willow." [11] The marriage between a Polish woman and a German man is condemned as the result of insouciance on the part of the German and cunning ploy on the part of the Pole, which in combination mark a victory for the Polish nationalist cause. The German men, in other words, are imagined as the potential victims in a game of reverse colonization, for instead of successfully germanizing the region, they become polonized. [12] In featuring such moments of defeat, the narratives of the Ostmarkenromane reveal collective colonial anxieties of impotence and subjugation in the German eastern colonies.

## Identifying the Polish Colonial Other

As James Blaut argues in his study of European colonial ideology, the period surrounding the turn of the last century was an age fascinated with spatial mappings of evolutionary difference. The world was thereby envisioned as hierarchically organized according to the range of proximities to a European civilizational center.[13] The following passage from an article in the *Grenzboten* reveals the anxiety aroused when – in the German version of this model – the spatialized developmental trajectory is followed too close to its imagined German nucleus:

> We assume a common human characteristic . . . but at the same time, we also assume that the ideal of humanity has only been realized to certain degrees and extents in the different races and peoples, such that there are quarter-humans, half-humans, and full-humans, and then in these categories, there are various varieties. The Mongols indeed stand as far away from us as Chamberlain describes; the Negroes and the Malays are not quite as distant – the Negroes are described as grown children by those who have studied them closely. However, we have to recognize the non-Aryan branches of the Caucasian family as humans, who participate in humanity in the true and highest sense of the term, and with whom it is possible to reach an understanding about the largest questions and the holiest concerns, such that we can share a common cultural heritage with them. That none of these peoples, not even the Germanic and half-Germanic enjoys such a richness of noble capabilities as the German is nonetheless true.[14]

While the author of this article finds it easy to assert and maintain a gross distinction between Mongols, Negroes, and Malays on the one side and Germans on the other, much more work is necessary in negotiating the boundary between the German self and the *adjacent* Others (be they Caucasian, Germanic, or half-Germanic). The author finds himself compelled to cede them status as fully human but then proceeds in his struggle to maintain a conceptual border surrounding the German *Volk*. The insistence upon an unequal distribution of nebulous "noble capabilities" is indicative of the crisis underlying such considerations. In this fluid spectrum of difference, where would the Pole be located?

In the adjacency of internal colonization, reverse-colonial anxieties were exacerbated by the threat of racial nonidentifiability. For the project of imagining and justifying the Polish regions as German colonial territory, constructing a radicalized – and racialized – conception of Polish difference was of central importance. Ann Laura Stoler has argued that "The colonialist politics of exclusion was contingent on constructing categories. Colonial control was predicated on identifying who was 'white' [and] who was 'native.' "[15] Stoler's work addresses this demarcational dilemma in the context of European/Malaysian miscegenation in the Dutch East Indies. The German/Polish relationship is additionally threatened by the lack of a delineable (that is, visible black and white) "precontact" racial dichotomy. Not only did hermeneutic uncertainty thwart the process of categorizing specific individuals; it also challenged the underlying claims to a racial difference of the magnitude necessary to justify colonial invention. [10]

The difficulties were not limited to the singular issue of race, because an ideal and absolute colonial Other also exhibited his or her absolute difference in forms of government, religion, and cultural practice. The Malaysian, for example, was non-Christian and lacked European models of statehood and monetary trade structures. The Poles, meanwhile, had shared with Germans centuries of a common Christian heritage, European government institutions, economic practices, and close cultural contact. Thus, in the profound adjacency of this colonial situation, there were ample opportunities in which the Pole could fluidly transgress the border between Self and Other in a threatening slippage of similarity.

## The Black Pole

At stake in the colonial *Ostmarkenroman* was the dual task of rendering the Pole visibly identifiable and of affirming the legitimacy of German intervention by firmly locating the Pole in a position of appreciable otherness. The first strategy taken by the colonial *Ostmarkenroman* in the conceptual establishment of an identifiable Polish race involved the construction of two visually discernable racial categories. Underlying, developmentally linked difference could then be mapped onto these. In a majority of *Ostmarkenromane*, a chromatic dichotomy is established rendering the Poles non-white. Here, class plays a large role in iconographic choice. For while Polish peasants are often portrayed in deindividualized groups, described as having a dark skin color and resembling North American "Indians" or "Gypsies," aristocratic individuals are frequently of sickly pale complexion with jet-black eyes and hair.

In Anne Bock's 1898 *Der Zug nach dem Osten* (The drive to the east), the narrative follows the point of view of the representative of the *Ansiedlerkommission* who has been sent to inspect a German estate. At dinner he singles out for attention the single Polish guest at the dining table: "At the other end of the table sat a man of medium height and slight build with black hair, black eyes, a black beard, clean-shaven chin and cheeks, and noticeably small hands, with which he handled his knife, fork, and spoon in an almost feminine dainty manner when he ate."[17] While this Pole's black hair, beard, and eyes would be a merely arbitrary set of attributes were he alone in possession of them, the text instead enforces an overburdened dichotomy of black and white, or of "black" versus "straw colored," "blond," and "flaxen." Polish figures in the novel become categorizable according to their common set of black features, be they articulated in detail, as in the above case of Herr von Kornatschewski, or reduced to a generalized adjectival: "the black Kascha stepped forward."[18]

The dichotomy of blond versus black is a central structuring device of the genre. The Polish seductress is almost always rendered in shades of black. Her appearance is occasionally elliptically reduced to the adjectival: "And then, on a beautiful spring day, the little black Bronislawa came to the farm."[19] More commonly, however, images and connotations of blackness are drawn from iconographies established in the representation of other recognizable racial groups, as when the German schoolteacher in Johannes Höffner's *Das Moor* (The Moor) meets the Polish woman with whom he becomes obsessed: "He was struck by her beauty. Her loose, black hair, the black eyes, heavy and passionate, and her large, gold earrings in the shape of half-moons gave her something Italian or gypsy-like. She wore a red silk blouse with dark ties and a black skirt."[20] This blackness of the seductive Polish woman allows the reader to identify her (and the threat she poses) even where the German male colonist in the text fails to do so.

In Clara Viebig's text, the "blackness" of the Poles is reinforced by representing their point of view and, from this position, perceiving the Germans as "white." When the Polish shepherd Dudek notices the arrival of the Bräuers to the colony, he stands shaking his fist: "New ones had arrived again – white invaders with yellow hair."[21] His opposition to the "whites" not only establishes Dudek's own position as non-white but also casts the entire encounter between German and Pole in the discourse of a colonial encounter. Leading the reader to identify temporarily with the Polish point of view has two functions. First, inside the mind of the Other one experiences an unmediated sense of the threat he intends to pose to the colonizing encroachers. At the same time, however, one is tempted to share in Dudek's sense of injustice. This seduction by the Other is a textual enactment of the very polonization whose threat provides the underlying logic of the novel.

Returning to a German perspective, then, brings with it a sense of relief, of having withstood a temptation. Peter Bräuer perceives the Poles working in the fields as nonwhite. In a projection of his Karl May fantasy, for Bräuer "the men looked reddish-brown, copper-colored like the Indians."[22] Polish women are even darker, with brown skin, black hair, and black eyes, initially mediated to the reader through an appeal to a familiar "gypsy" iconography: in the first encounter between Germans and Poles in the text, Peter Bräuer's wife looks out over the fields, sees the female Polish laborers, and gasps in horror: "Were those gypsies? She looked fearfully at her blond-headed children – gypsies are said to steal children! . . . Frau Kettchen's blue eyes surveyed the brown women . . . suddenly, one of the brown women stepped forward . . . close to the carriage."[23] This steady juxtaposition of white, blond, and blue-eyed features with the "darkness" of the native population is an overburdened strategy in Viebig's text, as it is typically throughout the genre of the *Ostmarkenroman*. This relentless repetition, an almost panicked need for the constant reinscription of chromatic difference, reveals an anxiety of racial containment – the dark versus light, blond versus black dichotomy must be constantly reinforced, for the distinction it hopes to discipline always threatens to collapse.

## The Breakdown of Blackness

While maintaining the chromatic dichotomy typical of the genre, Viebig's text introduces a shift in the depiction of the seductive Polish woman. The ambiguity of racial division across the fluid German-Polish frontier zone is textually enacted through the figure of Stasia, the young girl whom Bräuer's son Valentin marries. Initially, the reader is introduced to Stasia as the daughter of the forester Frelikowski; she speaks Polish, was raised and educated among Polish children, and is strongly identified with the Polish community. Valentin's father therefore initially refuses to condone a marriage between the two young people, chastising his son for even considering the possibility of marrying a Pole: "Are you crazy, boy? You want to marry a Polack?"[24]

Valentin is ultimately able to gain his parents' blessing, however, when he brings Stasia to their home. Here, she finds the opportunity to cast doubt upon her identity. She explains that although her mother is indeed Polish, her father is really a German; he has merely changed his name from "Fröhlich" to "Frelikowski" in response to the constant linguistic complications with the Poles in the community – the Bräuers now take quiet notice of Stasia's blond hair.

Stasia is a transgressive figure in the text. Perhaps half-German by blood, perhaps completely Polish by cultural affiliation, she introduces an ambivalent moment across the rigorously maintained racial dichotomy of "white" Germans and "black" Poles. Her physical appearance reflects this miscegenation, for Stasia has the black eyes of the "gypsylike" Polish women but the blond

86

hair of the Germans. Consistently, one of these two features is mentioned when Stasia appears in the novel, usually selected to mark her in contrast with her surroundings. Stasia's blond hair distinguishes her in the household of aristocratic Poles for whom she works, while her dark eyes differentiate her from the blue-eyed German community. Who is she really?

Soon after the engagement is finalized, the relationship between Valentin and Stasia begins to shift, revealing ruptures in its fundament. Stasia begins to bypass her planned meetings with her German fiancée, spending – as the reader discovers – an increasing amount of time with her Polish lover, Szulc. Valentin senses that something is not quite right, yet having no proof of Stasia's infidelity, he only grows increasingly obsessed and more willing to try to meet her growing demands. However, his efforts will all be unsuccessful, because – as the reader will discover – Stasia has only married Valentin for reasons of cultural politics. She knows that his attempts to win her affections will allow him to be led down the path of polonization.

Significantly, the Bräuers turn to their clergyman for advice regarding their son's relationship with Stasia. However, the Bräuers are not Protestant, but Catholic, and their church's spokesperson, Vicar Górka, is a Pole. Heavily invested in the chance to "polonize" Valentin, the vicar gives Valentin's mother ambivalent information about Stasia, together with carefully worded theological advice pressuring for a swift finalization of the marriage. Through this figure of a nationalistic Polish Catholic clergyman, individual acts of polonization are linked to the larger Polish nationalist cause. The sinister machinations of these highly stereotyped agitators orchestrate the narrative of almost every Ostmarkenroman. Typical actions are pressuring Polish children to disobey German-school language policies, converting Protestant Germans to Catholicism, and encouraging pretty Polish girls to pursue marriages with German men in order to polonize them. Given the understanding of a racial struggle for dominance taking place in the Eastern Territories, the rhetorical claim that the Poles were conducting their battle through a calculated, underhanded campaign of deception brought legitimacy for the intensification of German policies identifying and excluding them.

In considering the gendered colonial master narrative conveying this threat, I am guided by Susanne Zantop's investigation of the textual strategies of "pre-colonial" German literature and the "colonial fantasies" she observes them enacting.[25] Zantop shows how the depiction of individual, gendered relationships between colonizer and colonized allegorically served to stake larger claims about the essential nature of the colonial encounter in general. The master narrative involved the marriage between a male European colonizer and a colonized woman. Her love for him affirms the legitimacy of his presence. Their marriage evokes a patriarchal template of gendered power and control, which in turn conceptually organizes the relationship between the two cultures for the reader.

In the *Ostmarkenroman*, the male German colonizer pursues a "black" Polish woman with a seeming expectation that such a patriarchal relationship can be instituted – that he can civilize, domesticate, and control this primitive Other. However, he has been deceived. The relationship will ultimately end in tragedy, but only for him and not for his female counterpart, and the source of the marital rupture will be shown to have lain in her scheming ulterior motives. The German male colonial novice, it will become clear, has never really understood the actual nature of the relationship, because the Polish woman consciously performs an inauthentic, seductive act.

The colonial Other has somehow gained an oppositional agency in these texts. The Polish woman erects a facade – a passive screen upon which the colonizer is able to project his desire for legitimated power – behind which she plots his demise. If the German man is warned in advance, perhaps he can avoid this fate. Yet in order to do so, he must be able to reliably identify the enemy.

## Polnische Wirtschaft

Deviating from the "blackness" of the surrounding Polish population, the blond Stasia brings into representation the fear that a dependence upon a somatic chromatism in the conceptualization of difference (as otherwise so rigorously maintained in Viebig's text) will break down in the fluid adjacency of the eastern frontier. The novel, however, resolves the potential threat of this breach with the introduction of an alternative iconography of difference – one that functions reliably without appeal to racial coloration.

"Domestic degeneracy" is a discursive strategy of identification observed by Anne McClintock, "widely used to mediate the manifold contradictions in imperial hierarchy . . . where skin color as a marker of power was imprecise and inadequate."[26] Instead of physical traits, practiced degeneracy and filth of self and space render the colonial subject identifiable. In the case of German constructions of a colonial Poland, the long-standing iconography of *polnische Wirtschaft* (a term that literally translates as "Polish economy," "Polish business," "Polish housekeeping," *Wirtschaft* can also mean a tavern or pub) takes on a new, reinvigorated role.

First introduced by Georg Forster in his eighteenth-century travel writings from Poland [27] and broadly popularized with Gustav Freytag's 1855 *Soll und Haben* (Debit and credit), "Polnische Wirthschaft" became the title of Paul Oskar Höcker's *Ostmarkenroman* of 1896 and remains a pejorative term in common usage today. [28] Within the logic of the phrase, *Wirtschaft* is understood in its broadest sense as management of self and environment. [29] *Polnische Wirtschaft* then denotes an essentialized Polish *incapacity* for such management. Integrating attributes of race and space under the aegis of one sign, *polnische Wirtschaft* was to indicate gross agricultural mismanagement, neglected villages, and pestilent dwellings – all rendered inherent by-products of the filth, backwardness, laziness, and brutality adhering to the Poles. Scenes such as the following description of a Polish village from Erich Fliess's *Ostmarkenroman, Der Proboszcz* (The pastor), are accordingly de rigueur in the genre: "The lively village children, boys and girls, played noisily at the village marsh and on the dung heaps that were piled in front of all of the low huts made out of smeared mud. Some – the youngest – were only dressed in dirty shirts, and on their square, Slavic, louse-infested heads, they wore the fur-stuffed cloth hats of their progenitors." [30] While these louse-infested children play on dung heaps, the situation inside their houses does not offer respite from the filth. Traugott Pilf's short story "Der Raureif" depicts the hovel of a Polish woman who "lifted the filthy featherbed and took from under the rough sheets – which probably hadn't been washed since the summer – a few bread rounds that hadn't yet been baked. She had placed the dough in the charmingly scented, sweating warmth of the bed so that it would rise better. The baked bread was then placed on the damp clay floor to cool, even though the hens had just left their calling card there." [31] *Polnische Wirtschaft* was circular in its mode of signification and in its logic, for it created the degenerate environment that elicited the degenerate characteristics inherited by the next generation. The Pole is depicted as existing in a perpetual state – and self-perpetuating cycle – of backwardness, filth, idleness, and decay.

In Clara Viebig's novel the ambivalence introduced by colonial adjacency is ultimately resolved in this identifiable otherness of *polnische Wirtschaft*. The anxiety of racial fluidity and (non)identifiability, only partially containable through imaginations of chromatic difference and Polish "blackness," is relieved through a discursive strategy that ultimately proves to be much more powerful. For the iconography of domestic degeneracy rendered the Pole immediately identifiable and, in the very same gesture, delivered one of the strongest pleas for German colonial intervention. The Pole was living in an animalistic, barbaric state from which he was unable to free himself of his own accord. Not able to manage themselves or their environment, Poles were easily represented as being in great need of German civilizing efforts. This understanding of the Polish situation only allowed for one solution to the "Polish problem," one of exclusionary (or better, expulsion-based) colonization – because Polish degeneracy, *polnische Wirtschaft*, was contagious.

Conceptually related to the trope of *Verkafferung* familiar from colonial novels set in Africa (in which a white European is understood to succumb to the primitive force of his surroundings, to degenerate and "go native"), polonization is treated in these texts as a form of cultural, perhaps even biological, contagion. As such, it benefited from popular understandings of race at the turn of the last century. For despite Darwin's discrediting of Lamarck's previously paradigmatic theory of evolution, major elements of the latter maintained their hold in social discourse into the early twentieth century. Most influential were Lamarck's assumptions concerning the inheritability of acquired characteristics, as well as an environmentalist notion that an organism acquired such characteristics in adaptation to its environment. As Stoler argues, "this Lamarckian feature of eugenic thinking was central to colonial discourses that linked racial degeneracy to the sexual transmission of cultural contagions." [32] This explained the understood self-perpetuating circularity of *polnische Wirtschaft*. It also explained the vector of contagion: brought into the Polish domestic sphere, the German was most threatened with a natural pressure to adapt to this environment – and his children would be raised within it.

It is through the categories of *polnische Wirtschaft* that Stasia's true identity is unambiguously determined. Although the term itself never enters Viebig's text, it is literally rendered in the tavern (*Wirtschaft*) that Stasia and Valentin operate after their marriage. The establishment is filthy: the tables are sticky with spilled beer, cobwebs hang from the ceiling, and the floor is covered in layers of dirt. Stasia, meanwhile, encourages a predominantly Polish clientele of heavy drinkers, allowing them to run up large, unpaid tabs. Her Polish lover, Szulc, is also a regular guest, and although Valentin is struggling to learn Polish, he cannot understand their conversations. In terms of the national identity and moral degeneracy of their guests, the tavern's appearance, and its financial mismanagement, this is indeed a *polnische Wirtschaft*. [33]

Introducing the final crisis of the narrative, Valentin finally confronts his wife with accusations of an affair with Szulc. Stasia storms off to her father's home, refusing any further contact with Valentin and leaving him devastated. Completely obsessed with regaining his Polish wife, he watches her window night after night. His midnight stalkings culminate in a hallucinatory delirium, during which Valentin is sucked down into the marshy quagmire surrounding Stasia's house. Dying in a landscape ruined by poor irrigation, Valentine's death is doubly the result of *polnische Wirtschaft*.

*Das schlafende Heer* proceeds to deliver a catalog of colonial failures. Peter Bräuer will ultimately pack his family and their belongings back onto a wagon and return to the Rhine Valley. Hanns-Martin Doleschal, the failed "Hakatist," commits suicide after having been brutally attacked by the Poles he has provoked with his inflammatory rhetoric, and a further German colonist, Erich Kestner, will leave, anxious to sell his land to the Colonization Commission at a profit. Yet Viebig's text nonetheless ends on a programmatically optimistic note, as Helene Doleschal stands amongst her five flaxen-haired sons, gazing proudly over the fields of the coming harvest. For these five boys, this eastern Polish region is their *Heimat*, and the reader has every sense that they will stay on to successfully manage this territory, banishing the threat of racial contagion to the space beyond that which they bring under German control. In a time of contested approaches to *Polenpolitik*, Clara Viebig's *Ostmarkenroman* strongly supports a colonialist approach, while not only identifying the potential obstacles to this project but also indicating who is best suited to pursue its goals. This is decidedly not the Bräuer family.

For the anxieties introduced by colonial adjacency have also doubled back onto the identity of the colonizer himself. In the attempt to polarize a fluid continuity into an absolute difference, the question, who is German? returns. And in the post-*Kulturkampf* period in the Eastern Territories, the Bräuers' Catholicism is not an unimportant fact. Instead, it calls into question their own status as true Germans. After all, it was their Catholicism that placed the Bräuers under the influence of Vicar Górka's advice concerning the appropriateness of Valentin's marriage to Stasia.

Peter Bräuer's German identity is not only compromised by his religious denomination but also by his colonial naïveté. For Bräuer is repeatedly shown projecting the myth of Wild West adventure (in the manner of Karl May) onto the Polish territories. Idealizing America as a terrain of absolute freedom, Bräuer imagines himself able to deal with the "wild natives" (*die Wilden*) alone with the help of his revolver. In Posen, he complains, he must heed the state authority and established law granting the native Poles a certain (if unequal) set of political and personal rights.

In the gendered narrative of the *Ostmarkenroman*, the threat of reverse-colonizing polonization is identified in order that it might be contained. *Polnische*

*Wirtschaft* is contagious, but the threat of transmission is reduced to the singular vector of the seductive Polish woman: identifiable and thus avoidable. The threat to young Valentin is immediately apparent as he first enters the Polish region. He has been allowed to drive his own wagon, and as he appears over the horizon, a flock of Polish girls surround him, calling up their siren song, "Daj mi buzi" (Give me a kiss!), and stalling the forward movement of his wagon. Valentin has entered the space of contagion, and he will join the many German men who fail the test of resistance.

*Das schlafende Heer* is thus a novel without a hero – yet it creates the space for one in the imagination of the reader. It represents polonization as the threat of reverse colonization through the figure of the seducing Polish female and the national cause of eastern colonization as requiring the containment of her malicious contagion.

### NOTES

1. Clara Viebig, *Das schlafende Heer* (1904; repr., Berlin: Egon Fleischel, 1910), 269. In certain abridged editions of the novel published later in the century, this quote is reduced (cf. Paul Franke Verlag, n.d.). My translation does not convey the strong Rhenish dialect of the original: "Ich hab' en ganz hübsch Vermögen, aber am Rhein is dat gar nix, da sind ihrer viel, die Geld haben. Im Posenschen is et aber noch wat, die Polacken sind power. Un ich dacht': jedenfalls is et da genug für 'ne schöne Anfang. Als ich zum Valentin dervon sprach, war der gleich Feuer un Flamm'. De hat schon auf der Schul' immer gern Indianerbücher gelesen, und wat die Geschichten vom Karl May sind – hau, de kann schön schreiben! Die mocht' ich selber noch gern lesen! Da kriegt mer ja so en Lust!"

2. Viebig, *Das schlafende Heer*, 181. " 'Och, wär' ich doch nach Amerika verzogen, ganz weit weg, wo et noch Wilde gibt.' "

3. Lech Trzeciakowski, *The Kulturkampf in Prussian Poland* (New York: Columbia University Press, 1990), 11.

4. William W. Hagen, *Germans, Poles and Jews: The Nationality Conflict in the Prussian East, 1772–1914* (Chicago: University of Chicago Press, 1980), 175. See also Adam Galos et al., *Dzieje Hakaty* (Poznań: Instytut Zachodni, 1966), 69–70, 102–3. These accounts differ from that given by Richard Wonser Tims in his 1941 *Germanizing Prussian Poland, The H-K-T Society and the Struggle for the Eastern Marches in the German Empire, 1894–1919* (New York: Columbia University Press, 1941), 216–36. Tims claims that the rank and file of the organization was filled by German settlers. However, like Hagen, he claims that large farm owners were not well represented in the organization.

5. Sabine Grabowski, *Deutscher und polnischer Nationalismus. Der deutsche Ostmarken-Verein und die polnische Straz, 1894–1914* (Marburg: Herder Institut, 1998).

6. Hagen, *Germans, Poles and Jews*, 175.

7. "Sorgfältig ausgewählter Lesestoff" is the title of a pamphlet issued by the *Ostmarkenverein*. See Maria Wojtczak, *Literatur der Ostmark: Posener Heimatliteratur (1890–1918)* (Poznań: Wydawnictwo Naukowe Uniwersytetu im. Adama Mickiewicza w Poznaniu, 1998), 24–40, and Edyta Polczyńska, *Im polnischen Wind: Beiträge zum deutschen Zeitungswesen, Theaterleben und zur deutschen Literatur im Grossherzogtum Posen 1815–1918* (Poznań: Wydawnictwo Naukowe Uniwersytetu im. Adama Mickiewicza w Poznaniu, 1988).

8. Erich Liesegang, "Deutsche Volksbibliotheken für die Ostmarken," *Die Ostmark* 1 (January 1898): 1.

9. Reflecting the antiurbanity of the *Heimatliteratur*, these narratives are only seldom set in the large towns of the east, such as Posen or Thorn. See Peter Zimmerman, "Heimatkunst," in *Deutsche Literatur: Eine Sozialgeschichte*, ed. Horst Albert Glaser (Reinbek: Rowohlt, 1982), 8:154–68.

10. Carl Busse, *Im Polnischen Wind: Ostmärkische Geschichten* (Stuttgart: J. G. Cotta Nachf., 1906); Traugott Pilf, "Rauhreif," in *Geschichten aus der Ostmark* (Lissa i. P.: Oskar Eulitz, 1908), 5–22.

11. Traugott Pilf, "Sehend geworden," in *Geschichten aus der Ostmark*, 51. "Seine besondere Aufmerksamkeit wandte [der Pastor] den Mischehen zu, die nicht selten waren; Gleichgültigkeit und Leichtsinn, auch wohl berechnende Absicht brachten die ungleichen Bekenntnisse und die verschiedenen Rassen zusammen. Dass ein polnischer Mann ein deutsches Mädchen heimführte, kam nicht so oft vor; meist heiratete der Deutsche eine Polin; aber das eine war in beiden Fällen sicher, dass die Kinder katholisch wurden und polnisch sprachen. Und auch der deutsche Mann bog sich oder wurde gebogen und gebeugt zum Wasser der polnischen Sprache wie eine nachgiebige, biegsame Weide."

12. I borrow the concept "anxiety of reverse colonization" from Stephen Arata, "The Occidental Tourist: *Dracula* and the Anxiety of Reverse Colonization," *Victorian Studies* 33, no. 4 (Summer 1990): 621–50.

13. James M. Blaut, *The Colonizer's Model of the World: Geographical Diffusionism and Eurocentric History* (New York: Guilford Press, 1993).

14. "Entwicklung und Fortschritt, Zivilisation und Kultur," *Die Grenzboten* 59, no. 18 (May 3, 1900): 239. "Wir nehmen ein allgemein Menschliches an . . . Nur nehmen wir zugleich an, dass die Idee der Menschheit in den verschiednen Rassen und Völkern nur gradweise und teilweise verwirklicht ist, sodass es Viertelsmenschen, Halbmenschen und Vollmenschen und unter diesen wiederum verschiedne Spielarten giebt. Die Mongolen stehn uns in der That so fern, wie Chamberlain beschreibt; die Neger und die Malayen schon nicht mehr so fern; die Neger werden von denen, die sie genau kennen, als grosse Kinder beschrieben; die nicht arischen Zweige der Kaukasierfamilie aber werden wir als Menschen anerkennen müssen, die des Menschlichen im eigentlichen und höchsten Sinne des Wortes theilhaftig sind, und mit

denen eine Verständigung über die höchsten Fragen und die heiligsten Interessen möglich ist, sodass wir mit ihnen gemeinsame Kulturgüter haben können. Dass sich keins dieser Völker, auch der germanischen und halbgermanischen, einer solchen Fülle von edlen Anlagen erfreut wie das deutsche, bleibt dabei bestehn."

15. Ann Laura Stoler, "Carnal Knowledge and Imperial Power: Gender, Race, and Morality in Colonial Asia" in *Gender at the Crossroads of Knowledge: Feminist Anthropology in the Postmodern Era*, ed. Micaela di Leonardo (Berkeley: University of California Press, 1991), 53.

16. It also proved impossible to distinguish Germans from Poles in the Eastern Territories through statistics. In 1894 the *Alldeutsche Blätter* published a study that attempted to determine the number of "Sprach-und Rassenfremden im Deutschen Reiche" (linguistic and racial foreigners in the German Empire), a phrase further specified as follows: "We mean those who, by language or race are non-German" ("Wir meinen diejenigen, die nach Sprache oder Rasse undeutsch sind"). The study concluded that this number could not be determined: "The number of Slavs, Latins, etc., who, like the Jews, have taken on the German language as the language of everyday life, cannot be statistically captured at all" ("Die Zahl der Slaven, Romanen u.s.w. aber, die ebenso wie die Juden die deutsche Sprache als Umgangssprache angenommen haben, ist statistisch überhaupt nicht fassbar.") "Die Sprach- und Rassenfremden im Deutschen Reiche," *Alldeutsche Blätter* 12 (March 18, 1894): 50–51.

17. Bock, *Der Zug nach dem Osten*, 25. "[A]m unteren Ende der Tafel [war der Platz] eines mittelgrossen, schmächtigen Mannes mit schwarzem Haar, schwarzen Augen, schwarzem Schnurrbart, glattrasiertem Kinn und Wangen, und auffallend kleinen Händen, mit denen er fast damenhaft zierlich mit Messer, Gabel und Löffel beim Essen hantierte."

18. "[D]ie schwarze Kascha trat hervor." Bock, *Der Zug nach dem Osten*, 220; see also 11, 183, 220, 256, 278.

19. Pilf, "Rauhreif," 8. "Und dann kam in einem schönen Frühling die kleine schwarze Bronislawa auf den Hof."

20. Johannes Höffner, "Das Moor," in *Der Sinn des Lebens*, cited in Wojtczak, *Literatur der Ostmark*, 86. "Er war von ihrer Schönheit betroffen. Das lose, schwarze Haar, die schwarzen Augen, schwer und leidenschaftlich, und dazu die grossen goldenen Ohrringe in Halbmondform gaben ihr etwas Italienisches, Zigeunerhaftes. Sie trug eine rotseidene, mit dunklen Schnüren versetzte Bluse und einen schwarzen Rock."

21. Viebig, *Das schlafende Heer*, 28. "[D]ie geballte Faust schüttelte er gegen die kleine Kolonie. Da waren ihrer wieder neue hinzugekommen, – weisse Eindringlinge mit gelben Haaren."

22. Viebig, *Das schlafende Heer*, 67. "Die Männer sahen rotbraun aus, kupfern wie die Indianer."

23. Viebig, *Das schlafende Heer*, 16. "Waren das etwa Zigeuner? Ängstlich sah sie auf

ihre Blondköpfe – Zigeuner sollen doch Kinder stehlen! . . . Frau Kettchens blaue Augen musterten die braunen Weiber . . . plötzlich trat eine der Braunen . . . dicht an die Britschka."

24. Viebig, *Das schlafende Heer*, 285. "Biste geck, Jung? So en Polackenmensch willste heiraten?"

25. For a critique of Zantop's understanding of the "precolonial," see, for example, Nina Berman, "K. u. K. Colonialism: Hofmannsthal in North Africa," *New German Critique* 75 (Fall 1998): 3–27. There, she argues that Germans and Austrians were actively involved in the European colonial project as members of international scientific survey missions, as colonists and explorers for other countries, and so forth, bringing their experiences directly to the German reading populace.

26. Anne McClintock, *Imperial Leather: Race, Gender, and Sexuality in the Colonial Context* (New York: Routledge, 1995), 53.

27. Hubert Orlowski, *"Polnische Wirtschaft": Zum deutschen Polendiskurs der Neuzeit* (Wiesbaden: Harrassowitz, 1996), 53.

28. For a detailed history of the discourse of *polnische Wirtschaft*, see Orlowski, *"Polnische Wirtschaft."* Paul Oskar Höcker, *Polnische Wirtschaft* (Berlin: Deutsches Verlagshaus Bong, 1896).

29. "Schlamperei, Durcheinander, Unordnung . . . Diese Wendung beruht auf einem alten Vorurteil, nach dem die Polen (ähnlich wie die Balkanbewohner und andere Volksgruppen) in ihren Lebensverhältnissen als unordentlich, nachlässig angesehen werden." Günther Drosdowski and Werner Scholze-Stubenrecht, eds., *Duden, Redewendungen und sprichwörtliche Redensarten: Wörterbuch der deutschen Idiomatik* (Mannheim: Dudenverlag, 1998), 552.

30. Erich Fliess, *Der Proboszcz* (Leipzig: Richard Eckstein Nachf. [H. Krüger], 1908), 10. "Die muntere Dorfjugend, Buben und Mädchen, spielten und lärmten am Dorftümpel und auf den Dunghaufen, die überall von den niedrigen, aus Lehmpatzen errichteten Kabachen aufgeschichtet waren. Einige, die Jüngsten, waren nur mit einem schmutzigen Hemde bekleidet, dafür trugen sie auf dem viereckigen slavischen weichselzopfigen Schädel eine der pelzbesetzten Tuchmützen ihres Erzeugers."

31. Pilf, "Rauhreif," cited in Wojtczak, *Literatur der Ostmark*, 120. "[H]ob die schmutzige Federdecke und nahm von dem wohl seit Sommerzeit nicht gewaschenen groben Bettlaken einige runde Brote, noch ungebacken. Sie hatte den geformten Brotteig in die lieblich duftende und dunstende Bettwärme gelegt, damit er besser aufgehen sollte. Das fertige Brot wurde dann zur Abkühlung auf den feuchten Lehmfussboden gelegt, wenn auch dort eben erst die Hühner ihre Erinnerungszeichen hinterlassen hatten."

32. Stoler, "Carnal Knowledge," 72.

33. Walter Olma, "Das Polenbild im deutschen Heimatroman: Clara Viebigs Erfolgsroman *Das schlafende Heer* als Beispiel," in *Studien zur Kulturgeschichte des deutschen Polenbildes 1848–1939*, ed. Hendrik Feindt (Frankfurt a. M.: Harrassowitz, 1995), 120.

DAVID SIMO

# Colonization and Modernization

## The Legal Foundation of the Colonial Enterprise;
## A Case Study of German Colonization
## in Cameroon

While colonization – that is, the domination of foreign countries by force – has existed in all historical periods, the European colonization of overseas countries that started in the sixteenth century and culminated in the nineteenth was unique in its scale, style, objectives, and – of particular interest in this essay – legitimation apparatus and discourse. European colonization was the dissemination throughout the world of a process that was at the same time thoroughly transforming Europe itself – the process called modernization.

Michel Foucault has constructed a critical genealogy of modernity, by which he means the effect of modernization or the period within which it takes place.[1] In his works modernization is seen as a powerful mode of domination over human beings that is based on reason. It attempts to classify and regulate all forms of experience through systematic constructions of knowledge, discourses, and institutions. Colonization, as the export of this process, also attempts to install power through a system of rules. This system of rules is made to appear as the transformation of a chaotic and disorderly situation into one of rational order.

In the discussions and resolutions of the Berlin Conference, which took place from November 1884 through January 1885, the forces and institutions that were supposed to realize this transformation were named: religion, science, philanthropic movements, commerce, and administration. These have all been the subject of research.[2] Yet there is another force that is implicit in all of the conference's resolutions and aims: the law. The introduction of colonial jurisdiction as a means of control and domination and specifically as a means of education and domestication of the natives, intended to force them into the new dynamics of colonial society and make them useful in the exploitation and transformation of their country, has not been analyzed in the case of Cameroon.

I am not a lawyer and therefore do not embark on a legal discussion of colonial laws and jurisdiction. Rather, as a scholar of culture, I focus on the logic of discourses and their function as integral components of power and domination and as the expression and organizing force of conscious processes of thinking and acting.

## The Berlin Conference and Legitimation of Colonization in Africa

After the Vienna Conference in 1815, international conferences to settle conflicts became one of the main instruments of European diplomacy. By the 1880s various treaties had been concluded regarding the region of the "Eastern Question," the North African territories, and other regions. As the historian Wolfgang Mommsen notes, however: "the rest of Africa was not yet subject to any international agreement; from the vantage points of European politics, it was considered as a no man's land where everybody was justified in establishing informal or formal colonial control in so far as the territories in question had not already been appropriated by any of the established colonial powers, namely Great Britain, France and Portugal. In other words, most of Africa remained outside the jurisdiction of international law, and was at best only indirectly integrated into the operations of the concert of Europe."[3] The Berlin Conference aimed to end this situation and to shape a basis for a legally regulated occupation of Africa. This regulation appeared to consist of the banning of war and the elaboration of a ritualized and civilized modus of intercourse between states. It was the expression of reason, achieved through rational discussion, and was supposed to appear as coercive but nevertheless normal and acceptable to rationally thinking people. It was based on categories such as sovereignty, possession, and power, which were considered self-evident. As a setting for rational discussion, the conference had to address explicitly various issues related to such categories. Indeed, issues such as the nonparticipation of indigenous African populations and the question of these people's sovereignty were raised. The delegate from Great Britain, Edward Malet, addressed these issues after the inaugural speech of German chancellor Otto von Bismarck, who had ignored them. Malet reminded the audience that indigenous peoples were not represented at the conference, which would nevertheless make decisions of extreme importance to them. Likewise, the U.S. delegate, John Kasson, quoted the report of Henry Morton Stanley, who had traveled to the Congo region in 1874 and had stressed that the only parties exerting sovereignty over the territories he visited were indigenous tribes.[4]

The questions that Malet and Kasson raised should not be interpreted as moments of embarrassing frankness – that is, as antithetical to the dominant discourse in the conference. In fact they were rhetorical questions, and the answers provided were based on the same logic that structured the whole conference. Participants stressed that indigenous Africans did not need to be represented, since they could not, as barbarians, be treated as legal subjects. This argument was formulated most clearly by the Belgian delegate, Baron Auguste Lambermont: "With respect to these populations, who for the most part cannot be considered as being outside the community of the rights of man, but who in the present state of things are hardly suited to defending their interests themselves, the Conference must assert the role of an official protector. The necessity of insuring the preservation of the indigenous people, the duty of helping them to reach a higher political and social status, and the obligation of instructing them and of initiating them into the advantages of civilization are unanimously recognized. Africa's future itself is at issue."[5] Such a statement is the legal formulation of a practice, and we should take note of the effort to translate the practice into existing legal notions in order to legitimize it. Lambermont uses the notion of legal minority to describe the status of the indigenous populations. This notion is used in European legal discourse to describe a category of persons such as children, adolescents, or insane persons who need a guardian to act legally in their name.

Such projection of ontogenetical categories onto phylogenetic considerations is very common in imperialist discourse. It was already present in the writings of Bartolomé de Las Casas, who in 1551 sought to explain how Indians could be human beings yet be so different from Europeans. He explained that mankind was one but that some human beings were born earlier than others and had the responsibility to help the younger ones, just as a wild field with the potential to produce useful fruits must be cultivated. Difference between two peoples was explained as difference between various life stages or ages – Europeans being adults and Indians children.[6]

In Las Casas's text the use of ontogenetical differences to explain the relationship between Europeans and non-Europeans functioned as the basis for the religious and civilizing mission of colonization. At the Berlin Conference it served to transfer the sovereignty of the indigenous people over their own territories to European powers, who became "protectors" and could therefore act without asking their opinions. The indigenous populations were legally deprived of their status as subjects of history and instead became objects. Like children and insane persons, they were not considered as persons governed

by reason and could not act as autonomous subjects. The legal discourse functioned as power because its rules enforced what was rational, normal, and true
and therefore fixed a framework within which things had to be thought and
spoken about. But this legal discourse was not totally coherent. The colonial
powers transgressed against it or transformed it when it sometimes obstructed
their immediate political and economic goals.

In the months preceding the Berlin Conference, those who were proclaiming the legal minority of Africans had signed treaties and agreements that they
now used to claim possession of various African countries. In the months after
the conference, they signed more such treaties. From 1883 to 1907 individual
Germans or representatives of the German state signed ninety-five treaties and
contracts with various chieftains in Cameroon and used these treaties in their
negotiations with other European powers. [7] The most famous of these was
signed on July 12, 1884, by King Bell and King Akwa and by Johannes Voss and
Edward Schmidt, the latter two representing respectively the German firms
Jantzen & Thormählen and Woermann. The treaty was not signed directly by
German officials but merely by private German business representatives. Nevertheless, the German government recognized it as binding on the state and
used it to proclaim sovereignty over the territory. In spite of this legal flaw,
German officials claimed that the transfer of sovereignty was based on the will
of the Cameroonian people – the very people who were simultaneously argued
to be legal minors.

## The Introduction of Colonial Jurisdiction in Cameroon

As we have seen, the legal discourse used to found the colonial enterprise was
not free of contradiction. But it did help to force overseas expansion into a logic
of modernization – to rationalize it and fit it into the categories of reason. The
first imperial expansion in the sixteenth century had legitimized the colonial
enterprise in a different way. At that time the church was the highest authority
for deciding what was acceptable and for authorizing colonial conquest. It
was the Catholic Church, for example, that decided the status and treatment
of natives, and it did so according to its own interests and principles. For
example in 1537 Pope Paul III interpreted any attempt to deny Indians the
status of human beings and treat them like animals as an expression of the
devil's strategy to prevent the church from christianizing them. Indians were
thus declared human beings, against the will of the colonists who wanted to
treat them like the other natural resources at their disposal. Missionaries and

colonists had different interests; the church made a decision that legitimized the presence and action of its servants. The classical period of imperialism in the nineteenth century took place in a different context. The church was no longer the source of absolute truth. It was still an important power, but its categories were now at least partly in tension with the secular discourse of modernization. The legal formulation of this secular discourse was used to justify colonization and to organize colonial practice. Let us now analyze the use of legal instruments to establish colonial power in the protectorate of Cameroon.

In the novel *Le jardin des supplices* by the French author Octave Mirabeau (the same novel upon which Franz Kafka drew for his more famous story "In the Penal Colony"), the main character draws a distinction between Europe and the colonies. The setting is the early twentieth century. The main character describes Europe as a space where law and rules have restrained the liberty of individuals in such a way that life is no longer interesting there. In the colonies, by contrast, individuals are really free – they may even kill someone with impunity. In the language of this character, the term "individuals" refers only to Europeans, not to natives. The fundamental distinction between Europe and the colonies – in which the latter is defined as a colonial space of fewer regulations, less psychic repression, and less domination of the individual through social institutions – is very important. Here we see the dream of many Europeans who found the processes of bureaucratization and rationalization to be oppressive and who saw the colonies as a space where they could be free from these constraints, even finding the possibility of a total freedom without moral and rational control. During the first years of German colonial rule in Cameroon (or more precisely, in those regions of Cameroon that were actually under German control), German traders, soldiers, and civil servants seem to have found such a space. They acted so freely and so cruelly that Kaiser Wilhelm I, acting under pressure from the Reichstag, issued a number of decrees to reduce their zeal. These decrees were of no avail, as we shall see.

Let us turn to the question of how the protectorate was administered. Since the German constitution contained no provision for governing colonies, the Reichstag was asked in 1885 to adopt a Colonial Constitution (*Kolonialverfassung*). The Reichstag accepted the bill, after difficult debate, on April 10, 1886. Traders and colonial lobbyists in the German Colonial Society (*Deutsche Kolonialgesellschaft*) had influenced this Colonial Constitution. They hoped to exclude the Reichstag from control over the colonies, and therefore sought to place the greatest power possible in the hands of the kaiser. The first article of the Colonial Constitution did indeed concentrate authority in the kaiser, who had the power to issue decrees on almost all matters concerning the protectorates. The chancellor was given limited powers, most of which were actually delegated to him by the kaiser. The budget for administering the colonies had to be submitted to the Reichstag, however, and this was the only opening for that representative body to discuss the German government's actions in the colonies.

When the Germans came to Cameroon, there was already a European-inspired court of equity functioning in Duala.[8] This court had been established in the late 1850s by agreement between Europeans and local Africans for the peaceful settlement of disputes arising in the coastal region. The court, which was dominated by British traders, was suppressed by the Germans soon after the latter gained control of the territory. The Germans instead established two sets of courts: one for whites and one for local people. Already debating the colony's first budget, the Reichstag took up the question of what law ought to be enforced there. A bill in 1886 prescribed the application of the German civil and criminal law and procedure as practiced in the consular courts. At first this law applied only to whites.

Yet the German laws were never fully applied to whites or Europeans in the colony. For example, colonists argued that imprisoning a white convict would cause natives to lose respect for whites. The German Colonial Society took up the complaint of a white trader who was to be jailed together with Africans and had appealed to the Reichstag and asked the chancellor for a decision regarding such cases. As historian Harry Rudin has noted, "Of the whites charged with violation of the law a rather large number were usually acquitted. . . . Imprisonment was a far less common penalty than the imposition of a fine."[9] Many of these offenses concerned whites' physical violence toward Africans. Even after various decrees in the first decade of the twentieth century sought to strengthen the rule of law and protect natives in the German colonies, whites remained free to deal with natives in almost any way they liked, and this was the case right up until the end of German rule.

The natives, by contrast, saw themselves forced into new confines, with their freedoms newly constrained. Representatives of those peoples who had signed treaties with the Germans and now feared they would completely lose control of their way of life added a text to the treaties known as the *Wünsche der Kamerun Leute* (Wishes of the Cameroon people). In this text they sought to give expression to their will, to retain certain advantages they had originally expected, and to protect some customs:

Our wishes is that white men should not go up and trade with Bushmen, nothing to do with our markets, they must stay here in this river and they give us trust so that we will trade with our Bushmen.

We need no protection, we should like our country to annect with the government of any European power.

We need no attention about our Marriages, we shall marry as we are doing now.

Our cultivated ground must not be taken from us, for we are not able to buy and sell as other country.

We need no Duty or Custom House in our country.

We shall keep Bulldogs, Pigs, Goats, Fowls, as it is now, and no Duty on them.

No man shall take another man's wife by force, or else a heavy [fine(?)].

We need no fighting and beating without fault and no impression on paying the trusts without notice and no man shall be put to Iron for the trust.

We are the chiefs of Cameroons. [10]

This text was followed by the statement "This document was signed by the Consul as a sign of his agreement."[11]

A full discussion of this very interesting document is beyond the scope of this essay. Let us merely consider that it was an original formulation of the chieftains, added to the treaty that was written by Germans in German – a language these chieftains did not understand and in words that did not reflect their way of thinking and depicting reality. The document expresses both trust and distrust of Germans – trust that they will be willing to respect a signed agreement, but also distrust of the Germans' intentions. That distrust was based on decades of experience with European coastal traders. Local chieftains did not think that the very Europeans who eagerly insisted on the inviolability of written contracts might themselves break them. This was one of several misunderstandings, based on ignorance, that governed their whole intercourse with the Europeans, whom the chieftains believed they were using to increase their own power but who in fact, in the end, deprived the chieftains of authority. At the same time chieftains were struggling to maintain their own jurisdiction over their territory.

In the early days of the colony, German officials, with the assistance of native interpreters, adjudicated matters. These officials, it was claimed, took native customs into consideration.[12] It is hard to establish what that claim actually signified, given that the officials did not know those customs and were relying on interpreters who were presumably eager either to please their white masters or to favor the party with whom they personally sympathized. Moreover, communication through interpreters was always imprecise, since the interpreters had only superficial knowledge of one or both languages.

In 1892 the German authorities created a court system in Duala that was to render judgments in minor civil and criminal cases between natives. It was a court of first instance, and in the hands of native chieftains. Here, too, the Germans claimed that judgments conformed to local customs, but the reality was different. The chieftains had to take into account the changed environment, and the justice they practiced was necessarily different from that of their traditional ways. First, they now had to keep a record of the proceedings, which inevitably modified existing procedures. Second, new penalties, previously unknown, were now handed down – fines to be paid in cash (German marks) or prison sentences. The very possibility of appealing beyond the first instance to the German colonial governor was an innovation. Finally, this new, ostensibly customary court system had no jurisdiction in cases involving murder or other crimes punishable by death. All these novelties constituted a transformation of the traditional local way of handling legal problems.

Civil or criminal cases between Europeans and natives were not the subject of any law until the years 1894–96, only changing due to scandals that came to the attention of the Reichstag. The first of these were the so-called Leist and Wehlan cases. In 1893 Heinrich Leist served as acting governor in the absence of Governor Eugen von Zimmerer. During that time Dahomean soldiers revolted. They had served the German colonial administration efficiently in military campaigns against oppositional chiefdoms in the colony's interior. It was said that they had been bought in their home country; in German Cameroon they were forced to work without pay for five years. To keep their families alive, the soldiers' wives were forced to prostitute their honor to whites and blacks. Acting Governor Leist used these women to service his guests and to carry out forced gardening labor, to which they objected. When the Dahomean soldiers finally refused to allow their wives to continue working for Leist, his reprisal was cruel and humiliating. He ordered the women to be stripped naked, placed over barrels, and beaten in the presence of their husbands, who were made to stand in formation. At that point the Dahomean soldiers tried to kill Leist and failed; however, they did kill another German. Leist then hanged all those Dahomeans who were unable to escape and sentenced the women to hard labor on a distant plantation. Wehlan's case, while less extreme, involved the burning of a number of native villages and the sexual abuse of native women.

The Reichstag discussed both cases. The Social Democratic leader August Bebel charged Wehlan with torturing, starving, mutilating, and killing a large number of natives.[13] Some of the parliamentary delegates asked that Leist be put on trial. The trial, which took place after some time in a military court in Potsdam, resulted in a verdict of guilty, and Leist was removed from his office and offered a position of equal rank but lower pay. His sentence was typical for cases of European cruelty to natives, and serves as key evidence that ill treatment and even the killing of natives were considered minor crimes.

The Reichstag debates on the Leist and Wehlan cases led to publicity, which in turn forced the government to act. In a letter of February 14, 1894, from the director of the Colonial Department of the Foreign Office in Berlin, Dr. Paul Kayser, to the colonial governor of Cameroon, Kayser referred to the debate and explained the urgency of working out legal rules that would help prevent the misuse of power by colonial officials in Cameroon. One could not aim to codify everything the way it was done by "civilized" people, he explained, but it was possible to elaborate a clear framework in which jurisdiction could function. As an example of such a framework, he pointed to the New Guinea Native Laws of 1888. This first letter from the Berlin colonial administration on legal matters related to Cameroon is interesting for its distinction between jurisdiction for colonial subjects and jurisdiction for "civilized" people. The principles of law and justice, as understood in Europe, were extended to the colonies but were also transformed, losing their universality in favor of a special relativity in conceptions of justice – a relativity itself imagined and created in Europe. While the German colonial administration relativized the universality of justice, that relativism did not admit the validity of justice as practiced by natives; that was dismissed as no justice at all.

Kayser's letter led to a discussion that in 1896 produced the first decree from an imperial chancellor (at that time, Chlodwig Hohenlohe-Schillingsfürst) dealing with jurisdiction over natives in all African protectorates. This decree legalized flogging as the standard penalty for minor offenses as well as for special situations that were considered crimes in the colony when committed by a native (for example, "insolence toward his master" [freches Benehmen gegen seinen Herrn], "laziness at work" [Faulheit im Dienst]). The decree specified the conditions under which flogging was to be carried out, such as the sort of whip to be used, and also stated that children under sixteen, Arabs, Indians, and women (this last probably as a result of the Leist scandal) were not to be whipped. Elsewhere in the decree other penalties were specified. The entire decree aimed to make penalties more humane and to avoid future criticism in the Reichstag, especially from the Social Democratic and Center parties. The historical record shows that the Berlin colonial administration found it necessary to send many reminders to the Cameroon officials, urging them to observe the decree strictly – an indication that those aims were not easy to attain.

The decree had another aim as well: to give European plantation owners the means to force natives to work for them. The labor question remained a problem in Cameroon up to the end of German colonial rule. Various strategies were developed to compel natives to give up their way of life and work for Europeans. One such measure was the introduction of a head tax, later changed to a hut tax. Another means was of a legal nature. The government refused to force natives to work – but once those same natives were under a labor contract, their employer was given legal means to force them to work.[14]

In the years between 1894 and 1898 and again in 1901, an intensive discussion about creating a colonial penal law was held by the Colonial Council (Kolonialrat), a body of experts established in 1890 to advise the Colonial Department. Many members of this body had colonial connections and even personal colonial business interests. The discussion in the Colonial Council shows clearly that different visions of colonization were in operation and that these visions could not easily be harmonized. Those members with colonial connections advocated laws that would serve the interests of the German plantation owners, and so they proposed penal laws that would give plantation owners maximal power over the natives – even including the right to force those not under contract to work on the plantations. They considered colonization as a matter of exploiting the colony's resources, and they saw the natives as one of several means for doing so. This group therefore criticized the German administration's practices and emphasized the need to rid it of philanthropic and Christian considerations. Only then would the natives be freely available for the benefit of colonists. A typical example of this argumentation can be seen in the minutes of the Colonial Council, at the point where Dr. Julius Scharlach, a lawyer with colonial business connections, protested against the idea of extending a uniform system of justice to the people in the colonies:

Above all he [Scharlach] misses, as the highest principle, the recognition of the superiority of the whites. One cannot and ought not to speak of any equalization of the blacks. . . . [E]very violation of the personal dignity of whites must be met with the severest punishments. One cannot avoid the fact that the natives of our protectorates are our subjects, and moreover subjects of an inferior race. It is simply insupportable to demand that the natives be treated as our equals. That they are not, and that they are not capable of reaching our cultural level even after a hundred years of freedom – that is shown by, among other things, the current conditions in the Negro republic of Haiti.[15]

Other members of the Colonial Council advocated the creation of laws that would conform to principles of law, humanity, and justice. This second group was responsive to pressure from the churches, Reichstag, and international opinion, which had already criticized the treatment of natives in the German colonies. This group privileged the principles of the Enlightenment and of modernization: colonization was to be a civilizing mission, as the Berlin Conference had stressed. Those principles had several philosophical implications, as we have seen: that all mankind is one and that all people have the same natural capabilities and rights; that mankind is perfectible by way of continuous progress from a primitive situation to intellectual and cultural perfection; and that the nonsimultaneous is simultaneous – that is, that people living in the same period can belong to different stages of human evolution. This second group within the Colonial Council correspondingly argued that penal colonial law ought to treat natives as human beings and to be a means of educating them to a higher standard of civilization. One such member of the Colonial Council was Dr. Herzog, who responded to Scharlach's comments as follows:

The formal objections that the previous speaker raised against the draft of Article 11 may be in part justified. But he goes too far in his demand that the average black understand the laws; even the average German is not always capable of understanding the text of our law books. His [Herzog's] objections are, however, directed primarily against the professional position of the previous speaker. The one-sided establishment of German rule cannot be justified, in any case not from the standpoint of civilization. The position of the lawyer Dr. Scharlach reminds one of that of the Spanish conquistadors. Taking into consideration the natives' more naive than evil character, the committee believed it ought to create milder laws and in so doing emphasize the educational impulse more than the deterrent one. Also he, the speaker [Herzog], cannot simply accept as dogma that every white is a sacrosanct and superior person.

That depends, just as much in the colonies as here in Germany, on the dignity of the individual. [16]

The reference to the attitude of the conquistadors is interesting. Indeed, this discussion of the Colonial Council is a sort of repetition of another discussion that had taken place in 1551 in the Spanish town of Vallodolid. On one side were Las Casas, Francisco de Vitoria, and Francisco López de Gómara, who argued that Indians were human beings and had to be treated as such. On the other side were the humanist Juan Gines Sepulveda and the Spanish colonists, who argued that Indians were not human beings and could not benefit from the privileges attached to that status.

A second discussion in the Colonial Council that took place in Berlin in 1897 exactly reproduced the same opposition; only the categories of the discourse had changed. In 1551 the position of Las Casas had won because it was in accordance with the interests of the church. In 1897 the legal project that was, in the end, adopted represented a compromise between the two positions.

It was not an easy task to couple humanistic discourse and civilizing aims on the one hand with a colonial reality based on violence on the other. Perhaps that is why those proposed laws were never promulgated. Instead, the drafts were sent to the colonies for further discussion there. One of the various reactions came from the district judge (Bezirksrichter) in Duala on July 15, 1901. His general comment drew attention to the idea that it was necessary to be familiar with natives' customs and legal concepts precisely in order to ensure that such customs and legal concepts were not included in the colonial jurisprudence. The goal ought to be, instead, to move away from those customs and concepts by way of carefully elaborated, appropriate laws that aimed at gradually changing them. The judge advocated a legal method that could transform the existing native mentality into a new one – which was precisely why the existing mentality had to be thoroughly studied. The judge stressed the difference between issuing a law in Europe and in a colonial situation. In Europe the jurisprudence was the expression of the legal conception or philosophy of the people, while in the colony it was the introduction of something new, unknown, and foreign. It had an educational function and a political and administrative goal. It was not possible to separate the three functions in the colony as they were in Europe.

The reactions from officials in the various German colonies showed how impressed they were with the comments from the judge in Cameroon. One consequence was that some of the proposed legal articles could be immediately put into practice in Cameroon, even though they had not been officially promulgated. A second consequence was that the governor of Cameroon gained more power over the implementation of existing laws and the formulation of new measures. The first effect of this power was an instruction from the governor of October 15, 1910, that established a difference between common-law penalties and disciplinary penalties: the common-law penalties had to be decided according to the German penal code, while the disciplinary penalties – importantly, these were all related to labor contracts – had to be decided according to special colonial laws and regulations.

This solution, based on the concept of evolution, did not solve the fundamental methodological problem of imposing a foreign law – the very problem described by the judge in Duala. But it did serve to reconcile the contradiction between respecting Enlightenment principles and serving the interests of the colonists. A number of letters from the governor to colonial officials make clear that most of the officials abused this distinction intentionally by recategorizing common-law and other cases that had to be decided according to the German penal code as disciplinary procedures, giving the officials much more autonomy and power.

The years 1906 and 1907 are generally considered to be an important turning point in German colonial policy. The Colonial Office was created, and a banker, Bernhard Dernburg, was appointed its colonial secretary. Dernburg was interested in improving the economic situation in the colonies, and he was convinced that this was only possible if the natives' overall condition was likewise improved. He therefore started what was called his "humane native policy" (humane Eingeborenenpolitik). He took the criticisms from Social Democrats and others in the Reichstag regarding the treatment of the natives very seriously, especially those concerning colonists' unmonitored use of whipping as an everyday penalty. Governor Jesco von Puttkamer of Cameroon, who favored the interests of colonists, was replaced by Theodor Seitz, who was determined to improve all aspects of the colonial administration there. The Reichstag even took the position that colonists ought to receive government support only if they respected the inalienable rights of the natives and contributed to the natives' economic development and even self-determination. The last colonial secretary, Dr. Wilhelm Solf, declared in a speech at the coastal town of Kribi in Cameroon, on September 2, 1913, that colonies were to prosper with the natives and for them, not against them or in spite of them.[17]

Such declarations showed clearly that the practice of colonial rule in Cameroon and the other German colonies had been contrary to the long-proclaimed goals of colonization and even to various decrees, regulations, and laws that aimed to protect the natives from colonists' arbitrary practices. The Colonial Institute, founded in 1898 in Hamburg, sought to improve the number and quality of colonial personnel. Yet the number of whites taken to court in, for example, the period of 1909–10 – 114 – suggests that the new measures did not have much impact on the condition of natives.[18] In the years just before the First World War, the chancellor and kaiser Wilhelm II disregarded petitions from the Duala people concerning their forced removal from their land, in violation of signed treaties. Through to the end of German colonial rule, even colonial authorities lacked much will to protect the interests of natives and implement legal agreements in the colonies.

There were thus contradictions in which the extension of modernization overseas became entangled from its very beginnings. Based on universal assumptions yet modifying them constantly, in the end the system displayed a regime of reason that cohabited with its opposite. As in Kafka's penal colony, colonial jurisdiction introduced procedures and penalties that were familiar to Europe but belonged to its past.[19] The facts that cruel bodily punishment, which had disappeared in Europe at the beginning of the nineteenth century, was reintroduced under colonial jurisdiction and that class-specific and race-specific justice, rather than equality before the law, were once more practiced testify to the complexity of the process. Colonization sought to export the Enlightenment, but the whole process brought a regression to phenomena of premodern times in Europe that from that very Enlightenment standpoint were seen as regrettable. Europeans were supposed to combat local alleged wildness to establish a civilized order, but colonization in fact established a reign of violence and injustice. The Europeans, who had succeeded in a Promethean enterprise to transform almost the whole world, could not organize it in a humane and just manner. Mahatma Gandhi, when asked what he thought of Western civilization, reportedly responded, "I think it would be a very good idea." Indeed, European modernization is still on the periphery of empire: an idea that becomes perverted and often transformed into its contrary when it is practiced in reality.

### NOTES

1. See Michel Foucault, *Madness and Civilization* (New York: Vintage, 1973), *The Birth of the Clinic* (New York: Vintage, 1975), and *Discipline and Punish* (New York: Vintage, 1979). See also Steven Bert and Douglas Kellner, *Postmodern Theory: Critical Interrogations* (New York: Guildford Press, 1991).

2. See, for example, my earlier contribution to that research: David Simo, "L'intel-

ligentsia allemande et la question coloniale: Les fondements idéologiques et culturels de la colonisation allemande," in L'Afrique et l'Allemagne de la colonisation à la coopération 1884–1886 (le cas du Cameroun), ed. Kum'a Ndumbe III (Yaoundé: Edition Africavenir, 1986), 181–202.

3. Wolfgang J. Mommsen, "Bismarck, the Concert of Europe, and the Future of West Africa, 1883–1885," in Ndumbe, L'Afrique et l'Allemagne, 17.

4. Kange Ewane, "L'émergé et l'immergé dans la conférence de Berlin," in Ndumbe, L'Afrique et l'Allemagne, 10.

5. Kange Ewane, "L'émergé et l'immergé," 12. "A l'égard de ces populations qui, pour la plupart, ne doivent pas être considérées comme se trouvant en dehors de la communauté du droit des gens, mais qui dans l'état présent des choses, ne sont guère aptes à défendre elles-mêmes leurs intérêts, la conférence a dû assurer le rôle d'un tuteur officieux. La nécessité d'assurer la conservation des indigènes, le devoir de les aider à atteindre un état politique et social plus élevé, l'obligation de les instruire et de les initier aux avantages de la civilisation, sont unanimement reconnus. C'est l'avenir même de l'Afrique qui est en cause."

6. See Leon Poliakov et al., Über den Rassismus. Sechzehn Kapitel zur Anatomie, Geschichte und Deutung des Rassenwahns (Frankfurt: Ullstein, 1984), 69.

7. See Kum'a Ndumbe III, "Les traités cameroun-germaniques (1884–1907)," in Ndumbe, L'Afrique et l'Allemagne, 42–68.

8. Basic sources for the legal discussion that follows can be found in Julius Ruppel, ed., Sammlung der in Kamerun zur Zeit geltenden völkerrechtlichen Verträge, Gesetze, Verordnungen und Dienstvorschriften mit Anmerkungen und Register (1912; repr., Ann Arbor: University Microfilms, n.d.), and in Jean Pierre Dubois Djoko, "Die Gerichtsbarkeit in den deutschen Kolonien am Beispiel Kamerun. Übersetzung und Kommentar ausgewählter Dokumente aus dem Nationalarchiv Kameruns (Jaunde)" (master's thesis, University of Yaoundé, Cameroon, 1998).

9. Harry R. Rudin, Germans in the Cameroons 1884–1914: A Case Study in Modern Imperialism (London: Jonathan Cape, 1938), 201.

10. Cited in Rudin, Germans in the Cameroons, 423.

11. Cited in Rudin, Germans in the Cameroons, 423. "Dieses Dokument ist von dem Herrn Konsul zum Zeichen seines Einverständnis unterzeichnet worden."

12. Rudin, Germans in the Cameroons, 198.

13. Adolf Rüger, "Der Aufstand der Polizeisoldaten (Dezember 1893)," in Kamerun unter deutscher Kolonialherrschaft: Studien, ed. Helmuth Stoecker (Berlin: Rütten & Loening, 1960), 1:144.

14. See Adolf Rüger, "Die Entstehung und Lage der Arbeiterklasse unter dem deutschen Kolonialregime Kamerun," in Stoecker, Kamerun unter deutscher Kolonialherrschaft, 1:149–213, and Karin Hausen, Deutsche Kolonialherschaft in Afrika: Wirtschaftsinteressen und Kolonialverwaltung vor 1914 (Zurich: Atlantis, 1970).

15. "Vor allem vermisse er als obersten Grundsatz die Anerkennung der Superiorität der Weissen. Von einer Gleichstellung der Schwarzen könne und dürfe nicht die Rede sein . . . [J]edes Vergehen gegen die persönliche Würde der Weissen müsse mit den schwersten Strafen belegt werden. Über die Thatsache, dass die Eingeborenen unserer Schutzgebiete Unterworfene sind und zwar Unterworfene einer inferioren Race könne man doch nicht hinwegkommen. Es sei ein schlechterdings unmögliches Verlangen, die Eingeborenen als Unseresgleichen zu behandeln. Dass sie es nicht sind, und dass sie auch nicht im Stande sind, selbst in hundertjähriger Freiheit auf unsere Stufe der Kultur zu kommen, das lehrten unter anderen die gegenwärtigen Zustände in der Neger-Republik Haiti." Archives Nationales du Cameroun, FAI/292/Allgemeine Bestimmung betr. Ausübung der Gerichtsbarkeit 1894–1909, Bd. 1, Kolonialrath, 4. Sitzungsperiode (1895–1898), Nr. 22, Bl. 1f.

16. "Die formalistischen Bedenken, die der Herr Vorredner [Scharlach] gegen die Fassung des Artikels 11 geltend gemacht habe mögen theilweise berechtigt sein. Zu weit ginge er aber in seiner Anforderung, dass der Durchschnitts-Schwarze die Gesetze verstehen müsse; auch der Durchschnitts-Deutsche sei nicht immer in der Lage, den Text unserer Gesetzbücher zu verstehen. Seine Bedenken richten sich aber hauptsächlich gegen den fachlichen Standpunkt des Herrn Vorredners. Die einseitige Etablierung der deutschen Herrschaft lasse sich nicht rechtfertigen, jedenfalls nicht vom Standpunkt der Civilisation. Der Standpunkt des Rechtsanwalts Dr. Scharlach erinnere an denjenigen der spanischen Konquistadoren. Mit Rücksicht auf den mehr naiven als bösartigen Charakter der Eingeboren habe der Ausschuss geglaubt, mildere Gesetze schaffen und dabei mehr Gewicht auf das Erzieherische als auf das Abschreckende Moment legen zu sollen. Auch könne er, Redner, nicht ohne weiteres als Dogma hinnehmen, dass jeder Weisse eine geheiligte und überlegene Person sei. Auf die Würde des Einzelnen käme es doch in den Kolonien ebensoviel an, wie hier bei uns." Archives Nationales du Cameroun, FAI/292/Allgemeine Bestimmung betr. Ausübung der Gerichtsbarkeit 1894–1909, Bl. 2.

17. Engelbert Mveng, *Histoire du Cameroun* (Paris: Présence africaine, 1963), 317.

18. Rudin, *Germans in the Cameroons*, 201.

19. These are described in Foucault, *Discipline and Punish*.

# PART 3

# Colonial Racism and Antisemitism

PASCAL GROSSE

# What Does German Colonialism Have to Do with National Socialism?

## A Conceptual Framework

What does German colonialism have to do with National Socialism? To date this has been perhaps the most challenging question for much of the historical research on German colonialism. At stake, more often implicitly than explicitly, is the extent to which German colonialism is related to the upsurge of the National Socialist party and, later, regime in Germany and Europe between 1920 and 1945. Historians ask whether the German colonial empire served as an important or even indispensable precursor to the National Socialist racial state.

In the introduction to her book *Colonial Fantasies: Conquest, Family, and Nation in Precolonial Germany, 1770–1870*, Susanne Zantop addressed the possible intersections between German colonialism and National Socialism explicitly. She pleaded for a contextualization of the Holocaust in the larger historical framework of colonial fantasies, especially fantasies of conquest, mastery, and paternalism. However, rather than making a concise argument as to how German colonialism was intertwined with National Socialism, she was mostly concerned to delineate the contours of the problem:

> It would be wrong to conceive of colonial fantasies in terms of a linear, teleological development that began with a genuine curiosity about difference and ended in the Herero massacre of 1906 and the extermination of the Jews in the Third Reich. Of course there is always a danger of reading German history backward from the Holocaust. . . . While the Holocaust was certainly not the only possible outcome of German eighteenth- and nineteenth-century history, it is the outcome with which we must contend. We need to analyze and explain why it was not the enlightened models of tolerance and assimilation that prevailed, but racism, xenophobia, sexism, and aggressive expansionism. [1]

Zantop's exposition of the problem might be read as a research agenda for scholars of both German colonialism and National Socialism. According to her, three points are crucial for any argument of how German colonialism might be related to National Socialism. First, there is no straightforward link between the study of human difference from the eighteenth century onward and the physical extermination of racially defined groups in the twentieth century. More complex interpretations are needed to show the odd paths that those interested in anthropological difference took toward genocide(s). Second, though the Holocaust is not the end of German history, it nevertheless constitutes its defining moment. Therefore, any study of German colonialism cannot avoid addressing the question of what the implications of Germany's colonial engagement were in the larger context of modern German history, and specifically in the context of National Socialism. Third, historians of German (and European) colonialism have to confront the ambiguity that most colonial systems displayed enlightened tolerance and humanitarianism alongside racially inspired attitudes of dominance and subjugation. Consequently, morally inspired judgments that draw upon dichotomies such as "good and evil" and the like are inappropriate, as are efforts to establish direct historical continuities or discontinuities between dialectics that were inherent in enlightened discourses on anthropological differences and their subsequent interpretations.

To address the question of how German colonialism might have shaped the emergence of the National Socialist racial state means establishing a link between two historical periods in German history that are judged to have a completely opposite impact on the nation's historical memory. Whereas National Socialism has been the historical watershed for Germany's collective memory and political culture ever since 1945, until the last decade, with a few significant exceptions, German historiography tended to dismiss German colonialism as an ephemeral phenomenon with little or no residual meaning for German society and culture. [2] German colonialism has not come entirely to the forefront of historiographical interest, at least not in Germany itself, but research on this subject has recently intensified. Nevertheless, situating German colonialism in the context of Germany's general history remains a task undone. The main reason for this shortcoming seems to be that historians in Germany have not translated adequately the notion of "Empire" as used in research in France and Britain – as the conflict-laden common denominator of expansionist, exploitative, missionary, and humanitarian aspirations overseas as well as migration patterns over time and space – into the specific historical context of Germany in the nineteenth and twentieth centuries. This, in turn, is due to a self-centered nationalist approach to German history that still prevails. [3]

Some more (or less) prudent attempts have been made to relate Germany's colonial history to National Socialism. These historians have not always borne in mind that the search for possible common denominators in a straightforward comparative approach simplifies the historical specificity of both phenomena to be compared. Marxist scholarship, for instance, predominantly advanced by the extensive research on German colonialism in the former German Democratic Republic in the 1960s and 1970s, held that imperialism and National Socialism were both expressions of late capitalist society. [4] While there can be no doubt that capitalism, with its inherent need for resources, markets, and labor, played an important role in the shaping of nineteenth- and twentieth-century imperialism, such overarching concepts can neither satisfactorily account for why fascism failed to develop in other leading expansionist societies in the West nor explain key particularities of National Socialism, such as the prominence of racial politics. Using a quite different approach, a few scholars have singled out circumscribed atrocities in the course of Germany's colonial history, such as medical experiments in concentration camp–like institutions or the near annihilation of the Herero and Nama during the war in German Southwest Africa, and have interpreted these instances as direct precursors to the politics of genocide and the Holocaust. [5] While there are some apparent structural similarities between these events, these arguments assume, at least implicitly, the same ideological and political intentions regarding the politics of genocide. More convincing would be the establishment of a more specific, and also causal, link between the colonial order and the structure of National Socialist rule.

Hannah Arendt's work on totalitarianism still offers the single most influential intellectual framework for theorizing a linkage between the era of imperialism and National Socialism. [6] According to Arendt, during the late nineteenth century European imperialism served as the laboratory of amalgamated racial doctrines and anonymous bureaucratic policy. At the beginning of the twentieth century, these ideas were reimported back to Europe, where they were fused with a kind of newly racialized anti-Semitism and reinforced by the experience of World War I. Though Arendt's work offers a dynamic model for explaining the transfer of racial ideologies from a colonial to a European context, her work inevitably raises more questions than it answers. For instance Arendt refers mostly to British and French, rather than German, colonial activities to substantiate her thesis. But the key problem remains Germany's singularity, for why – among the many European extreme right-wing national movements that emerged after World War I – did Germany's National Socialist variant come to power? And once in power, why did it establish a racial order with all the ultimate consequences of its ideological core, despite Germany's relatively short colonial experience? If German colonialism led in some causal way to National Socialism, then the German colonial order must have been different from that of its European rivals. After all the dominant colonial powers, Great Britain and France, remained democracies and stood in opposition to the dictatorships that came to power in most of interwar Europe. Such lingering questions point to one of the major tensions inherent in this kind of comparative approach.

What I would like to offer here is a framework for approaching the possible connections between German colonialism and National Socialism. Rather than argue for a direct linkage between the two, I want to dispose of the problematic logic of continuity or discontinuity that still organizes historical thinking on the topic. I propose an approach based on correspondences between the two historical events instead of assuming direct lines of causality leading from one to the other. The substance of those correspondences seems to lie in a shared governing structure based on a common biopolitical intellectual foundation – namely, eugenicist ideas of racial selection, racial reproduction, and territorial expansion, which I call the "racial order."[7] In the colonial context, eugenics not only implied the racialization of all aspects of the colonial experience in terms of biological categories, but, more important, also introduced policies of racial reproduction.[8] By racial reproduction I mean the German colonial state's intention of allowing procreation only among particular racially defined groups as a means of establishing and perpetuating white supremacy, which ultimately led to the formation of a "racial state." I scrutinize this particular correspondence in three crucial areas: the drive to reformulate the relation between race and space in the early twentieth century; the emergence of racialized citizenship as a new concept of nationality; and violence and genocide in relation to the idea of an impending global "race war."

I moreover argue that rather than viewing Germany's colonial experience overseas as a necessary precondition for National Socialist racial politics, we need to look elsewhere for what distinguishes the German colonial experience from, for example, that of Great Britain and France. There was probably not any innate difference among those metropoles' forms of colonial rule, but there certainly was in their experiences of decolonization. While the major colonial powers underwent a process of decolonization much later and as a result of independence movements in the colonies themselves, Germany was stripped of its colonial possessions as a direct consequence of its defeat in World War I, which left a complete vacuum in the sphere of expansionism exactly when expansionist aspirations had reached their height. I therefore suggest that Germany's postcolonial experience – what might be called "colonialism without colonies" – became the fundamental factor in the interwar radicalization of pre–World War I ideas and practices of expansionist biopolitics.

## Race and Space

What was the spatial focus of nineteenth- and twentieth-century German expansionism? Historical research has traditionally considered eastern Europe to be the geographical target of Germany's expansionist drive, while writing off overseas colonialism as a marginal episode. Nevertheless, aspirations for colonial adventures overseas existed well before the onset of formal German colonialism in the 1880s.[9] The historiographical attention to the East obviously derives its validity from the experiences of the two World Wars, during which Germany sought to extend its national territory permanently on the European continent, in particular in eastern Europe, while efforts to enlarge overseas territories seemed to be sidelined. It is interesting to note that this same historiography has been reluctant to describe the German historical experience in eastern Europe since the eighteenth century as "colonialism." Only recently, some research has challenged that dismissal of the concept of colonialism to analyze German politics in eastern Europe.[10] Certainly, eastern and southeastern European history since the eighteenth century could be adequately conceptualized in this way, at least in part, given that Germany played a prominent role there through formal and informal colonial activities.

Most Germans were not concerned with colonialist adventures, whether overseas or on the European continent. Germany's colonial aspirations were largely class specific. The key proponents of overseas colonialism were located in certain segments of the bourgeoisie (Bürgertum): the intelligentsia, bureaucracy, and tradespeople. Before 1914 overseas colonialism became an important representation to these people of their own growing importance in society, and it became a means of usurping the aristocratic Prusso-German state. Conversely, interests of the old and new aristocratic Prussian elites, both in the agricultural and in the industrial sector, relied heavily on the European East. Germany's expansionist drive from unification until the end of the nine-

teenth century therefore mirrored to some extent tensions between the bourgeoisie and aristocracy in the Prusso-German state. In the Wilhelmine era the
institutionalization of radical Right politics in powerful extraparliamentary
lobbies such as the Pan-German League, the German Colonial Society, the
Navy League, and many others could partially overcome those sociopolitical
divides and turn German expansionism into a common national goal with
the intention of appealing to the masses, at least at the level of rhetoric. [11]
From the beginning of the twentieth century onward, the goals of enlarging
Germany's share of global influence, markets, and labor both overseas and
on the continent were no longer competing priorities, but rather two sides
of the same coin. The particular roles of German bourgeois elites in German
politics prior to World War I, their transformation after World War I, and their
eventual support for the National Socialist regime are all vital to any argument
linking German overseas colonialist aspirations to the drive to form a compact
racialist empire in Europe. [12]

From the 1880s through the war aims of September 1914, overseas and continental expansionism were linked by the prevailing military and political doctrine that the nascent German overseas empire could grow only through a
victorious war against the other colonial powers on European soil. [13] During
this time a more aggressive bourgeois expansionism had the potential of sub-
verting the existing international order. Any war between the European powers also implied revisiting the existing global order and international colonial system. Indeed, during both World Wars the realization of the ambitious
colonization project in Africa depended partly on the victory over France and
eventually also Great Britain. Rather than positing an antagonism between
Germany's continental and overseas expansionism, we should see them as
two complementary, interrelated, and often ambivalent developments in the
history of German expansionism. Germany, the only major European power
besides Italy whose expansionist drive was directed both overseas and on the
continent itself (matched in this regard only by the United States), saw specific
tensions in its politics that differed from those of traditional overseas colonial
powers such as Great Britain, France, and the Netherlands and also from those
of the continental colonial powers Austria, Russia, and the Ottoman Empire.

We can see the complementarity of continental and overseas expansionism
in the shared ideological core of biologism. Since the late nineteenth century,
German expansionism both in eastern Europe and overseas was linked to a
new, biopolitically inspired discourse that the Pan-German movement publicly
dominated, but which drew followers from beyond that movement as well. [14]

This biologism can also be seen as a fundamental, general "eugenic consensus" among the German bourgeoisie. [15] Whereas for eastern Europe biopolitics was equated with *Volkstum*, a term referring to the preservation of the German *Kulturnation* inside and outside the formal boundaries of the German state, for the overseas empire the discourse revolved around the category of "race" (*Rasse*). In the contemporary biological understanding of society, however, culture and race were essentially synonymous. That is, "culture" signified an expression of biologically inherited and unchangeable traits, while physical markers, such as skin color, represented merely the visible signs of a defined and permanent cultural state. In this sense "cultural" politics in the East and racial politics in the colonies often referred to the same underlying ideas: those of late nineteenth-century biologism.

The innovative synthesis between spatial expansionism and biopolitics is readily evident in colonial racial policies, in contrast to the less obvious biologistic foundations of eastern European expansionism. This was largely because the colonial racial discourse was new, straightforward, and outspoken. But colonial racial policies were not meant to be an end in themselves. Instead, they were intended as a means of establishing and preserving dominance – that is, ensuring white supremacy over distant possessions. Of course such doctrines remained trapped in ambivalent assumptions about the true nature of racial differences, which is the reason why the persons involved in these practices and institutions were forever working to catch up with goals created by their own imaginations. The idiosyncrasies inherent in the establishment of a colonial racial order became apparent not least when the ultimately unresolvable question of who should be classified as "native" was posed. [16] In a settler society such as German Southwest Africa, the negotiations between inclusion in and exclusion from an imagined corporate and homogenized white-settler society produced a system of gradations of whiteness. [17] While the black-white dichotomy lay at the foundation of the white supremacist discourse of European rule over Africans, the idea of gradations of whiteness undermined that very dichotomy. Here we see a close correspondence between the shaky racial order of a German colonial society and the fragility of the allegedly inclusive notion of the German *Volksgemeinschaft* of the Third Reich.

In the wake of World War I, German colonialism's synthesis of territorial expansion and a biopolitics of race was one available model for expansionist aspirations both overseas and on the continent. That synthesis was an attempt to correlate geography with political, cultural, and economic power, expressed in terms of culture and/or race. The ultimate aim of the Nazis' reorganization of race and space became evident during World War II with their plans to completely redraw the eastern European ethnogeographical map. The persecution and extermination of eastern European Jewry was their central goal; in addition, the Nazis sought to homogenize – that is, to cleanse – the existing ethnically mixed eastern European landscape. This, in turn, produced overwhelming migrations of civilians who had been designated German or non-German back and forth between the German fatherland and its eastern European colonial annexes. German administrators were barely able to handle these migrations, which in part came to their paradoxical conclusion with the "expulsion" of the Germans from the newly formed Eastern European countries right after World War II. The Nazis envisaged a classical colonial system with an Aryan-German oligarchy and a non-Aryan, mainly Slavic, enslaved work force whose only justification for living was to derive from the ability to work (*Tüchtigkeit*). The plans to reestablish a compact colonial empire in the heart of the African continent that emerged from the National Socialist bureaucracy at the beginning of World War II were presumably driven by the same desire to implement an old-fashioned slavery-like regime. [18] However, the old doctrine that such overseas ambitions could only be realized through a military victory on the European continent still held true, and so these colonial plans were confined to the bureaucratic drawing board until spring 1943 and then, as the final victory did not arrive, finally dismissed.

## Racialized Citizenship and Racial Reproduction

The legal counterpart of the attempts to reformulate the relationship between race and space was the concept of racialized citizenship. Racialized citizenship emerged from the colonial context after 1900 but also paralleled efforts in Imperial Germany to ethnicize citizenship in the eastern regions. [19] Racialized citizenship comprised the legal framework for granting a graded system of membership in the community of German citizens (*Staatsangehörigkeit*) as well as granting full-fledged rights in the public sphere (*Staatsbürgerschaft*) along racial and/or ethnic boundaries. Such legal efforts were not ends in themselves; rather, they reflected the deep-seated cultural change from an assimilationist to a dissimilationist stance in German legal and demographic politics. This dissimilationist stance was, moreover, not particular to German colonialism; it mirrored the agenda of the day in international colonialism from the turn of the century. [20]

Right from the start of German colonial rule, colonial law introduced a basic distinction between whites, who held almost all the rights of citizens, and so-called "natives," essentially colonial subjects without full citizenship, who were roughly equated with nonwhites.[21] "Natives" could become German citizens by marrying German men, by being born to German fathers, or by naturalization. In the years thereafter, the concept of racialized citizenship took on a more distinct shape.

A few years before 1900, colonial civil servants in German Southwest Africa debated how to bar racially mixed descendants of German fathers from becoming Germans with the same rights as German colonists. In 1905, 1906, and 1912 local colonial administrations or the central colonial administration issued bans on mixed marriages for German Southwest Africa, German East Africa, and Samoa, respectively. In the German metropole itself, however, sexual relations and marriages between German citizens and colonial subjects, mostly involving men from Togo and Cameroon, were not at all regulated, although it can be assumed that the number of such marriages exceeded the number in the colonies.[22] In 1912 and 1913, when the Reichstag debated revisions to the German citizenship law, the colonial administration called for limiting German citizenship to whites. Nationalist lobbies such as the Pan-German League and the German Colonial Society supported such a limitation and furthermore advocated a bill against (colonial) miscegenation (Reichsmischlingsgesetz). These are strong indications that the focus of attention regarding colonial mixed marriages and their demographic consequences was shifting from the colonies to the metropole. The discussions among civil servants, scientists, and politicians in and out of the colonial administration regarding how to bar nonwhites from full German citizenship in the years prior to Nazi rule did not so much reflect an actual state of affairs but rather inflated possible future demographic developments into a scenario of impending racial decline. In the end, however, the government of that day refrained from inserting race into the law as a category to define the German nation – not because of conviction, but rather mainly because of legal and diplomatic reservations about the possibility of accurately defining nonwhites and "natives."

Even though the eugenicist concept of racialized citizenship was not formally enacted in the 1913 revision of the citizenship code, it already posed a challenge before World War I to two basic principles of traditional bourgeois society. First, because mixed-race children of German men were no longer considered German, the bans on racially mixed marriages undermined the concept of patriarchal lineage and loosened ties formerly thought unbreakable between the family unit and the German nation.[23] Second, because radical eugenicist thinking focused on sexual intercourse rather than marriage per se, colonial eugenicist discourse detached procreation from its social and legal contexts and subordinated male sexuality to the dictates of racial reproduction – that is, ethnically pure reproduction.[24] In sum, the pre–World War I discourse on racially mixed marriages, miscegenation, and sexual restrictions along the color line should be understood as the crystallization of new eugenic thinking that was on the upswing in Germany and western Europe during and after the war.[25] In Germany the colonial situation sharpened and focused the visions of eugenic discourse in an exemplary fashion before that discourse was clearly delineated in the metropole. It remains striking, however, that the regulation of German men's sexual drives in distant parts of the world seemed so completely irrelevant to the German metropole itself.

It could be argued that National Socialist restrictions on German citizenship did not go beyond what had already been discussed prior to World War I.[26] The Nuremberg Laws, for example, introduced the distinction between a *Reichsbürger* – that is, a person holding full rights as a citizen, and a *Staatsangehöriger*, a second-class German citizen who merely held German nationality. The latter group encompassed mainly those non-Aryan Germans who held German citizenship but could not be expatriated easily because they resided in German territory. However, it is important to note that the Nuremberg Laws regulated marriages and proscribed all sexual intercourse between non-Aryans and Aryans, including Aryan men. In this sense the dictates of racial purity trumped male sexual freedom and circumscribed the prerogatives otherwise enjoyed by Aryan men under National Socialism. During World War II the Germans brought racialized citizenship to the conquered parts of Europe, racializing their victims in legal terms.[27]

Despite correspondences between the colonial situation and the policies of fully racialized citizenship in Germany during the National Socialist dictatorship, it is crucial to bear in mind that colonial and National Socialist citizenship policies were each implemented against very different political backdrops. In the pre–World War I colonial context, the concept of racialized citizenship was gradually evolving and served mainly as the colonial administration's strategy for imposing the utopia of white supremacy in some distant places overseas. Conversely, the racialization of citizenship in mainland Germany after 1933 did not serve as a strategy for imposing colonial rule, but rather it was aimed at ethnically cleansing the German population in a legal framework that was propagated as an act of popular self-defense. The concept of racialized citizenship was the most marked and readily distinguishable effect of the early twentieth-century eugenicist discourse on racial purity, yet it could take on different expressions depending on historical circumstances. [28]

## Genocide and the "Race War"

Perhaps the strongest correspondence between German colonialism and National Socialism stems from violence and atrocities based on racial criteria. Does the near annihilation of the Herero and Nama during the war in German Southwest Africa, which was carried out in fulfillment of General Lothar von Trotha's "extermination order,"[29] represent systematic genocide in a total war setting as the consequence of specific structural conditions put in place by the German (colonial) state? Or was violence in the colonial situation merely a means – though particularly aggressive – of resolving conflicts produced by exploration, conquest, the exploitation of resources, and ensuing cultural clashes known from colonial histories anywhere overseas? To date the answer to this question remains open, as it can only be addressed by a comparative approach that looks in detail at colonial warfare in other settings at that time, such as elsewhere in Africa, in Indochina, in the Dutch East Indies, or in the Ottoman Empire. This line of inquiry – asking whether German colonialism was fundamentally different, and in particular more violent, than that of other European powers – itself has a history dating back to World War I. Already at the time of the Paris Peace Conference in 1919, the Entente powers produced memoranda and collections of evidence that were intended to prove the Germans' incapability of ruling over "indigenous people" and to justify stripping Germany of its colonies. [30] However, evidence for that fundamentally different style of colonialism has been scarce and largely relies on isolated measures such as the mixed-marriage bans.

It is important to note possible differences between German colonial atrocities and atrocities committed under National Socialist rule. For instance one can argue that the extermination of European Jewry and other biologically or ethnically defined groups was meant to be a definite "Final Solution" with no other outcome, while in the colonies genocide or near annihilation of circumscribed groups was one of several forms of cultural encounter and conflict. This argument seems to hold particularly true for nineteenth-century colonies with a large number of European immigrants aiming at establishing neo-European nations, such as those in the United States, Australia, New Zealand, and South Africa. After the turn of the century, the eugenicist response to colonial policies was, however, to criticize the senseless loss of "valuable" lives thought to be indispensable for exploiting the colonies' natural resources. Indeed, the colonial administration made strong efforts to identify colonial subjects according to particular biological criteria in order to tap them more efficiently as a labor force, both in tropical colonies such as Togo and in settlement colonies such as German Southwest Africa. [11] Ultimately, the correspondence between colonialist practices of violence and extermination policies during National Socialism lies not so much in the intentional physical extermination of racially defined groups, but rather in the drive to select, in systematic fashion, groups of the population according to racial criteria as a foundation of the racial state. Under these circumstances physical extermination can become an option, but it is not a goal in itself as it was in the case of the Holocaust.

While much has been written about links between German colonial warfare and the Holocaust, another link between European colonialism and National Socialism has been much less discussed yet appears more securely founded: the perception of war in Europe as "race war." In German historiography the term "race war" has often referred to the Holocaust, and in some cases also to the eastern European theater of World War II, where the Nazis sought to redraw the ethnogeographical map. [12] Long before National Socialism, however, "race war" referred to the colonial context and implied the supposedly fundamental antagonism between white colonists and nonwhite colonial subjects. In the years preceding World War I, German politicians also began applying the concept of an impending "race war" to the European context as a result of developments during the European arms race. In the course of that arms race, the Allies "discovered" colonial subjects, so to speak, as a new strategic factor in a future war with Germany and recruited 650,000 nonwhite soldiers from around the world to face the Germans on the European battlefields. [13] These colonial subjects were to serve as paid mercenaries who were to compensate for the Allies' demographic deficit vis-à-vis Germany. The German military administration, supported by the nationalist lobbies such as the German Army League and Pan-German League, made propagandistic use of the Allies' plans. They themselves expected to introduce German colonial subjects into war in the colonies, not in Europe. After France, Britain, and Russia did in fact deploy their colonial subjects as soldiers and workers on European soil to defeat Germany and its allies, "racial affront" became the dominant intellectual model. In no European country did the public discourse on the use of colonial soldiers in Europe carry the racial connotations than it did in Imperial Germany. In these discursive battles Germany stylized itself as the sole protector of the racial order in Europe and the colonial order overseas. For the German elites, then, World War I represented not only a fight for Germany's rightful share of world power, but also a struggle against the whole world in the name of the white race. Faced with colonial subjects as combatants, Germany saw itself fighting, in this sense, a classical colonial war on European soil.

World War I led not only to the deployment of colonial soldiers in Europe and the accompanying propaganda; it also set in motion new patterns of colonial migration between the colonies and the metropole. Until then most colonial subjects came to the metropole temporarily, for example as seamen, students, or participants in colonial exhibitions or parades. Their presence in Europe was therefore geographically restricted (for example, to the vicinity of ports, with their traditional ethnic mixture) or confined to single individuals who lived in isolation from their countrymen and did not form ethnic communities. Although the quantitative impact of post–World War I colonial migration is not known, its quality definitely changed: people came for social, economic, and political reasons and often settled in Europe permanently. Furthermore, interwar Europe became the meeting place for worldwide anticolonial movements, with and without ties to communism, and for African Americans inspired by Pan-Africanist politics and bohemian art and leisure and who sought a better life than what was available in the United States. In short, post–World War I metropolitan societies became more ethnically diverse by virtue of colonial subjects' claims to political and economic participation.

Germans' only actual experience with this new pattern of colonial migration took place during and after the occupation of parts of the left bank of the Rhine by the French army between 1920 and 1935. Until the mid-1920s colonial soldiers – predominantly from the Maghreb – belonged to the occupation force. The main German response to the French occupation was a hugely inflated propaganda campaign between 1920 and 1924 against the "Black Disgrace on the Rhine."[34] The campaign denounced France as an unsuitable colonial power and called for Germany's own reinstatement as such. In highly symbolic fashion, the use of colonial soldiers in the French occupation reversed, on German soil, the colonial situation between whites and blacks.

In that episode and in others, Germans expressed their reaction to non-white individuals' presumed infiltration of European societies in biological terms, especially as the threat of miscegenation. The idea of Germans being the guardians of the white race, of course, already carried strong biological implications, particularly targeted against any kind of race mixture. Rather than exploring the biological and sociological implications of race mixing in an open-ended manner, however, most scientific and political commentary sought to demonstrate that the consequences of race mixing for white societies were negative. Race mixture, implicitly and explicitly, became the antipode to race purity, propagated through the same discourse. It was evident that miscegenation between Europeans and colonial subjects in continental Europe was quantitatively a minor phenomenon. Nevertheless, the concept of biological infiltration from the outside world came to pervade ideas of change, threat, subversion, and destabilization of the existing order, and racial miscegenation became the catchphrase for those ideas.

The inclusion of the colonial world in prewar European military planning, the use of colonial soldiers against Germany, and the subsequent colonial migration in Europe have to be considered together as developments that shaped Germans' perceptions of intra-European politics as "race war." This perception itself suggests a link between European colonialism and National Socialist racial politics. In Germany's immediate postcolonial history between the two World Wars, the vacuum created by the loss of the colonies encouraged Germans' belief in their country's role as protector of the white race in Europe and the traditional colonial order. The idea of "race war," launched prior to World War I, survived throughout the interwar period. Perhaps World War I's most important contribution to this logic was the conclusion that a future "race war" would not be confined to overseas but rather would need to be fought in Europe itself, not only against the colonial subjects of the traditional colonial metropoles but also against the colonial or semicolonial people living in eastern Europe.

German colonialism and National Socialism share important characteristics: both called for a racial order based on racial reproduction as the foundation of the state; both sought, at least in part, to replace the classic nation-state with a racial state; both implied the dissolution of the bourgeois family through the complete subordination of sexuality to racial purity; and both entailed an expansionist drive to reproduce this racial order elsewhere. What does German colonialism ultimately have to do with National Socialism? The most singular significance of German colonialism lies exactly in what makes it appear as a likely precursor to National Socialism: the emergence of modern colonial racial politics as a model for the formation of an expansionist bourgeois racial state, in accordance with the liberal biopolitical paradigms of the day. This is especially true after 1900, when a strong bourgeois reformist movement embraced German overseas expansionism and infused it with the spirit of eugenics. Moreover, efforts to disentangle social relations between colonizers and colonized on racial grounds went hand in hand with efforts to import the racial order of the colonial world back into the body of Germany. Through their attempts to organize the world as a dichotomy between whites and "coloreds," colonial racial politics stirred up new tensions concerning whether the interests of the nation should be subordinated to race – tensions that were never resolved before the outbreak of hostilities in World War I.

Nevertheless, despite the clear parallels between colonialism and National Socialism, I conclude that German colonialism was less a prerequisite for the emergence of National Socialist racial politics than an expression of the same intellectual eugenicist model at an earlier time and in a different historical setting. For the crucial problem remains that there is no convincing evidence to date that German colonial rule differed from that of other colonial powers. Formalized bans on mixed marriages do not alone indicate a "special path" (Sonderweg) leading from German colonialism to National Socialism. Neither does the fact that many eugenically inspired German colonialists were later to be found eagerly working for the National Socialist regime. Their cooperation or collaboration with National Socialism does not in itself indicate causality or meaningful, structural continuity across different epochs. And while German colonialism imagined an ideal state organized around the inclusion and exclusion of specific, racially defined collectives, it was only under National Socialism that the exclusion of racially defined groups ultimately gave way to their physical extermination as an end in itself.

Rather than making claims of continuity, we would do well to focus on what distinguished Germany from other European colonial powers: the traumatic defeat in World War I and the "premature" end of its colonial rule. After the Allies stripped Germany of its colonial possessions, Germans engaged in a dialectic of "colonialism without colonies" that perpetuated pre-1880s escapist colonial fantasies of a powerful imperialistic Germany and mixed them with militarized fantasies of dominance through racial reproduction that had developed during Germany's short-lived formal colonial rule. Radicalized by the experience of defeat in a total war, this fusion functioned as the paradigm for the Nazi revision of the postwar order – a revision that eventually led to World War II.

The transition period between the pre–World War I arms race and the dispossession of Germany as a colonial power is crucial to understanding the relationship between German colonialism and National Socialism, and it has yet to be further developed in conceptual terms. It is true that many aspects of Germany's immediate postcolonial history were neither specific nor surprising. Like decolonization processes in other European countries, the loss of overseas empire left a political and cultural vacuum in Germany. During the nineteenth century, colonies had become psychological and social attributes of great powers' wealth and achievement. The persistence of procolonial sentiment throughout the interwar period in Germany, the aim of which was simply to reestablish a traditional colonial empire, is not surprising and indeed existed in all postcolonial European powers. Colonialist activities after 1920 drew support from the wider German protests against the peace settlement and from the feeling that Germany's prewar colonial record had been unjustly criticized. Colonialist agitation provided a platform both for the new right-wing power holders who were to run the National Socialist state and for the old colonial experts from the Kaiserreich.

There were some aspects that are specific to the German case of decolonization and that were not shared later by the major European powers of the time such as Great Britain, France, and the Netherlands when they lost their overseas possessions. First, in contrast to other European experiences, decolonization for Germany came about with no power conflict between colonizers and colonial subjects, but rather through diplomacy. Germany's decolonization was therefore an issue among the European powers and the United States and not shaped by the situation coloniale. German politicians responded by seeking to antagonize and create tensions among the Allies. Second, that particular aspect not only underpinned the self-righteous argument that German colonists and administrators had not mistreated colonial subjects, but even that the inhabitants of the former German colonies wished to have the Germans back as their rulers. German politicians' and German society's experience of decolonization of an overseas empire was not shared by any other European power after World War I (setting aside the specific decolonization processes of Austria and the Ottoman Empire as continental colonial powers). Germany was thus cut off from new developments within the international colonial system and in particular from changes in social relations in the colonies and Europe brought about by colonial migration. The true importance of the persisting colonial imaginary after World War I was that this imaginary was not counterbalanced by new experiences in the field or by any actual colonial policies (other than diplomatic efforts to regain the colonies). Germany's "colonialism without colonies" in the interwar period made possible uninhibited projections and plans driven by ideology and sentiments of the lost empire and lacking the checks inherent in practical conflict and negotiation. Third, the German colonial movement readily embraced National Socialism even before the Nazi Party took power. In many other European colonial powers, ardent colonialists and white colonists reemigrating to the metropole often took traditionalist and conservative political positions, especially during the post–World War II process of decolonization. The rapprochement of the German colonial movement with the political right wing was different, and it deserves specific mention. The Nazis, with their strong anticapitalist and antiliberal support, were not natural allies for the traditionally bourgeois and socially exclusive circles of colonialists, who had reservations about appealing to the masses. Yet National Socialists and colonialists met in the arena of racial politics. Both gave issues of race paramount importance for explaining current affairs and redirecting the future of Germany and the world.

Germany's postcolonial history began with World War I. However, many elements of Weimar and National Socialist postcolonial politics were already present before Germany was stripped of its colonies: the belief in the need to fight a European war to extend its colonial possessions; the reorientation of racial politics in eugenic terms as a means to establish power; and the opening of colonial politics to a wider public. German colonial history in the interwar years was the logical extension of the baggage with which Germany entered the war – that is, ideas of reorganizing space and race in Europe and overseas, as German radical nationalists had advocated before the war. As it happened, the war left Germany without a colonial empire but with a role as self-appointed guardian of the racial order in Europe and the colonial order elsewhere. This very line of thought lay at the heart of the idea of a German "Empire" between World War I and the end of World War II, both on the European continent and overseas.

NOTES

I would like to thank Jeffrey Schneider for his helpful critique of earlier versions of this essay and Lora Wildenthal for her patience and editorial skills.

1. Susanne Zantop, *Colonial Fantasies: Conquest, Family, and Nation in Precolonial Germany, 1770–1870* (Durham: Duke University Press, 1997), 16.

2. This tendency is particularly obvious in the master narratives of German history such as Hans-Ulrich Wehler, *Von der "Deutschen Doppelrevolution" bis zum Beginn des Ersten Weltkrieges 1849–1914*, vol. 3, *Deutsche Gesellschaftsgeschichte* (Munich: C. H. Beck, 1995), and Thomas Nipperdey, *Machtsstaat vor der Demokratie*, vol. 2, *Deutsche Geschichte 1866–1918* (Munich: C. H. Beck, 1992), in which the German colonial experience is almost exclusively discussed in terms of diplomatic and military strategy.

3. Sebastian Conrad's recent plea for transnational perspectives in German historiography argues against this longstanding, narrow interpretation of German his-

tory. Sebastian Conrad, "Doppelte Marginalisierung: Plädoyer für eine transnationale Perspektive auf die deutsche Geschichte," *Geschichte und Gesellschaft* 28 (2002): 145–69.

4. Horst Gründer, "Kolonialismus und Marxismus: Der deutsche Kolonialismus in der Geschichtsschreibung der DDR," *Geschichtswissenschaft in der DDR*, vol. 2, ed. Alexander Fischer and Günther Heydemann (Berlin: Duncker & Humblot, 1990), 671–709. An example from the old Federal Republic is Peter Schmitt-Egner, *Kolonialismus und Faschismus: Eine Studie zur historischen und begrifflichen Genese faschistischer Bewusstseinsformen am deutschen Beispiel* (Giessen: Andreas Achenbach, 1975).

5. Wolfgang Uwe Eckart, "Arzneimittelerprobung in der ehemaligen deutschen Kolonie Togo: Zum Gewaltverhältnis von Kolonialpolitik, Kolonialmedizin und pharmakologischer Erkenntnisbildung," *Forum Wissenschaft* 1 (1989): 29–35; Wolfgang Uwe Eckart, *Medizin und Kolonialimperialismus* (Paderborn: Schöningh, 1997); Gunter Spraul, "Der 'Völkermord' an den Herero: Untersuchungen zu einer neuen Kontinuitätsthese," *Geschichte in Wissenschaft und Unterricht* 39 (1988): 713–39.

6. Hannah Arendt, *The Origins of Totalitarianism*, new ed. (New York: Harcourt Brace Jovanovich, 1973).

7. For an extensive discussion on the links between German colonialism and the emergence of eugenics, see Pascal Grosse, *Kolonialismus, Eugenik und bürgerliche Gesellschaft in Deutschland, 1850–1918* (Frankfurt: Campus, 2000); English edition, *Colonialism, Eugenics and Civil Society in Germany, 1850–1918* (Ann Arbor: University of Michigan Press, forthcoming).

8. Eugenics is not to be confused with social Darwinist notions such as the survival of the fittest and the extermination of the weak. Most German eugenicists strongly criticized social Darwinism and viewed their own task as quite different: the selective breeding of the fittest ("die Leistungsfähigsten") within the framework of racial purity.

9. Hans Fenske, "Ungeduldige Zuschauer: Die Deutschen und die europäische Expansion 1815–1880," *Imperialistische Kontinuität und nationale Ungeduld im 19. Jahrhundert*, ed. Wolfgang Reinhard (Frankfurt: Fischer, 1991), 87–123; Zantop, *Colonial Fantasies*.

10. Kristin Kopp, "Contesting Borders: German Colonial Discourses and the Polish Eastern Territories" (PhD diss., University of California at Berkeley, 2001) and Kristin Kopp's essay in this volume.

11. Geoff Eley, *Reshaping the German Right: Radical Nationalism and Political Change after Bismarck*, rpt. (Ann Arbor: University of Michigan Press, 1991).

12. David Blackbourn and Geoff Eley, *The Peculiarities of German History: Bourgeois Society and Politics in Nineteenth-Century Germany* (Oxford: Oxford University Press, 1984).

13. See especially Chancellor von Caprivi's remarks before the Reichstag on May 12, 1890, where he argued that in the case of a European war the peace treaty would

decide the future distribution of colonial territories overseas. Cited in *Koloniales Jahr-buch* 3 (1890): 95. The most important study of war aims is still Fritz Fischer, *Griff nach der Weltmacht: Die Kriegszielpolitik des kaiserlichen Deutschland 1914–1918* (Düsseldorf: Droste, 1961).

14. Roger Chickering, *We Men Who Feel Most German: A Cultural Study of the Pan-German League 1886–1914* (Boston: Allen & Unwin, 1984).

15. Geoff Eley, "Die deutsche Geschichte und die Widersprüche der Moderne: Das Beispiel des Kaiserreiches," *Zivilisation und Barbarei: Die widersprüchlichen Potentiale der Moderne*, ed. Frank Bajohr (Hamburg: Christians, 1991), 17–65.

16. Cornelia Essner, " 'Wo Rauch ist, da ist auch Feuer': Zu den Ansätzen eines Rassenrechts für die deutschen Kolonien," *Rassendiskriminierung, Kolonialpolitik und ethnisch-nationale Identität*, ed. Wilfried Wagner (Münster: Lit, 1992), 145–60.

17. Robert Aitken, "Exclusion and Inclusion: Gradations of Whiteness and Socio-Economic Engineering in a Settler Society: German Southwest Africa, 1884–1914" (PhD diss., University of Liverpool, 2002).

18. Alexandre Kuma N'Dumbe, "Pläne zu einer nationalsozialistischen Kolonial-herrschaft in Afrika," *Aspekte deutscher Aussenpolitik im 20. Jahrhundert*, ed. Wolfgang Benz and Hermann Graml (Stuttgart: Deutsche Verlags-Anstalt, 1976), 165–92; Alex-andre Kuma N'Dumbe, *Hitler voulait l'Afrique: Le projet du IIIe Reich sur le continent africain* (Paris: L'Harmattan, 1980); Horst Kühne, *Faschistische Kolonialideologie und Zweiter Welt-krieg* (Berlin: Dietz, 1962); Wolfe Schmokel, *Dream of Empire: German Colonialism, 1919–1945* (New Haven: Yale University Press, 1964).

19. Dieter Gosewinkel, *Einbürgern und Ausschliessen: Die Nationalisierung der Staat-sangehörigkeit vom Deutschen Bund bis zur Bundesrepublik Deutschland* (Göttingen: Vanden-hoeck & Ruprecht, 2001), esp. 263–337.

20. Grosse, *Kolonialismus*, 26–31.

21. The following remarks are based on Grosse, *Kolonialismus*; Lora Wildenthal, *German Women for Empire, 1884–1945* (Durham: Duke University Press, 2001); Cornelia Essner, "Zwischen Vernunft und Gefühl: Die Reichstagsdebatten von 1912 um kolo-niale 'Rassenmischehe' und Sexualität," *Zeitschrift für Geschichtswissenschaft* 45 (1997): 503–19; Helmut Bley, *Kolonialherrschaft und Sozialstruktur in Deutsch-Südwestafrika, 1894–1914* (Hamburg: Leibniz, 1968); Franz-Josef Schulte-Althoff, "Rassenmischung im kolonialen System: Zur deutschen Kolonialpolitik im letzten Jahrzehnt vor dem Er-sten Weltkrieg," *Historisches Jahrbuch* 105 (1985): 52–94.

22. Pascal Grosse, "Zwischen Privatheit und Öffentlichkeit. Kolonialmigration in Deutschland, 1900–1940," *Phantasiereiche: Der deutsche Kolonialismus in kulturgeschicht-licher Perspektive*, ed. Birthe Kundrus (Frankfurt: Campus, 2003), 91–109.

23. Lora Wildenthal, "Race, Gender and Citizenship in the German Colonial Em-pire," *Tensions of Empire: Colonial Cultures in a Bourgeois World*, ed. Frederick Cooper and Ann L. Stoler (Berkeley: University of California Press, 1997), 263–83.

24. Grosse, Kolonialismus, 184–91.

25. See, for example, Paul Weindling, Health, Race and German Politics between National Unification and Nazism (Cambridge: Cambridge University Press, 1989); Richard Wall and Jay Winter, eds., The Upheaval of War: Family, Work and Welfare in Europe, 1914–1918 (Cambridge: Cambridge University Press, 1988); William H. Schneider, Quality and Quantity: The Quest for Biological Regeneration in Twentieth-Century France (Cambridge: Cambridge University Press, 1990); Peter Weingart, Jürgen Kroll, and Kurt Bayertz, Rasse, Blut und Gene: Geschichte der Eugenik und Rassenhygiene in Deutschland (Frankfurt: Suhrkamp, 1988).

26. See, for example, Helmuth Stoecker, ed., Drang nach Afrika: Die deutsche koloniale Expansionspolitik und Herrschaft in Afrika von den Anfängen bis zum Verlust der Kolonien, 2nd, rev. ed. (Berlin: Akademie, 1991), 184; Fatima El Tayeb, Schwarze Deutsche: Der Diskurs um "Rasse" und nationale Identität 1890–1933 (Frankfurt: Campus, 2001), 15–17.

27. Gosewinkel, Einbürgern, 404–20.

28. See the detailed comparison between the colonial mixed-marriage bans before 1914, the Nuremberg Laws of 1935, and the Kolonialblutschutzgesetz of 1940 in Birthe Kundrus, "Von Windhoek nach Nürnberg? Koloniale 'Mischehenverbote' und die nationalsozialistische Rassengesetzgebung," Phantasiereiche: Zur Kulturgeschichte des deutschen Kolonialismus, ed. Birthe Kundrus (Frankfurt: Campus, 2003), 110–31.

29. See the English version of the "extermination order," in, for example, introduction to The Imperialist Imagination: German Colonialism and Its Legacy, ed. Sara Friedrichsmeyer, Sara Lennox, and Susanne Zantop (Ann Arbor: University of Michigan Press, 1998), 13.

30. Brian Digre, Imperialism's New Clothes: The Repartition of Tropical Africa, 1914–1919 (New York: Peter Lang, 1990).

31. For a detailed discussion, see Grosse, Kolonialismus, 96–144.

32. See, for example, Michael Burleigh, Die Zeit des Nationalsozialismus: Eine Gesamtdarstellung (Frankfurt: S. Fischer, 2000), 656–768, and Gosewinkel, Einbürgern, 404–20.

33. Christian Koller, 'Von Wilden aller Rassen niedergemetzelt': Die Diskussion um die Verwendung von Kolonialtruppen in Europa zwischen Rassismus, Kolonial- und Militärpolitik (Stuttgart: Franz Steiner, 2001).

34. Robert C. Reinders, "Racialism on the Left: E. D. Morel and the 'Black Horror on the Rhine,'" International Review of Social History 13 (1968): 1–28; Keith L. Nelson, "The Black Horror on the Rhine: Race as a Factor in Post–World War I Diplomacy," Journal of Modern History 42 (1970): 606–27; Sally Marks, "Black Watch on the Rhine: A Study in Propaganda, Prejudice and Prurience," European Studies Review 13 (1983): 297–334; Gisela Lebzelter, "Die 'Schwarze Schmach': Vorurteile-Propaganda-Mythos," Geschichte und Gesellschaft 11 (1985): 37–58; and Koller, Wilden, 201–335.

MARCIA KLOTZ

# The Weimar Republic

## A Postcolonial State in a
## Still-Colonial World

Postcolonial studies is generally understood as a history and theorization of
the oppressed. It focuses on the places and peoples who were on the receiving end of the colonial stick, and it generally traces their struggles to develop
economic, psychological, and national sovereignty in the wake of the extreme
brutality of colonial relations. Yet discussions of postcoloniality also include
the histories of colonizing powers. The rich, though often conflictual, multi-
culturalism of contemporary Paris or London certainly finds its place in postcolonial discussions, because it is clearly incomprehensible outside of the historical context of empire. Given these two standard understandings of the
postcolonial, it might seem counterintuitive to think of the Weimar Republic
as a postcolonial state, for it fits into neither of these narratives. Germany's
former colonial subjects were never liberated from German colonial rule to
embark on a search for the kind of postcolonial identity that occupied Frantz
Fanon or Albert Memmi. Nor did they travel to Berlin or Hamburg in especially significant numbers, which is to say that, although German metropoles
often boast a broad diversity of immigrants from many different regions today,
newcomers from Namibia, German East Africa, the Pacific Islands, or other
areas formerly colonized by Germany are no more numerous than those from
other areas. For the period to be treated here, the Weimar years, the number
of former subjects of German overseas rule living in Germany was quite small
indeed. In what sense, then, can we think of the Weimar Republic as a topic
of postcolonial scholarship, and what do we stand to gain from such an approach?

This question can best be addressed, I propose, by approaching the term
"postcolonial" in a very general manner, as a historical perspective that sheds
light on a given historical topic by orienting it toward its colonial past. Thinking of the years between the Great War and Hitler's rise to power in these terms
entails situating that era within a study of larger global shifts. It means viewing

135

the Weimar Republic much as a painter might, by trying to sketch the empty space around it rather than simply tracing its outline. From this perspective the well-known Weimar national identity crisis, for example, might be framed less in terms of the various economic and political domestic crises with which we are familiar and more in terms of how understandings of the world in which Germany found itself were changing. National identity, after all, is not determined solely by membership in the kind of imagined community Benedict Anderson has written about. That imagined community is itself defined according to an imagined outside, a "world" in which the nation takes on meaning.

In 1914, when the Great War broke out, the world that established the meaning of German national identity had long been structured by the dichotomy of colonial rule: imperial powers on this side, areas either colonized or destined to become so on the other. That understanding of the globe was radically disrupted when European nations turned their enormously destructive weapons away from colonial targets and onto one another. As the war drew to a close, it was clear that the global understanding that had structured the colonial globe was forever gone; it was not at all clear, however, what new global order would arise to take its place. As the loser in that war and the loser, in turn, of its status as a colonial power, Germany played a special role in these global shifts, becoming Europe's first postcolonial nation in a world trying desperately to maintain the colonial structure that had so long held it together. This essay examines the role that colonial globe played in the German experience of both the Great War and its aftermath.

## Colonialism and the Great War

If the First World War did not definitively demolish the colonial global vision, it most certainly weakened the center-periphery structure of the imperial world, which is why 1914 is generally considered the end point for the so-called belle époque of colonialism. The Great War itself can hardly be understood without recourse to colonial history, and not only because colonial rivalries played an important part in the events leading up to its outbreak. Colonial history was also decisive in determining how the belligerents fought and how they readied themselves, ideologically and militarily, for the conflict. This was especially relevant in their integration of what was to become the decisive piece of technology in the conflict: the machine gun. [1] From the 1880s on, it was clear to colonial officials everywhere that rapid-fire weapons had completely redefined modern warfare. In any number of colonial conflicts, machine guns had granted Europeans victory when they were clearly outnumbered by courageous and well-trained fighters. As Hilaire Belloc put it in his often-cited poem, "The Modern Traveller":

I shall never forget the way
That Blood stood upon this awful day
Preserved us all from death.
He stood upon a little mound
Cast his lethargic eyes around,
And said beneath his breath:
"Whatever happens, we have got
The Maxim Gun, and they have not."[2]

Yet military elites on both sides of the conflict were reluctant to add the machine gun to their arsenals, dismissing its many enthusiastic proponents precisely because most of them had served in the colonies. As John Ellis attests, "the machine gun became associated with colonial expeditions and the slaughter of natives, and was thus by definition regarded as being totally inappropriate to the conditions of regular European warfare."[3]

The few machine guns that were in use in 1914, of course, quickly determined the course of battle, establishing the long trenches that were to remain stationary for most of the following four years. Yet even as generals on both sides of the conflict raced to add as many rapid-fire weapons to their arsenals as possible, they refused to change their training procedures for recruits. Throughout the war conscripts were taught to attack in long lines with single-fire rifles, following an officer who would supposedly lead them across no-man's-land to bayonet the enemy at close quarters. Soldiers were trained to fight in a war considered honorable and fitting for white soldiers but deployed in one that had, up to that moment in history, been viewed as fitting only for the darker-skinned victims of white rule.[4]

A major component in the war propaganda on both sides of the battle lines consisted of accusations that the enemy was responsible for importing the colonial game into Europe. On the Allies' side war campaigns relied heavily on tropes of "barbarism" versus "civilization," whose meanings had been established through long centuries of colonial rule. They condemned the German invasion of Belgium, Luxembourg, and France as an act of "barbarian" aggression. Sexual violence quickly established itself as the preferred metaphor to depict that aggression, just as colonial uprisings had been effectively allegorized through the rape of white women. [5] In England Louis Raemaeker's political cartoons repeatedly represented the occupied nations as vulnerably thin, lily-white female figures in torn white robes, the victims of rape, torture, humiliation, abuse, and dismemberment at the hands of long-armed, animalistic "Huns." [6] In France, as Ruth Harris has shown, there was a vigorous national debate about what should be done with French and Belgian women made pregnant by German rapists. [7] Was abortion justified at such an extreme moment of crisis in order to root out what was called "the child of the barbarian"? Or should one trust that the mother's blood would sufficiently civilize the unborn child before birth? This debate echoed the long-standing disagreements between conservative and liberal colonialists in all imperial powers. Those who wanted to abort the offspring of German rapists joined Joseph Conrad's Kurtz in his call to "exterminate the brutes," while those who wanted to save the unborn product of rape essentially argued for the civilizing mission to save the barbarian German fetus's soul. Thus was the colonial debate brought back home to Europe, fully internalized within the very bodies of French and Belgian women.

Attacks on German "barbarism" were linked not only to the "primitive" peoples but also to the brutality of the colonizer. During their first offensive, German soldiers were said to have chopped off the hands and arms of children so that they might not grow up to become enemy fighters. [8] This charge invoked famous memories of the cruel reign of King Leopold; piles of hacked-off arms and hands were the most commonly invoked image used in the campaign to end the rubber trade's rule of terror in the Congo. [9] Even the common epithet used to denigrate Germans as "Huns" during the war traced its genealogy to the colonial experience. In the famous *Hunnenrede* (Hun Speech), Wilhelm II had sent German soldiers to quell the Boxer Rebellion with an admonition to take no prisoners, so that the Chinese might, in the coming millennia, remember Germans with the same reverence that the name Attila the Hun inspired in Europe. This particular propaganda trope identified Germany with colonial abuses, thereby identifying the Allied powers themselves with the hapless victims of the rubber gatherers in the Congo, the Chinese rebels, and the feudal Europeans who fell to Attila's marauding army. Germans were barbarians – imperialistic barbarians.

German propaganda likewise relied on colonial tropes, though to different ends. They responded to the rape accusations with posters that portrayed occupation troops cheerfully helping the local women of Belgium or France with their laundry or bouncing children on their knees while grateful, aproned mothers looked on from the background. There was much outrage in the German camp that the French and British had the audacity to deny that Germans were civilized, for was Germany not a white nation, located at the very heart of Europe? A 1916 poster by Louis Oppenheim, for example, is titled "Wir Barbaren!" and features a graph that shows Germany to be more literate, producing more books, and spending more money on social welfare than either France or Britain. Portraits of Dürer, Beethoven, Kant, Bismarck, Gutenberg, Humboldt, and Goethe adorn the bottom of the poster.[10] This strategy likewise echoed German colonial discourse, repeating a trope that had been used since the 1880s, when Friedrich Fabri had argued that a nation with so monumental a culture as Germany's had both a right and a responsibility to participate in the mission of civilizing the globe.[11]

When German propagandists went on the offensive, however, they appealed more to the social Darwinist element in colonial ideology. They made much of the fact that both Britain and France had conscripted colonial troops from Africa, Indochina, and India to fight in the heart of Europe. It was the black soldiers among these who received the most attention in German propaganda. France deployed roughly 140,000 French West African troops in the war, of whom an estimated 31,000 lost their lives.[12] German representations of the colonial troops who fought under the French flag were complex and often contradictory. On the one hand the "Senegalese fighters," as they were called (despite the fact that they actually came from a number of different French colonies), were feared as physically superior to whites precisely because of their "primitive" status; they were supposedly not yet weakened by the enervating luxuries of modern civilization, as were their European contemporaries.[13] On the other hand German commentators also expressed disdain for the "colored mob" (farbiges Gesindel) and condemned France for betraying the white race by mobilizing "primitive barbarians" against "civilized Europeans."[14] German propagandists also professed sympathy for the "Senegalese" soldiers, claiming they were being used as cannon fodder, forced to lead the attacks, and spurred on by threatening machine guns at the rear that would decimate them should they not advance. Rumors circulated that the black soldiers were cutting off fingers, noses, and other body parts from wounded or dead Germans to take home as souvenirs – repeating the accusations about German troops dismembering children in Belgium.[15] Sandra Mass has compellingly argued that this campaign resulted in a displacement among German soldiers, whose rational fear of bodily fragmentation was recast as a horror of sharing the battlefield with dark-skinned opponents.[16]

Colonial tropes thus served a variety of functions, yet they established the foundation for much in the propaganda campaigns on both sides of the conflict. Moreover, even the war's critics articulated their reservations about the conflict in terms borrowed from colonialism. Romain Rolland, for example, was indignant that Europeans, having proclaimed civilization to the peoples of the world, were now making a mockery of that very concept by turning their guns against one another and calling on their dark-skinned colonized subjects to rescue them. By allowing themselves to sink into bellicose relations, he feared, the nations of Europe were voluntarily giving up their power; global leadership would now necessarily pass to other peoples. [17] Sigmund Freud expressed similar concerns in an essay depicting the profound disillusionment into which the war had cast him and his contemporaries:

> True, we have told ourselves that wars can never cease so long as nations live under such widely differing conditions. . . . And we were prepared to find that wars between the primitive and the civilized peoples, between those races whom a color-line divides, nay, wars with and among the undeveloped nationalities of Europe or those whose culture has perished – that for a considerable period such wars would occupy mankind. But we permitted ourselves to have other hopes. We had expected the great ruling powers among the white nations upon whom the leadership of the human species has fallen, . . . to succeed in discovering another way of settling misunderstanding and conflicts of interest. [18]

While Freud, speaking here, as it were, for his entire generation, had come to accept as inevitable wars between "civilized" and "primitive" peoples, he was not prepared for belligerence between "the white nations" themselves. The war had unmasked the conceit that had justified European claims to the "leadership of the human species" on the basis of technological and scientific progress, showing it to be absolutely insufficient without similar progress in diplomacy and civil relations. [19]

As the war drew to a close, it was not at all clear whether colonialism would survive the conflict. After the Bolshevik Revolution, Lenin delivered a proposal for peace to be based on "the liberation of all colonies; the liberation of all dependent, oppressed, and non-sovereign peoples."[20] The United States rejected Lenin's proposal, fearing not only that it would bring a socialist revolution to the war-weary peoples of Europe, but also that Lenin might undermine "the stability of the future world order by applying the self-determination principle to the colonial world."[21] Woodrow Wilson countered with his famous Fourteen

Points, repeating most of Lenin's proposals but with the important difference that self-determination was to be a guiding principle only for white European peoples. Colonial rule, according to Wilson's model, would remain intact. When the Committee of Ten finally met at Versailles, the Japanese delegation proposed that the League Covenant include a clause proclaiming an international commitment to the principle of racial equality.[22] Though their proposal was summarily dismissed, the very fact that it had been put forth at all shows the extent to which the ideological underpinnings of colonialism had been shaken.

The war's end in 1918 thus brought a moment in world history when the colonial global imaginary, destabilized by the depletion of wealth and population among the rulers of empire, might well have toppled. Instead, a decision was made to prop it up again by emphasizing and reinforcing the ideology of the civilizing mission. As Article 22 of the Versailles Treaty stated: "To those colonies and territories which as a consequence of the late war ceased to be under the sovereignty of States which formerly governed them and which are unable to stand by themselves under the strenuous conditions of the modern world, there should be applied the principle that the well-being and development of such peoples form a sacred trust of civilization."[23] This renewed commitment to the civilizing mission did not translate into any concrete guidelines for more humane colonial policies. In fact the only real change that resulted from it was the constitution of the League of Nations – an international body to which grievances could be addressed if not necessarily acted upon – and the removal of Germany's colonies, supposedly because of colonial abuses.[24] Germany was also denied a place in the League itself, that "community of nations" deemed civilized enough to care for the peoples of the world. In Thorstein Veblen's words, Germany would be as welcome in the League as "a drunken savage with a machine gun."[25]

Thus did Germany become a postcolonial nation in a still-colonial world. The effects on the common populace were quite dramatic. Most Germans, of course, cared little for Germany's overseas territories, which had never turned a profit and were hardly affordable in the lean postwar years. Nevertheless, the loss of those colonies served an important symbolic function – a reminder of the new global order and Germany's diminutive status within it. In a world that had for centuries been divided between colonizers and colonized, it seemed to many that Germany, no longer held to be "civilized" enough to be a colonizer, was now being reckoned among the colonized.

Meanwhile, the French were also coming to terms with the reconfigured colonial globe but in a very different manner. Clemenceau, haunted by anxieties that war might again develop between Germany and France, feared that Germany would be in a position of advantage because the German population outnumbered the French by some twenty million people. The colonies, however, added a vast reservoir of manpower to the French army. When France deployed colonial troops to occupy the Rhine Valley in 1921, the intent, in part, was to demonstrate to the Germans, as General Charles Mangin put it, that "France does not stop at the Mediterranean, nor at the Sahara; . . . she extends to the Congo; . . . she constitutes an empire vaster than Europe, and which in half a century will number 100 million inhabitants."[26]

The hysterical German response to that deployment, coordinated by groups such as the Fichte League and the Pan-German League, has been well-documented.[27] Claiming that "black savages" were raping and murdering white women and girls in the heart of Europe, these right-wing groups mounted a successful international appeal, spawning petition drives and protests attended by tens of thousands in Great Britain, Sweden, the United States, and South Africa. While that campaign has rightly been derided as an example of German racism and hence viewed as a kind of foreshadowing of the Nazi racist state, we can also view it as symptomatic of Germany's postcolonial status in a yet-colonial global order. The fear of reverse colonization – the anxiety that the abuses dealt out to the colonized might one day be revisited upon the colonizer in turn – had been a dominant theme in colonial discourse. The deployment of African troops on German soil terrified precisely because it brought to life a ghost that had long haunted the practitioners of empire: Africa colonizing Europe.

The hysteria that this colonial occupation elicited was part of a larger shift in how people all over the world understood the world in which they lived. From T. S. Eliot's The Wasteland to Lothrop Stoddard's fearful Rising Tide of Color Against White World Supremacy to Oswald Spengler's internationally successful The Decline of the West, the Jazz Age was characterized by grim fears that the wizened and ailing intellectual and aesthetic traditions of Europe could not compete with more energetic, youthful cultures of peoples of color. These anxieties reflected the profound shift in geopolitical power wrought by the war. Even the conflict's victors, Great Britain and France, had lost their position of global hegemony to the United States and Japan by virtue of their devastated economic and industrial bases and their severely depleted populations. Although it took some time for people to become aware of the fact, the center-periphery organization of the colonial globe, in which the European continent had occupied the undisputed middle point, had died in the battlefields of the Great War.

## The Colonial World According to Hitler

Yet while all of Europe could be said to have lost the war, Germany lost it quite literally. It is hence not surprising that fears of reverse colonization, of a world turned on its head, were expressed more passionately there than anywhere else. It is in this context that a postcolonial approach has something to contribute to the ultimate question of the Weimar Republic – that of its catastrophic conclusion. What Hitler had to offer the German people was a global vision in which Germany was secured a position of respect and importance – a position based, in the final analysis, on its racial standing.

Colonial themes clearly structured Hitler's own understanding of the globe. The dichotomy that structures the world vision of *Mein Kampf* sets Jews against Aryans, of course, but it is important to note that this binary is not defined, as one might expect, according to racial characteristics. Instead, Hitler narrates the distinction between Jews and Aryans according to two parallel but very different histories of colonialism. Hitler defines "Aryans" in pseudoanthropological terms as those *Kulturträger* (carriers of civilization) who have always colonized other *Völker*, generally enslaving them but always to the productive end of founding new civilizations.

> Aryan tribes (often in a really ridiculously small number of their own people) subjugate foreign peoples, and now, stimulated by the special living conditions of the new territory (fertility, climatic conditions, etc.) and favored by the mass of the helping means in the form of people of inferior kind now at their disposal, they develop the mental and organizatory abilities slumbering in them. Often, in the course of a few millennia or even centuries, they create cultures which originally completely bear the inner features of their character, adapted to the already mentioned special qualities of the soil as well as of the subjected people. [28]

Aryan expansionism thus represented the positive model of colonialism that Hitler would reclaim in the future.

But there was also a negative form of colonialism for Hitler, one that had been practiced against the Aryan peoples themselves. This is where the Jews came in, for it was the Jews who had set one European nation against another in the Great War, the Jews who had set one class against another, the Jews who had allowed African troops to occupy the Rhineland. In a Germany already inflamed with fears of reverse colonization, Hitler gave a face to those fears, and it was a Jewish face. In its most cunning form, according to *Mein Kampf*, Jewish colonization adopted an ideological disguise, misleading the German worker with the false egalitarianism of Marxist doctrine. In that guise the Jewish colonizers threatened the future of the entire globe:

> The Jewish doctrine of Marxism rejects the aristocratic principle in nature; instead of the eternal privilege of force and strength, it places the mass of numbers and its dead-weight. If, with the help of the Marxian creed, the Jew conquers the nations of this world, his crown will become the funeral wreath of humanity, and once again this planet, empty of mankind, will move through the ether as it did thousands of years ago. . . . Therefore I believe today that I am acting in the sense of the Almighty Creator: *By warding off the Jews I am fighting for the Lord's work.*[29]

This is perhaps the most often-cited passage in *Mein Kampf*, for here Hitler comes closest to an open declaration of the genocide that he would eventually bring to the Jews of Europe. There can be no doubt, of course, that it articulates a paranoid delusion. Yet it is also important that the form that delusion takes is a *colonial* form and that it is seen from the point of view of *the colonized* – not the colonizer. It is the perspective, for example, of a native of the New World, someone who might have welcomed the missionaries for the sake of their doctrine that all men are brothers in the eyes of the Lord, only to lose her or his entire people to illness, enslavement, and exploitation. While the colonizers had preached egalitarianism, their actions betrayed altogether different motives, resulting in the radical depopulation of whole continents. Similarly, the Jews might preach egalitarianism in its Marxist guise, but they only did so, for Hitler, in order to gain inroads that would allow them to enslave, exploit, and eventually decimate their hosts. The brownshirts thus fought, according to Hitler's delusional understanding of the globe, to *decolonize* Germany, and with it the world, to free the Aryan peoples from the colonization of the Jews. If they failed, the entire globe would be transformed into a depopulated, lifeless sphere, spinning silently and without meaning through black, empty space. For Hitler, one could either colonize or be colonized; there was no middle ground. In the postcolonial Weimar Republic, located in a yet-colonial world that seemed to offer Germany no place, such words, tragically, found all too many listening ears.

By situating the Weimar Republic in relation to its colonial past and the colonial present of its contemporaries, I hope it is clear that I do not intend to suggest any validity for such a world view or to excuse Germans' willingness to follow Hitler. The point is rather to follow the circulation of colonial tropes, to note the lingering power of the ideology of empire in times and places that seem quite separate from it. Colonialism was alive and well in the battlefields of the Great War. We cannot understand how that war was fought and experienced, both by the soldiers and by those behind the fronts, without recourse to the world wrought by colonialism. Likewise, colonial ideology was instrumental in the Weimar years, lighting a world stage where many Germans believed themselves to have been cast in the role of victim. In point of fact, of course, the position of Germans in the Weimar Republic was not parallel to that of colonized people in other parts of the globe, but that reality had little effect on popular fears or perceptions. The tropes of empire are malleable and multifaceted, as is the call to cast off its onerous yoke. The radical, emotional appeal for decolonization could and did serve liberatory ends around the globe, but it also played a part in the genocidal rhetoric of Adolf Hitler.

### NOTES

1. John Ellis, *The Social History of the Machine Gun* (New York: Pantheon, 1975).

2. "The Modern Traveller," as quoted by Ellis, *Machine Gun*, 94.

3. Ellis, *Machine Gun*, 57.

4. Much has been written about the disillusionment of these soldiers and the war neurosis in which many took refuge. See Paul Lerner, "Psychiatry and Casualties of War in Germany, 1914–1918," *Journal of Contemporary History* 35 (2000): 13–28, and *Hysterical Men: War, Psychiatry, and the Politics of Trauma in Germany, 1890–1930* (Ithaca: Cornell University Press, 2003); Peter Riedesser and Axel Verderber, "Maschinengewehre hinter der Front": Zur Geschichte der deutschen Militärpsychiatrie (Frankfurt am Main, 1996); Bernd Ulrich, "Die Desillusionierung der Kriegsfreiwilligen von 1914," in *Der Krieg des Kleinen Mannes*, ed. Wolfram Wette (Munich: Piper, 1995), 110–35; and Robert Welden Whalen, *Bitter Wounds: German Victims of the Great War, 1914–1939* (Ithaca: Cornell University Press, 1984). For similar accounts of British sources, see Joanna Bourke, *Dismembering the Male: Men's Bodies, Britain, and the Great War* (London: Reaction Books, 1996); Elaine Showalter, "Rivers and Sassoon: The Inscription of Male Gender Anxieties," in *Behind the Lines: Gender and the Two World Wars*, ed. Margaret Randolph Higonnet, Jane Jenson, Sonya Michel, and Margaret Collins Weitz (New Haven: Yale University Press, 1997), 61–69; Eric Leed, *No Man's Land: Combat and Identity in World War I* (Cambridge: Cambridge University Press, 1979); and Paul Fussell, *The Great War and Modern Memory* (New York: Oxford University Press, 1975).

5. Jenny Sharpe, *Allegories of Empire: The Figure of Woman in the Colonial Text* (Minneapolis: Minnesota University Press, 1993).

6. *Raemaeker's Cartoons: With Accompanying Notes by Well-Known English Writers* (New York: Doubleday, Page, 1917).

7. Ruth Harris, " 'The Child of the Barbarian': Rape, Race and Nationalism in France during the First World War," *Past and Present* 141 (November 1993): 170–206.

8. Nicoletta F. Gullace, "Sexual Violence and Family Honor: British Propaganda and International Law during the First World War," *American Historical Review* 102, no. 3 (June 1997): 714–47. Gullace emphasizes that the stories about dismemberment in the British press generally focused on female victims and were often of a sexual nature. See also Harris, " 'The Child of the Barbarian,' " 184.

9. Some of these horrifying images are reproduced in Adam Hochschild, *King Leopold's Ghost: A Story of Greed, Terror and Heroism in Colonial Africa* (Boston: Houghton Mifflin, 1999).

10. *German Propaganda and Total War: The Sins of Omission* (London: Athlone Press, 2000), 47. For a primary example, see Johannes Mayrhofer and Matthias Erzberger, *Unter uns "Barbaren": Briefe aus dem Weltkrieg* (Leutkirch: J. Bernklau, 1917).

11. Friedrich Fabri, *Bedarf Deutschland der Colonien? Eine politisch-ökonomische Betrachtung* (Gotha: Friedrich Andreas Perthes, 1884).

12. Gregory Martin, "German and French Perceptions of the French North and West African Contingents, 1910–1918," *Militärgeschichtliche Mitteilungen* 56 (1997): 31–68; Charles Balesi, *From Adversaries to Comrades-in-Arms: West Africa and the French Military, 1885–1918* (Waltham MA: Crossroads Press, 1979); Myron Echenberg, *Colonial Conscripts: The "Tirailleurs Sénégalais" in French West Africa, 1857–1960* (Portsmouth NH: Heinemann, 1991); Joe Lunn, " 'Les Races Guerrières': Racial Preconceptions in the French Military about West African Soldiers during the First World War," *Journal of Contemporary History* 34, no. 4 (October 1999): 517–36; and Marc Michel, *L'Appel a l'Afrique: Contributions et réactions a l'effort de guerre en AOF (1914–1919)* (Paris: Publications de la Sorbonne, 1982).

13. Sandra Mass, "Das Trauma des weissen Mannes: Afrikanische Kolonialsoldaten in propagandistischen Texten, 1914–1923," unpublished manuscript.

14. Martin, "German and French Perceptions," 57.

15. Martin, "German and French Perceptions," 58; Mass, "Trauma," 12. It should be noted, however, that these accusations were not specific to the black fighting troops. Similar accusations were made against the Russian soldiers on the eastern front.

16. Mass, "Trauma," and Sandra Mass, "Fragments of Identity: White Feminists and the 'Black Horror' Propaganda in the Early Weimar Republic," paper delivered at German Studies Association Annual Meeting, Houston, Texas, October 2000.

17. *Demain: Pages et Documents* 11–12 (November–December 1916): 266.

18. Sigmund Freud, "Thoughts for the Times on War and Death" (1915), in *Collected*

*Papers*, ed. Ernest Jones, trans. Joan Riviere (London: Hogarth Press, 1924), 4:287–317; quotation on 289.

19. See also Walter Benjamin's meditations on this topic in "Theorien des deutschen Faschismus: Zu der Sammelschrift *Krieg und Krieger*: Herausgegeben von Ernst Jünger," Walter Benjamin, with Theodor W. Adorno and Gerschom Scholem, *Gesammelte Schriften*, ed. Rolf Tiedemann and Hermann Schweppenhäuser (Frankfurt am Main: Suhrkamp, 1980), 3:238–47.

20. Vladimir Lenin, "Fourth Letter: How to Achieve Peace," *Letters from Afar*, in *Collected Works* (Moscow: Progress Publishers, 1964), 23:333–39.

21. Secretary of State Robert Lansing, as quoted in Arno J. Mayer, *Political Origins of the New Diplomacy 1917–1918* (New York: Howard Fertig, 1969), 304.

22. Mark Mazower, *Dark Continent: Europe's Twentieth Century* (New York: Alfred Knopf, 1999).

23. Arthur Pearson Scott, *An Introduction to the Peace Treaties* (Chicago: University of Chicago Press, 1920), 100.

24. I hope it is clear that I use "supposedly" here not because I doubt the validity of the accusations against German colonial rule. German atrocities were real, heinous, and numerous. I mean to suggest only that the Versailles condemnation of Germany served to whitewash the atrocities of other colonial powers.

25. Thorstein Veblen, *Elimination of the Unfit* (1917, rpt. Saugatuck CT: 5 X 8 Press, 1950), 5.

26. As cited in Keith L. Nelson, "The 'Black Horror on the Rhine': Race as a Factor in Post–World War I Diplomacy," *Journal of Modern History* 42, no. 4 (December 1970): 613.

27. See Tina Campt, Pascal Grosse, and Yara-Colette Lemke-Muniz de Faria, "Blacks, Germans and the Politics of Imperial Imagination," in *The Imperialist Imagination: German Colonialism and Its Legacy*, ed. Sara Friedrichsmeyer, Sara Lennox, and Susanne Zantop (Ann Arbor: University of Michigan Press, 1998), 205–29; Sally Marks, "Black Watch on the Rhine: A Study in Propaganda, Prejudice and Prurience," *European Studies Review* 13, no. 3 (July 1983): 297–334; and Reiner Pommerin, *Sterilisierung der Rheinlandbastarde: Der Schicksal einer farbigen deutschen Minderheit, 1918–1937* (Düsseldorf: Droste, 1979).

28. Adolf Hitler, *Mein Kampf*, trans. Ralph Manheim (Boston: Houghton Mifflin, 1939), 400.

29. Hitler, *Mein Kampf*, 83–84; emphasis in original.

SUSANNAH HESCHEL

# Theology as a Vision for Colonialism

## From Supersessionism to Dejudaization
## in German Protestantism

The relationship between German colonialism and the German Protestant church has only recently begun to be investigated by historians and theologians.[1] How the Christian message was altered to encourage the formation of German colonies, how the gospel was preached in colonial settings, and how the colonial experience altered theological trends back home in Germany are all topics deserving greater study, as are questions of the impact of racial thinking on missionary efforts and racism's reconfiguration of theology. Debates among German theologians concerning whether there should be racially separate Christian churches for missionized Africans and whether baptism erased racial difference, for example, were clearly informed by racist discourse and colonialist experience. In addition to missionary work Christian theology served more generally to justify Germany's imperialist desires, giving moral sanction to land seizures, deportations, enslavement, and brutality. This essay addresses the question of why Christianity so easily became used by European colonizers.

Christianity was well suited to serve as a religious justification for colonialism, I argue, because at its core Christian theology is a colonialist theology. Colonialism stands at the heart of Christianity's origins within Judaism. Christianity colonized Judaism, taking over its central theological concepts of messiah, eschatology, apocalypticism, election, and Israel as well as its Scriptures, its prophets, and even its God and denying the continued validity of those ideas for Judaism. In consequence a unique relationship exists between Christianity and Judaism; no other major world religion has colonized the central religious teachings and scriptures of another faith and then denied the continued validity of the other, insisting that its own interpretations are exclusive truth. Not even Islam, which claims to be God's final revealed truth, denies the ongoing validity of Christianity and Judaism as religions of the Book; Muhammad came to see his mission as restoring the pure religion of Abraham, not abrogating or superseding it.

Through the Christian doctrine of supersessionism, Judaism came to function in Christian theology as the Other, whose negation confirms and even constitutes Christianity. Yet its colonization of Judaism is not a conquest, in which Judaism is destroyed or sublated, but, as Jean-Luc Nancy writes, "a specific type of conflict that is best defined as the conflict between an integrity and its disintegration." [2] The conflict is reflected by Paul, who writes in Romans 11:28: "As regards the gospel, they are enemies of God for your sake; but as regards election they are beloved, for the sake of their ancestors." Enemies of Christianity, deniers of its faith, Jews are beloved for having unwittingly provided the very basis that constitutes Christianity. Without Judaism's concept of election there would be no Christianity, yet by refusing to accept Christianity the Jews become enemies who must be forced to submit. In its theological structure, then, Christianity created a colonialist model that provided an easy validation for subsequent geographic colonial ventures. At the same time, in colonizing Judaism Christianity was unable to erase it; Judaism is taken within, becoming the unwilling presence inside the Christian realm, a presence that is deeply troubling and gives rise to a variety of strategies within Christian theology to contain, redefine, and, finally, exorcise that presence.

The colonization process I am examining is neither the transformation of Christianity into a state religion under Constantine nor the colonization of Jews as people. Rather, I am concerned with Christian theological discourse and ways in which Jewish ideas were colonized by Christian Scriptures and doctrinal traditions. The theological strategies Christianity developed for coping with Judaism come to the forefront most intently in the modern period in liberal Protestant theology, responding to several factors. As Jonathan Hess has argued, the initial experiments in German colonialism were vectored inward – undertaken politically, economically, and mythically in relation to the Jewish population in Germany. [3] Susanne Zantop argues that "it was precisely the lack of actual colonialism that created a pervasive desire for colonial possessions and a sense of entitlement to such possessions in the minds of many Germans." [4] The long, drawn-out debates over Jewish emancipation in Germany, Hess writes, functioned "as a symbolic substitute for a foreign colony," and "fantasies of external colonial expansion are already inscribed into the project of internal colonization." [5] Jews were conscious of their position in relation to Christianity, calling themselves, as late as 1819, "prisoners of war, shvuye milḥama, in the hands of foreign [Christian] powers." [6]

The gradual emancipation of the Jews made their presence in Germany palpable, arousing resentments that were expressed through acts of hostility, including social ostracism, violence, and distrust of the government. [7] The involvement of theologians in the debates over Jewish emancipation in the late eighteenth and nineteenth centuries came at the same time that those same theologians were launching the quest for the historical Jesus – a quest that forced them to recognize that Jesus was a Jew in his personhood and his teachings. Was Jesus indeed the founder of Christianity, as theology claimed, or was he a Jew preaching a reform of Judaism and a greater religiosity, as history demonstrated? Theology and history stood in conflict; which was to be the victor? In the realm of theological fantasy, Judaism was not simply the Other; it was the colonized object whose presence within Christianity produced an anxiety about authenticity. Was Christianity its own creator or the daughter religion of Judaism? Where were the boundaries between the two religions? Where was the "Jewish" to be found within Christian theology, and how could it be extirpated without losing the heart of Christian teaching?

That the problem of Jesus's Jewishness was not limited to esoteric theological debates is reinforced by the simultaneous rise of the quest for the historical Jesus and modern antisemitism, linked by the identification of Germans with Christ. Theodore Ziolkowski has argued for Goethe's Werther as a Christ figure and notes Goethe's own distinction between the Jesus of history and the dogma of Christianity. [8] That Werther's suicide sparked a mass wave of suicides in Europe is evidence of the identification with his passion. Political disloyalty could be represented through the figure of Jesus as well; when Karl Gutzkow was put on trial for treason in 1835 for his notorious novel about religious doubt, *Wally die Zweiflerin*, among the damning passages read aloud at the court trial in Mainz was a long description of Jesus as a Jew. [9] The German nation could not be represented through a Jewish Jesus, who was both Jewish and mortal, but only through a historically transcendent, unique Christ. German nationalists' representation of Germany in terms of the Christ story grew stronger in the twentieth century. Some divorced Christ from the Jesus of the Bible, making him instead an "eternal idea" not limited by biblical history, just as they presented the German nation as a transcendent idea unbound by political conventions. Germany was identified in the Nazi era as Christ: crucified during World War I and resurrected by Adolf Hitler, who was described by some theologians and church leaders in messianic terms as the Second Coming: "In the Person of the Führer we see the One sent by God, who places Germany before the Lord of history . . . we believe he is come for us as Christ." [10]

Christian anxieties over the presence of Judaism at the very heart of its religion, and the implications of that presence for a dissolution of Christianity's existence as the religion of Jesus, were goaded by Jewish historians, who were eager to dismantle Christian hegemony over European culture and to emancipate themselves from the position of the politically and culturally colonized. The process of gaining emancipation was not simply a matter of attaining political rights for Jews, but an emancipation of the Jewish presence within the Christian. That emancipation of Jewish presence, which functioned in Jewish theological literature as a kind of revolt of the colonized, marks the first generation of scholars in the field of Jewish Studies (*Wissenschaft des Judentums*) in mid-nineteenth-century Germany and continued to influence the work of scholars into the Weimar era. It also explains the politics behind the excessive attention to this topic by modern Jewish historians, including Isaac Jost, Abraham Geiger, Heinrich Graetz, Levi Herzfeld, Joseph Derenbourg, Daniel Chwolsohn, Leo Baeck, Joseph Eschelbacher, and Felix Perles, among others. Study of the Jewish context of early Christianity was no apolitical scholarly endeavor, but rather was motivated by a Jewish colonial revolt against Christianity, which proceeded as an effort to assert the Jewish presence within Christianity all the more strongly as an act of dismembering the colonizer from the inside. By affirming Jesus's Jewishness and demonstrating the irrefutable parallels between Jesus's teachings and those of the rabbis of his day, Jewish historians sought to sever the connection between Christianity and the New Testament: the New Testament was a Jewish book, and Christianity was merely a collection of subsequently imagined dogma about it. If liberal Protestantism, in rejecting the dogma, miracles, and everything supernatural claimed by the New Testament and subsequent Christian theology, claimed to be the religion *of* Jesus rather than the religion *about* Jesus, then Jewish historians replied by demonstrating that the religion of Jesus was Judaism – liberal Pharisaic Judaism. Thus argued, for example, Abraham Geiger, one of the founders of the field of Jewish Studies as well as of Reform Judaism. Liberal Pharisaism did not disappear with the destruction of the Jerusalem Temple in 70 CE, but went underground, and was being revived by the Reform Judaism of nineteenth-century European Jews.

Starting in the mid-nineteenth century, Jews had begun to take a strong interest in the figure of Jesus, claiming him as a Jew as a means to justify their own emancipation in German society. In the 1860s Geiger wrote a passage that became notorious among Protestant theologians: "He [Jesus] was a Jew, a Pharisaic Jew with Galilean coloring – a man who shared the hopes of his time and who believed that these hopes were fulfilled in him. He did not utter a new thought, nor did he break down the barriers of nationality. . . . He did not abolish any part of Judaism; he was a Pharisee who walked in the way of Hillel." [11] Liberal Pharisaism, Geiger argued, had deteriorated into rigid rabbinic legalism as a consequence of Christian anti-Jewish persecution but was being revived by Reform Jews. Christians wishing to follow the faith of Jesus, Geiger implied, ought to convert to liberal Pharisaism – namely, Reform Judaism.

Christian reactions were swift and outraged. Geiger had elevated Hillel, Franz Delitzsch wrote, "in order to rank Jesus below him. . . . Hillel, however, left everything as he found it. . . . All history, on the other hand, proclaims what Jesus has become." [12] Geiger's comparison of Jesus with the Pharisees would endanger the position of Jews in Germany, Delitzsch warned; your words, he warned Geiger, "sound to me ten times more horrific than the crucifixion." [13]

Unable either to refute or to ignore Geiger's historical research showing the parallels between the sayings of Jesus and those of the rabbis recorded in the Mishnah, Targum, and Midrash, Protestant New Testament scholars were left with the uncomfortable recognition that Jesus had not in fact taught anything unique or different from the Judaism of his day. That was anathema to them. For Heinrich von Treitschke, in his essay that launched the antisemitic outbreak of the late 1870s, the writings of Jewish historians constituted "a dangerous spirit of arrogance" and "a fanatical fury" against the Christianity that constituted the backbone of German nationhood. [14] Both Jesus's lack of theological originality and his immersion in the cultural and religious world of Judaism, uncovered in the quest for the historical Jesus, stimulated a Christian backlash – an effort to repudiate and eradicate all traces of Judaism from Christianity. This was not undertaken as a liberation of the colonized Judaism, however, but as a regurgitation, a theological bulimia of the Jewish from within Christian theological teachings.

Christian anxiety about separating Jesus from Judaism arises from the central aporia of Jesus: his historical reality as a Jew and his theological reality as the founder of Christianity. Various scenarios were presented: Jesus began his ministry as a Jew hoping to raise the spiritual level of his fellow religionists, but he came to realize the degeneracy of Judaism and ultimately repudiated it; the Jews failed to recognize Jesus as their God-sent messiah because they were too mired in their moral and spiritual depravity to recognize that he was the Son of God; Jesus was deliberately sent to the Jews as part of a divine plan to destroy Judaism; Jesus was born in Aryan Galilee, and the violent Jews of southern Judea captured and murdered him once he entered Jerusalem. At the end of his *Life of Jesus*, Ernest Renan writes that the accomplishment of Jesus in Galilee was to overcome his Jewishness, as evidenced by the hostile reception he received in Jerusalem, where he "appears no more as a Jewish reformer, but as a destroyer of Judaism. . . . Jesus was no longer a Jew." [15] The Jewish historian Leopold Dukes wrote, in language typical of Jewish scholars, "To the question, What did Christianity take from Judaism, we answer in one word: everything." [16] Christian historians, by contrast, typically argued, in the words of Augustus Neander, "In the outset, how unlike Christ was the legal spirit of Pharisaism, with its soul-crushing statutes, its dead theology of the letter, and its barren subtleties!" [17]

It was in the context of attempting to rescue Jesus's difference from Judaism that Protestants at the turn of the century turned to racial theory, hoping that even if Jesus's teachings were the same as those of his fellow rabbis, in his person, his race, he was unique. By the time of World War I, theological debates were underway concerning whether Christianity, a Jewish religion imposed on Germany, had any place in German society, whether Jesus was an Aryan, and whether the Old Testament should be eliminated from the Christian Bible. In opposition to those who advocated a revival of Teutonic myths and rituals, Protestants offered a dejudaized version of Christianity.

Zantop argued that the rise of Nazism brought with it a revival of colonial longings. For Christian theologians it spurred an effort to dejudaize – not to end Christianity's occupation of Judaism, but Judaism's occupation of Christianity. By eradicating the Judaism within (eliminating the Old Testament from the canon, purging the New Testament of all Jewish references, declaring Jesus to have been an Aryan), they believed they were purifying Christianity, making it acceptable on nationalist and Nazi terms. The genocide of the Jewish was a Christian expurgation, a cleansing, a longing for virgin theological territory. In colonialist terms it meant eliminating the savage for the sake of civilization, making room for civilization to spread itself. It was not an effort at acquiring new colonial territory (converts to Christianity through missionary effort), but an expulsion and extermination based on a theological axis of morality/degeneracy analogous to the colonial axis of civilization/savagery.

The expurgation was institutionalized in 1939. On May 6 of that year several hundred Protestant theologians – professors, bishops, and pastors, all sympathetic to the German Christians (*Deutsche Christen*) – gathered at the Wartburg castle, with its strong Lutheran and German nationalist heritage, to inaugurate the Institute for Research and Eradication of Jewish Influence in German Church Life (*Institut zur Erforschung und Beseitigung des jüdischen Einflusses auf das deutsche kirchliche Leben*). [18] Proposals to create a dejudaization institute had circulated in 1938 among leaders of the German Christian movement, and its establishment six months after the *Kristallnacht* pogrom of November 9–10, 1938, was an expression of approval of that pogrom and an effort to carry out its goals within the church as well, to produce a *judenrein* Christianity.

In order to achieve a thorough dejudaization (*Entjudung*) of Christianity, institute members set to work immediately, publishing a dejudaized hymnal and New Testament, a catechism proclaiming Jesus the messiah of Aryans, and a slew of theological materials detailing the violent degeneracy of Judaism. "We know that the Jews want the destruction of Germany," [19] proclaimed Walter Grundmann, professor of New Testament at the University of Jena and academic director of the Institute, in 1938. Like other antisemites, Grundmann explained his assault on Judaism as self-defense: "To this day the Jews persecute Jesus and all who follow him with unreconcilable hatred." [20]

In the institute's dejudaized New Testament, *Die Botschaft Gottes*, passages describing Jesus's genealogical descent from Old Testament figures as well as any references to Zion, Jerusalem, and the Temple were removed. (The Old Testament had already been eliminated from the Bible.) To distance Jesus from Judaism, the Sabbath was called *Feiertag* and Passover was called *Osterfest*. Apocalyptic ideas were removed, as were terms such as "sinner," "righteous ones" (*Gerechte*), and "repentance." Records show that hundreds of thousands of copies of the dejudaized Bible and hymnal were sold to churches throughout the Reich.

The Institute published its hymnal in 1941, under the title *Grosser Gott Wir Loben Dich!* (Great God we praise you!). The book contained 339 hymns, all purged of references to the Old Testament or Judaism, and several presenting a militarized tone. Jewish words, such as "Amen" and "Hallelujah," were eliminated. In the second stanza of the classic Lutheran hymn "Ein Feste Burg" (A mighty fortress is our God), the hymnal removed the words "Herr Zabaoth" (Lord of hosts) and substituted "der Retter in Not" (the savior in time of need). The hymn itself was retitled "Heilig Vaterland" (Sacred fatherland), and the accompanying drawing of a castle highlighted a line containing warlike imagery from the hymn's first stanza: "Ein feste Burg ist unser Gott, ein gute Wehr und Waffen" (A mighty fortress is our God, a trusty shield and weapon). Another hymn, "Lobgesang" (also known as "Grosser Gott Wir Loben Dich!" and used as the hymnal's title) proclaimed:

Heilig, heilig, Herre Gott [which replaced "Heilig, Herr Gott Zabaoth!"]
Heilig, Herr der Kriegesheere!
Starker Helfer in der Not

The well-known Bach hymn "Wachet auf, ruft uns die Stimme" (Wake up, the voice calls us) was drastically altered. The first two stanzas were eliminated entirely, since the first contained references to "Jerusalem" and "Hallelujah" and the second stanza spoke of "Zion" and "Hosianna." The third stanza was retained, but the word "Hallelujah" was replaced with "Lob und Danklied" (Song of praise and thanks). "Stille Nacht" (Silent night) retained the reference to Bethlehem, since Grundmann had determined that a second Bethlehem existed in gentile Galilee, but the word "Hallelujah" was removed. Sales of the hymnal were excellent: churches throughout the Reich, north and south, in cities and villages, purchased copies for their congregations.

Institute members included faculty in Protestant theology from universities throughout the Reich and German scholars known for their publications in the field of Jewish Studies. They, in turn, brought about changes in the curriculum at their universities. At the University of Jena, Hebrew was no longer required, but doctoral dissertations had to incorporate racial theory and the doctrines associated with the aryanization of Christianity. Other disciplines such as physics also had Aryan theorists, but Aryan theology became genuinely central to the field of theology. Its success was due to the ability of the German Christians to take control of the institutional hierarchies of most of the regional churches in Germany by the mid-1930s. In addition most of the proposals put forward by the German Christians were not new; Adolf von Harnack, for example, had called for the elimination of the Old Testament two decades before, and the degeneracy of Judaism and Jesus's opposition to it were long-established themes in Protestant theology.

Grundmann wrote in 1942: "Should one be upset about Germany's attitude toward the Jews, Germany has the historical justification and historical authorization for the fight against the Jews on its side! To prove this statement is the special concern of this work; and later research cannot alter anything about this statement! So this work serves the great fateful fight of the German nation for its political and economic, spiritual and cultural and also its religious freedom."[21] Johannes Hempel, professor of Old Testament at the University of Berlin and member of Grundmann's institute, also declared in 1942, "the opposition between the Third Reich and the Jews [is] a struggle over life and death."[22] Hempel served as editor from 1927 to 1959 of the distinguished

*Zeitschrift für alttestamentliche Wissenschaft*, from whose title he eliminated the phrase "and the Evidence from Post-Biblical Judaism" in 1936.

What was declared theologically was intended politically and socially as well. These church figures did not simply respond to antisemitic measures decreed by the Nazi government; they proposed them. In 1932, for example, the German Christians called for a ban on marriages between Germans and Jews, anticipating the 1935 Nuremberg Laws. [23] According to the minutes of meetings held in February 1936, at which the Thuringian German Christians explained their views to representatives of other regional churches, one of the founders of the German Christian movement and the future director of the institute, Julius Leffler, called for murdering the Jews:

> In Christian existence there can be at any time a change of heart toward the Jew, and there must be. I can and must and am obligated as a Christian in my heart to have a bridge and find a bridge to the Jew, and still I must follow, as a Christian, the laws of my *Volk*, which are often very brutal, so that I succeed in the hardest conflict with the Jew. . . . If I also know that "Thou shalt not kill" is a commandment of God, or "As a Christian, you should love the Jew," because he is also a child of the eternal Father, so I can also know that I must kill him, I must shoot, and I can only do this if I am allowed to say: Christ. [24]

The *Entjudungsinstitut*, as it was colloquially known in church circles, flourished through the war years, coming to an end only in the fall of 1945 when church leaders in Thuringia declined to maintain it for the stated reason of financial limitations. Members of the institute retained their positions as academics and church leaders in both East and West Germany, some of them rising to positions of prominence, and German Christian ideas continued to circulate after the war in German theological writings. Some lost their positions at universities during denazification proceedings, but none lost a position within the church. After the war it was easy for institute members to claim that their work had been purely scientific, not Nazi, and that it fell within the rubrics of the classical Christian theological effort to define itself in opposition to Judaism.

Zantop sees colonialism emerging in Germany on the imaginative level. She writes: "Since a colonial discourse could develop without being challenged by colonized subjects or without being tested in a real colonial setting, it established itself not so much as 'intellectual authority' (Said) over distant terrains, than as mythological authority over the collective imagination." [25] The colonialist motifs she finds in literary rhetoric have parallels in the theological literature, particularly in the narratives of the Jesus story. For example, the lone discoverer, the courageous individual, the visionary genius is paralleled by the portrayal of Jesus as a spiritually unique genius who stands above others, a model for Christians. [26] By contrast, the Jews around Jesus, failing to recognize him as incarnate God, are portrayed as suffering from a religious degeneracy that is characterized by a moral weakness expressed in religious legalism and passivity in the face of Jesus's spiritual challenge. Such contrasts are typical characterizations found in the highly influential third edition of David Friedrich Strauss's *Life of Jesus* and in the numerous lives of Jesus written during the 1860s and '70s by Ernest Renan, Daniel Schenkel, Theodor Keim, and Karl von Hase, among others.

Treitschke, Zantop notes, speaks of a mature, virile German state taking possession of virgin territories. [27] Elsewhere she describes an "erotics of conquest" in German literary texts via "the insertion of the 'German' male as the superior mind and superior body . . . untainted by colonial experience (Herder) and hence a potentially better 'father-' or 'husband-' colonizer (Kant)." [28] Christianity, too, is described as untainted and virginal: Gustav Volkmar, a prominent member of the Tübingen School, writes, "The Judaism that formed the religious background to Jesus and Christianity was not the Pharisaic Judaism dominant during the Second Temple era, but the 'virgin womb' of the God of Judaism." [29] He is the God worshiped by Judaism but not the creator of Judaism. God's virginity, unlike Mary's, means that Christianity has no older sibling; it is God's only child. According to Volkmar, "The Pharisees represent a wish to deceive oneself and, on top of it, God, [a wish] which turned out to be more than an ever-growing despair, the tighter and more hardened the shackles of the idolatrous power, which one hoped to evade through hypocrisy." [30] Pharisaic religion is described as rigid, petrified, degraded, cankered, disfigured, wrathful, and violent and even as a cadaver; Pharisaism is a religion of materialism, deception, hypocrisy, abomination, and shackles; it murders the conscience, gentleness, and true religious spirit and, in the end, persecutes Jesus with enraged frenzy, to cite just a few of the adjectives used in German Protestant literature. [31]

Jesus was sent to the Jews because their religion had sunk so low, but because they were so mired in it, they were unable to recognize Jesus as the messiah and raise themselves out of their degenerate state. In Adolf von Harnack's classic formulation *Das Wesen des Christentums*, while Jesus's message was also proclaimed by the Pharisees, they "were in possession of much else besides.

With them [religion] was weighted, darkened, distorted, rendered ineffective and deprived of its force by a thousand things which they also held to be religious and every whit as important as mercy and judgment. . . . The spring of holiness . . . was choked with sand and dirt, and its water was polluted." With Jesus, "the spring burst forth afresh, and broke a new way for itself through the rubbish." [32] The purity of Jesus and the pristine quality of Christianity's message, untainted by Judaism, parallel the colonialist fantasies of virginity and virility.

For the philosemites, Germany could use Christianity to rid itself of the foreign presence of the Jews by encouraging their conversion. It would at least be an alternative to the deportation of the Jews proposed by the late eighteenth-century biblical scholar Johann David Michaelis. For him, as Hess describes, it would be best to send this "unmixed people of a more southern race" off to German colonial "sugar islands." [33] Judaism requires Christianity to cleanse it and bring a "return to the freer and nobler ancient Mosaic constitution," as Christian Wilhelm Dohm wrote in his essay supporting Jewish emancipation. [34] Conversion of Jews to Christianity was offered as a means by which Jews could liberate themselves from their Jewishness – until the rise of modern antisemitism created the notion that conversion would not liberate Jews but contaminate Christianity.

How could a Nazi be a Christian and worship a Jewish God? Grundmann posed and then answered this question in a manner typical of institute members: "Our *Volk*, which stands in a struggle above all else against the satanic powers of world Jewry for the order and life of this world, dismisses Jesus, because it cannot struggle against the Jews and open its heart to the king of the Jews." [35] Not to worry, he wrote. While a few Nazis had been duped by propaganda from Jews such as Moses Mendelssohn and others who claimed that Jesus was a Jew, New Testament scholarship had identified the false interpolations in the gospels made by Jewish Christians to hide the fact that Jesus was a Galilean of non-Jewish descent, most probably an Aryan. [36] That the Jews sought his death was further evidence that Jesus did not teach in accord with their principles.

Ridding Christianity of Jewishness proved not to be as simple to accomplish as its advocates had thought. Eliminating the Old Testament from the canon still left the presence of Jews in the New Testament in concepts such as "messiah" or "prophet" and in positive references such as that of Jesus preaching in the synagogue or in the statement that "salvation comes from the Jews" (John 4:12). Ridding the empire of the colony is not an easy task; there are always the remains of the day, the remnants of Jewishness that continue to cling to the Christian.

As much as Christianity may seek to eradicate Judaism in order to establish its own self-sufficiency, it cannot eradicate a more troubling awareness: that Judaism has its own intimate knowledge of Christianity and its origins and preserves that knowledge as long as it exists. Judaism is Christianity's archive, holding the memory of Jewish life in first-century Palestine, when the Pharisee preacher Jesus explained his message to his fellow Jews. To understand the words and deeds of Jesus, it is necessary to place them in the Jewish context, to locate them in the archive of Jewish debates over the Temple, Sabbath observance, and the end of times.

As Christianity originates within Judaism, it is Jewish sources that preserve evidence of its originality or lack thereof. Was Jesus teaching something new or simply repeating the common ideas of the rabbis of his day? Had the Jewish texts of the era not been preserved, the question would be moot. Judaism, then, is Christianity's archive in Jacques Derrida's sense of the word – the "archiviolithic force" that "not only incites forgetfulness, amnesia, the annihilation of memory, as mneme or anamnesis, but also commands the radical effacement, in truth the eradication, of that which can never be reduced to mneme or to anamnesis, that is, the archive." [37] The aporia of Christianity is its claim that Jesus founded a new religion, despite his being immersed throughout his life in the practices and beliefs of Judaism. It is his historical reality as a Jew that must be eradicated by Christian theology if its claim to be a new religion is to have any meaning. His Jewishness must be relegated to the archive, the storage that provides the contextualization for Jesus's religious messages, even as its context must be annihilated for Jesus's originality to have meaning. Thus, by the logic of the phenomenon, the Christian theologian cannot recognize Christianity's archive without destroying Christian theology itself.

For Judaism to be transformed into a prefiguration of the Christian also creates a dilemma. Augustine's solution was that the church preserve the existence of Jews not for their sake, but as witnesses, in their state of misery, to the higher truth of Christianity. Yet that preservation was not only for the sake of the Jews; the church required the Jewish presence as its archive. Israelite history and the divine revelation of the Old Testament were taken as the earliest level of Christian history, but only as a secretive proto-Christianity, with the biblical patriarchs unable to reveal their Christian identity in their own day because the Jews were spiritually incapable of understanding it. The prefigural reading of the Old Testament dissociated it from the history of Jews through its sanctification as Christian redemptive history (Heilsgeschichte). In The Wretched of the Earth, Frantz Fanon argued: "Colonialism is not satisfied merely with holding a people in its grip and emptying the native's brain of all form and content. By a kind of perverted logic, it turns to the past of the oppressed people, and distorts, disfigures, and destroys it." [38] Yet in the Christian case, and perhaps in other examples of colonialism as well, the destruction of the colonized Judaism was primarily necessary for the Christian's own self-regard. The Talmud was purged, expurgated, burned, and reviled, yet it was the church that preserved the extracanonical apocalyptic texts and the writings of Josephus and Philo. And Jewish intellectual life and culture flourished despite the colonial oppression.

Volkmar's metaphor, that the Mother womb from which Christianity emerged was "the virgin womb" of the God of Judaism, expresses the archive of German Protestantism quite clearly: Christianity was derived from Judaism and superseded it, but Judaism was not the offspring of God, who remained a virgin until giving birth to His first child, Christianity. Christianity is the first-born son of the virgin, Christ himself. Yet even in denying that Judaism is a divinely revealed religion, Volkmar is unable to remove it from Christian genealogy. It is the archive as circumcision, in Derrida's term, Judaism leaving its indelible presence in the flesh of Christian theology. [39]

## NOTES

1. See the recent studies: Ulrich van der Heyden, ed., Mission und Moderne: Beiträge zur Geschichte der christlichen Missionen in Afrika (Köln: Köppe, 1998); Ulrich van der Heyden and Jürgen Becher, eds., Mission und Gewalt: Der Umgang christlicher Missionen mit Gewalt und die Ausbreitung des Christentums in Afrika und Asien in der Zeit von 1792 bis 1918/19 (Stuttgart: Steiner, 2000); Werner Ustorf, Mission im Nationalsozialismus (Berlin: Selignow, 2002); Werner Ustorf, Sailing on the Next Tide: Missions, Missiology, and the Third Reich (Frankfurt a. M.: Peter Lang, 2000).

2. Jean-Luc Nancy, "The Deconstruction of Christianity," in Religion and Media, ed. Hent de Vries and Samuel Weber (Stanford: Stanford University Press, 2001), 117.

3. Jonathan Hess, "Sugar Island Jews? Jewish Colonialism and the Rhetoric of 'Civic Improvement' in Eighteenth-Century Germany," Eighteenth-Century Studies 32, no. 1 (1998): 92–100.

4. Susanne Zantop, Colonial Fantasies: Conquest, Family, and Nation in Precolonial Germany, 1770–1870 (Durham: Duke University Press, 1997), 7.

5. Hess, "Sugar Island Jews," 98.

6. Rabbi Moses of Pressburg, Sefer Eleh divre ha-berit: kovets ha-haramot u-fiske ha-

halakhot neged rishone ha-Reformim be-Hamburg, kolel igrotehem shel gedole ha-dor, ha-Hatam Sofer, 'Akiva Eger u-she'ar hakhme Yisra'el (1819; rpt., Jerusalem: Sifriyat mekorot, 1969), 26.

7. Christhard Hoffmann, Werner Bergmann, and Helmut Walser Smith, eds., *Exclusionary Violence: Antisemitic Riots in Modern German History* (Ann Arbor: University of Michigan Press, 2002).

8. Theodore Ziolkowski, *Fictional Transfigurations of Jesus* (Princeton: Princeton University Press, 1972), 46.

9. Karl Gutzkow, *Wally the Skeptic*, trans. Ruth-Ellen Boetcher Joeres (Bern: Herbert Land, 1974). See Geiger's reference to Wally in his letter to M. A. Stern, March 31, 1836, in Abraham Geiger, *Nachgelasse Schriften*, ed. Ludwig Geiger, (1876; rpt., New York: Arno Press, 1980), 5:89. Marilyn Massey calls attention to Gutzkow's novel, especially its indication of the religious mood in the era of the controversy over D. F. Strauss's first *Life of Jesus*. See Marilyn Massey, *Christ Unmasked: The Meaning of The Life of Jesus in German Politics* (Chapel Hill: University of North Carolina Press, 1983).

10. Siegfried Leffler, *Christus im Dritten Reich der Deutschen: Wesen, Weg und Zielsetzung der Kirchenbewegung Deutsche Christen* (Weimar: Verlag Deutsche Christen, 1935), 29f., as cited in Kurt Meier, *Die Deutschen Christen: Das Bild einer Bewegung im Kirchenkampf des Dritten Reiches* (Halle a. d. S.: M. Niemeyer, 1964), 8. For other, similar statements, see Gerhard Besier, *Die Kirchen und das Dritte Reich: Spaltungen und Abwehrkämpfe 1934–1937* (Munich: Econ Ullstein List, 2001), 256.

11. Abraham Geiger, *Das Judentum und seine Geschichte: In zwölf Vorlesungen* (Breslau: Schlettersche Buchhandlung, 1864), 117–18.

12. Franz Delitzsch, *Jesus und Hillel: Mit Rücksicht auf Renan und Geiger* (Erlangen: Andreas Deichert, 1866), 7, 11.

13. "Geigers Antwort an Franz Delitzsch," *Jüdische Zeitschrift für Wissenschaft und Leben* 10 (1872): 309.

14. Heinrich von Treitschke, "Unsere Aussichten," in *Der Berliner Antisemitismusstreit*, ed. Walter Boehlich (Frankfurt a. M.: Insel, 1965), 10, 11.

15. Ernest Renan, *The Life of Jesus*, trans. Charles Edwin Wilbour (New York: Carleton, 1864), 224–25.

16. Leopold Dukes, "Qu'est-ce que le Christianisme a pris au Judaisme, ou de la morale dite chretienne," *Archives Israelites* 10 (1849): 14.

17. Augustus Neander, *The Life of Jesus Christ in its Historical Connexion and Historical Development*, trans. John McClintock and Charles E. Blumenthal (New York: Harper, 1850), 35.

18. "When Jesus Was an Aryan: The Protestant Church and Antisemitic Propaganda," in *Betrayal: The German Churches and the Holocaust*, ed. Robert Ericksen and Susannah Heschel (Minneapolis: Augsburg Fortress Press, 1999), 68–89. The best study of the *Deutsche Christen* is Doris L. Bergen, *Twisted Cross: The German Christian*

Movement in the Third Reich (Chapel Hill: University of North Carolina Press, 1996).

19. Walter Grundmann, "Das Heil kommt von den Juden: Eine Schicksalsfrage an die Christen deutscher Nation," *Deutsche Frömmigkeit* 9 (September 1938): 1.

20. *Deutsche mit Gott: Ein deutsches Glaubensbuch* (Weimar: Verlag Deutsche Christen, 1941), 46. The foreword of this book was signed by Grundmann, Wilhelm Buechner, Paul Gimpel, Hans Pribnow, Kurt Thieme, Max Adolf Wagenführer, Heinrich Weinmann, and Hermann Werdermann.

21. Walter Grundmann and Karl Friedrich Euler, *Das religiöse Gesicht des Judentums: Entstehung und Art* (Leipzig: Georg Wigand, 1942), Vorwort (unpaged).

22. The larger context of his comment is as follows: "Je stärker das rassische und völkische Erwachen sich durchsetzt und je energischer in der politischen Lage der Gegensatz zwischen dem Dritten Reich und dem Judentum als ein Kampf auf Leben und Tod hervortritt, desto schärfer wird auch der Blick für den politischen Gehalt der Religion des alten Testaments, insbesondere seiner Zukunftserwartung." Johannes Hempel, "Chronik vom Herausgeber," *Zeitschrift für alttestamentliche Wissenschaft* N. F. 18 (1942–43): 212. See the biography of Hempel by Cornelia Weber, *Altes Testament und völkische Frage* (Tübingen: Mohr Siebeck, 2000).

23. See the "Principles of the Religious Movement of German Christians," issued in June 1932, in John Conway, *The Nazi Persecution of the Churches* (New York: Basic Books, 1968), 339–41.

24. Thüringisches Hauptstaatsarchiv Weimar, Bestand C 1400.

25. Zantop, *Colonial Fantasies*, 7.

26. Zantop, *Colonial Fantasies*, 173.

27. Zantop, *Colonial Fantasies*, 199.

28. Zantop, *Colonial Fantasies*, 101.

29. Gustav Volkmar, *Die Religion Jesu und ihre erste Entwicklung nach dem gegenwaertigen Stande der Wissenschaft* (Leipzig: F. A. Brockhaus, 1857), 52. Quoted in Susannah Heschel, *Abraham Geiger and the Jewish Jesus* (Chicago: University of Chicago Press, 1998), 161.

30. Volkmar, *Die Religion Jesu*, 60.

31. Michael Wirth, *Die Pharisäer: Ein Beitrag zum leichtern Verstehen der Evangelien und zur Selbstprüfung* (Ulm: Stetten, 1824), iii; Joseph Langen, *Das Judenthum in Palaestina zur Zeit Christi* (Freiburg i. B.: Herder, 1866), 189; "Pharisäer," in *Biblische Realwörterbuch zum Handgebrauch für Studirende, Candidaten, Gymnasiallehrer und Prediger*, ed. Georg Benedict Winer (Leipzig: Carl Heinrich Reclam, 1847–48), 2:244–48; and Christoph von Ammon, *Die Geschichte des Leben Jesu* (Leipzig: Vogel, 1842–47), 3:225; Renan, *Life of Jesus*, 299.

32. Adolf von Harnack, *Das Wesen des Christentums* (Leipzig: J. C. Hinrichs, 1900), 30–31.

33. Hess, "Sugar Island Jews," 92.

34. Christian Wilhelm Dohm, *Über die bürgerliche Verbesserung der Juden* (Berlin: Friedrich Nicolai, 1781), as cited in Jonathan Hess, "Memory, History, and the Jewish Question: Universal Citizenship and the Colonization of Jewish Memory," in *The Work of Memory: New Directions in the Study of German Society and Culture,* ed. Alon Confino and Peter Fritzsche (Urbana-Champaign: University of Illinois Press, 2002), 52.

35. Walter Grundmann, "Das Messiasproblem," in *Germanentum, Christentum und Judentum: Studien zur Erforschung ihres gegenseitigen Verhältnisses: Sitzungsberichte der zweiten Arbeitstagung des Instituts zur Erforschung des jüdischen Einflusses auf das deutsche kirchliche Leben vom 3. bis 5. März 1941 in Eisenach,* ed. Walter Grundmann (Leipzig: Georg Wigand, 1942), 2:381.

36. Walter Grundmann, "Mendelssohn und Hamann," in *Germanentum, Christentum und Judentum: Studien zur Erforschung ihres gegenseitigen Verhältnisses: Sitzungsberichte der dritten Arbeitstagung des Instituts zur Erforschung des jüdischen Einflusses auf das deutsche kirchliche Leben vom 9. bis 11. Juni 1942 in Nürnberg,* ed. Walter Grundmann (Leipzig: Georg Wigand, 1943), 3:1–48.

37. Jacques Derrida, *Archive Fever: A Freudian Impression,* trans. Eric Prenowitz (Chicago: University of Chicago Press, 1996), 12.

38. Frantz Fanon, *The Wretched of the Earth,* trans. Constance Farrington (New York, Grove Press, 1968), 210.

39. Derrida, *Archive Fever,* 26.

# PART 4

# Nazi Visions of Africa

ELISA VON JOEDEN-FORGEY

# Race Power in Postcolonial Germany

## The German Africa Show and
## the National Socialist State, 1935–40

While the marked effect of empire on British society and politics is well established, the long-term impact of overseas colonization on Germany is still generally deemed insignificant. The notion that colonialism was inconsequential to the larger narrative of German history is based on the way that "impact" is often understood: namely, as direct and statistically measurable. For colonization to have an impact there would need to be, for example, large numbers of persons traveling between colony and metropole. At the very least there would need to be evidence that the majority of the metropolitan population was enthusiastic about colonies or could find them on a map. Neither was true in the German case. Instead, German colonization is notable for its relatively small scale (though the African territories alone were four times as large as Germany proper), its short life-span (a little over thirty years), and its financial failure (from the viewpoint of the national economy, considering the need for metropolitan subsidies). Nevertheless, the intensity of colonial crises and reform debates shows that colonization constituted at times a national trauma, one that forced people to rethink long-held assumptions about how to exercise power. One consequence of this was the emergence of a specific idea of power – "race power" – that combined nineteenth-century racialism with lessons learned from colonial political praxis.[1] In this essay I examine the long-term impact of race-power ideas as reflected in the brief history of the German Africa Show (Deutsche Afrika-Schau), a traveling exhibition supported by the NSDAP (National Socialist Democratic Workers Party) that employed blacks in Germany during the Third Reich.[2]

The German Africa Show is evidence that a new and enduring vision of power as race power emerged from the process of colonization. "Race power" was an idea that was not only based in racialist concepts of the community and its health, but also defined by certain rituals of power that were dependent upon proper relationships between race and space. Persons who envisioned policies in terms of race power understood true power as something that could only be gained, maintained, and exercised through distinct forms of governance toward persons who were conceived as radically alterior, existing in a wholly separate and incommensurable moral universe irrespective of their place of residence or claim to citizenship. Ideas of governance informed by race power emphasized the legal and geographic separation of "alien races" and the use of raw forms of state coercion and violence toward them. Forms of race power were institutionalized in colonial governance and in metropolitan policies toward resident colonial subjects.

The possibilities opened up by race-power praxis were never restricted to the colonies. By the turn of the century they began to form Pan-German ideas for governing a Germanic "tribal empire" (*Stammesreich*) in Europe – essentially a reinterpretation of Europe in terms of a Germanic settler colony. [3] These thinkers demonstrated a heightened sensitivity to what they considered to be improper colonial mixing, including "mixed marriage," and an image of the international world as a "racialized globe." [4] They also began to codify the process through which unwanted colonial subjects on the continent would be structured out of the racialized moral community, through citizenship provisions, "race-appropriate" bodies of law, relocation onto reservations, mass deportations to overseas territories, and forced sterilization. [5]

The history of the German Africa Show was formed by the historical tension between colonial and Pan-German understandings of race power, between persons who sought to exercise race power overseas and those who were interested in reorganizing the European continent in terms of race geography. These two different racialist traditions determined two very different policies toward Africans in Germany once Germany's colonies had been lost. Colonial revisionists hoped to use resident former colonial subjects as propagandists for Germany's colonial cause. Radical racist groups such as the NSDAP had no toleration for "race aliens" in Germany proper. They saw the presence of Africans in Germany as indicative of insufficient attention given to race matters by the imperial state. In the postwar context of heightened race anxieties during the so-called "Black Horror on the Rhine" and of a prevalent sense that the proper racial order had been inverted (by the Versailles Treaty, which treated Germany as an "object" rather than a full subject of international law, and the "reverse colonization" of the Rhine with French colonial soldiers), Adolf Hitler blamed the Jews for Weimar's black presence: "more than seven million [Germans] languish under foreign domination and the vital artery of the German people runs through the hunting ground of African Negro hordes. . . . It was and is the Jews who bring the Negro to the Rhine always with the same concealed thought and clear goal of destroying by the bastardization which would necessarily set in the white race which they hate."[6] If "the Jews" had attempted to colonize Germany with African soldiers, they had already successfully colonized France, according to Nazi ideologue Alfred Rosenberg. In his words France had "led the emancipation of the Jews" and was pursuing a policy of "mongrelizing" Europe with blacks, so much so that France would soon be "hardly definable as a European state, but more an offshoot of Africa, led by the Jews."[7] Hitler and Rosenberg, like other radical racialists, characterized "the Jews" as anticolonizers, masters not of racial order and robust imperialism but of intermixing chaos and cosmopolitan degeneracy. They were the forces of pollution instead of purity, whose main aim was to invert the colonial-style hierarchies that Nazis believed were both natural and necessary to German historic dynamism.

## The German Africa Show

The German Africa Show began as a private venture, organized by blacks in Germany sometime between August 1934 and November 1935 as a response to the financial difficulties resulting from an increase in overt racial discrimination after the NSDAP assumed power. It ended as an official organ of state propaganda, supported by the Foreign Office, the Office of Colonial Policy, the German Workers Front (DAF), the Society for the Study of Natives (*Gesellschaft für Eingeborenenkunde*), and the Propaganda Ministry. After the show was officially canceled in 1940, some performers received small sums of money through the Colonial Veteran's Aid (*Kolonialkriegerdank*) until at least 1943.[8]

Though the troupe would grow in number through the 1930s, it usually included about thirty members. Some performers were children, about a third were women, and many were German citizens. Kwassi Bruce, one of the show's founders, had come to Germany from Togo at the age of three for the 1896 Colonial Exhibition in Berlin. Like him, many performers in the show had served in Germany's colonial troops during the First World War.[9] Several of the performers had worked in Weimar theaters and variety shows before 1933, so they were well acquainted with the popular tastes of German audiences and the draw of colonial nostalgia. Many of the performers were married to white Germans and had children. Joseph Boholle, for example, had three adult children in 1935, one of whom had two children of his own. His family thus represented three generations of Germandom. Another show member, Erika

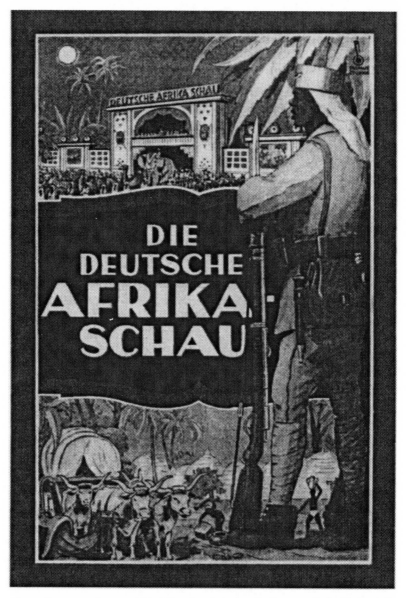

Fig. 1. Front cover from an Africa Show brochure (BA-Berlin R1001 6382, Blatt 244A). Reprinted with the permission of the German Federal Archives.

Diek, was the daughter of Mandenga Diek, who had received citizenship in Hamburg in 1896.[10]

The show was thus never a collection of persons new to Europe. Rather it consisted predominantly of persons well integrated into the German and the wider European economic and social orders who claimed these worlds as their own. Nevertheless, for financial and (later) ideological reasons, the show relied on popular stereotypes about Africa and its radical alterity. The performers appeared on stage in costumes representing the absurd pastiche of images of Africa that circulated in Germany at the time. The cover of a 1937 German Africa Show program, for example, uses a montage technique in order to suggest that the colonies have come "home" to Germany (see fig. 1).

Here we see an African colonial soldier standing with his rifle tall above a landscape teeming with people and wild animals, all emerging from a World Expo–style entranceway that reads "German Africa Show." Such exotic chaos seems to have been popular from the outset. One Bremen newspaper described the show as follows:

> A black soldier beats the hollow drum; he pulls you into this village, which exhibits a wonderful collection of many products from Africa's natives [Eingeborenen], the Masai, the Samoans [sic], as well as preserved animals. The show offers us a truly impressive picture already at first sight. Blacks who entered into the struggle for Germany [that is, the World War] under General von Lettow-Vorbeck and who can show several medals remind us of the time when the Negroes stood up for their German masters with rare fanaticism, and successfully opposed the inflammatory propaganda that Germany had no capacity to be a colonizing people [Kolonialvolk].[11]

During one particular showing the audience was promised an "African Fakir with his spear and war dance on sharp nails" as well as acrobatics, fire eating, and a variety of "native" dances. The performance opened with a lecture on "old Africa" by the performer Jimmy Overgrand and frequently closed with a speech and slide show by Kwassi Bruce. Finally the spectators were invited to visit an exhibition area, where they could meet the performers, view preserved animals, tour native villages, and purchase colonial souvenirs.[12]

At first glance the Africa Show may appear to be of little relevance to the grand narrative of German history and thus of little consequence to our understanding of National Socialist ideology and practice. Indeed, compared with other institutions of racial control, the Africa Show had a number of unusual features: it was a highly public affair; its members were mostly compensated for their work; and the living conditions were relatively good. The show's larger historical relevance rests on three peculiar qualities. First, the Africa Show is one of the few examples of official state policy toward blacks in Nazi Germany (the other key example being the sterilization of the children of French colonial soldiers and German civilians who were born during the Rhineland occupation). Second, the political and ideological pressures on the Africa Show were exerted by the upper ranks of the Nazi state hierarchy and therefore can tell us something about how the Nazi leadership was thinking about race on a global scale. Finally, Nazi discourse surrounding the show demonstrates the links between Nazi ideology and Germany's past colonial praxis that were rarely expressed explicitly.

State support for the Africa Show in 1935 was consistent with several trends in the long-term history of Africans in Germany. During the colonial period the state had kept close watch on Africans in Germany, attempting to control as much of their movements as possible because of the potential political threat they posed. [13] The state also sponsored ethnographic exhibitions (Völkerschauen) and subsidized the costs of employing, educating, and housing visiting Africans. These trends continued into the Weimar Republic, when colonial organizations tracked Africans in Germany and occasionally offered them jobs or small grants. The idea of sponsoring a wandering theater troupe was therefore nothing new; it could be embraced without much reflection.

Networks extending back to the colonial era in fact facilitated the first contact between what would come to be known as the Africa Show and a member of the German colonial elite. On November 18, 1935, Kwassi Bruce and Adolf Hillerkus, the directors of a traveling "Negro Village" (Negerdorf), met with Edmund Brückner, the former governor of Togo and head of the Colonial Department of the Foreign Office, in order to propose that the colonial organizations support their enterprize. [14] Brückner remarked that the proposal "seems to offer a way to provide a group of unemployed natives living in Berlin and its environs with a profitable activity." [15] Like many old colonials, Brückner was concerned about the negative impact that Nazi race policies might have on former colonial subjects. Bruce and Hillerkus were aware of this colonial revisionist concern and framed their proposal according to the weltanschauung of old colonial officialdom, whose members occupied key positions in the colonial organizations of the Third Reich. [16] As documented by Brückner's notes, they argued that: Africans in Germany had earned membership in German society by virtue of their service as colonial soldiers; as former "comrades in

172

the protectorate" (*Schutzgenossen*), they deserved jobs; and it was more desirable to employ former colonial subjects than to let them become burdens to society.

The arguments of this proposal would later be used to convince skeptical party officials and were eventually advanced by the highest echelons of the Nazi Party. In a March 30, 1936, circular sent to all district leaders (*Gauleiter*), future secretary of the führer Martin Bormann noted that

> about fifty *Neger* from our former colonies live with their families in Germany. These natives are almost entirely without secure jobs, and when they find work, the employer is treated with such hostility (*angefeindet*) that he is forced to let the *Neger* go. I point out that these *Neger* must be offered a means of living in Germany. It must also be taken into consideration . . . that some of the *Neger* remain in contact with their homelands (*Heimat*) and will report there about their treatment in Germany. The Foreign Minister and I have therefore agreed that it must be determined which *Neger* to be put under special protection for their deployment for Germany [that is, as colonial propagandists]. These will then be given a permit from the Foreign Office roughly stating that there are no reservations about their employment.[17]

Not surprisingly, Bormann concludes with a request for secrecy so that "the support of these *Neger* [would] not be misinterpreted." Nazi officials working in departments with no colonial ambitions whatsoever seem to have tolerated the show (albeit temporarily), because colonial revisionism was perceived to have gained a certain propagandistic value during the 1920s. More than a decade of active colonial propaganda had also shaped the party's general stance toward the efforts to regain overseas territories; Hitler and other party members were convinced that colonization should eventually become a goal of Nazi foreign policy.[18]

In soliciting the party's support, Bruce and Hillerkus sought to negotiate the tension between colonial aspirations and the Nazi program of constructing a strictly "Aryan" society. Before their meeting with Brückner, the Africa Show had begun to encounter popular resistance in the increasingly racialized public sphere. In Berlin, for example, a city official ordered that before the *Negerdorf* could appear at the Christmas Market, Bruce and Hillerkus had to present him with a license from the Foreign Office assuring that he would receive no complaints from "certain Party offices."[19] Bruce and Hillerkus also may have sought official backing as a means of protecting themselves against harassment from zealous party members while providing a livelihood for the other performers in a climate otherwise hostile to the employment of "non-Aryan" Germans. [20]

In its inaugural year the Africa Show operated more or less independently. The Foreign Office, the Society for the Study of Natives, and the German Labor Front each played but a minor role in the show's affairs. Only gradually would it become an example of what Alon Confino has called an official "vehicle of memory," one that served to focus public attention on a version of the past that was considered particularly important to the state and its goals. [21] The show's initial independence indicates that it was not immediately embraced as a vehicle for state propaganda and that in these early years the state did not feel the need to track closely the movements and cultural production of Africans in its midst. But the period of independence did not last long. The state took over the show's management in 1936, when various mishaps, including a fatal accident, called attention to the potential chaos that a wandering troupe could cause. The Labor Front fired the show's owner for financial mismanagement and replaced him with Hillerkus. Bruce was named the show's operation manager. [22] From then on the German Africa Show was no longer a private commercial enterprise but an organ of the state, and the show's discursive apparatus would be reshaped in explicitly National Socialist terms.

While the exhibition initially addressed the concerns of the colonial revisionist movement, the context in which the Africa Show appeared eventually conformed to the racial policies of the National Socialist state. Despite Bormann's directive, even those blacks in Germany deemed deserving of special permits were by no means guaranteed security against Nazi race policies or eager party functionaries at the local level. The Africa Show must be understood in the context of two modes of remembering the past: colonial revisionism and radical racism. Despite the tensions between these groups and their different emphases (for instance, the early Africa Show was criticized by skeptical Nazis for inadequately regulating the performers' mobility), the colonial enthusiasts ultimately proved amenable to Nazi priorities. Many had even shared such priorities well before the party was founded, albeit in a form that focused on colonial territory as the stage for race power. As governor of German Southwest Africa in 1905, for example, Friedrich von Lindequist had signed the first German colonial law against mixed marriages. As director of the Society for the Study of Natives in the 1930s, he argued that the Africa Show was created "for race-political considerations, to take the natives [Eingeborenen] off the streets, seal them off as much as possible, and strictly control them." [23]

Colonial revisionists could tolerate the public appearance of Africans and other "race aliens" in large measure because their old brand of imperialist racism had always combined race thinking and political pragmatism, with emphasis on the latter. They had even grown used to tolerating the presence of a few Africans in the metropole during the Imperial and Weimar periods, so this presence in the 1930s was not particularly threatening. Since the Nazis sought to exercise race power not in the colonies but in Germany, those of an anticolonial bent believed that even a few racial Others could infect the wider "Aryan" population with degenerate ideas or genes. Generally younger than the colonial revisionist leadership, they only experienced colonialism in its "improper" form – that is, "in reverse." They had no lived memory of the comfortable geographic split between metropole and colony, and therefore they less readily displaced their race anxieties onto any preexisting or future colonial terrain, with the brief exception of the Madagascar Plan. Germany itself was for them the focal point of race anxieties and of their resolution. They saw the presence of all non-Aryans not only as a threat to the *Volk* but also as a living reminder of the collapsed colonial world of Weimar, when the race threats of the colonial world appeared at Germany's doorstep. Since in their minds the past had to be completely overcome in order for Germany to rise again to greatness, the living metropolitan memories of this past (that is, people) had also to be "overcome." These party members gradually joined forces to protest the state's support of the Africa Show, which they saw as support for the flouting of Germany's past racial corruption at a time when the state was radicalizing its race policies in the name of Aryan purity.

As Nazi racial purists grew increasingly uneasy with the public appearance of blacks, Hillerkus and Bruce were replaced by a "Captain" Schneider.[24] Lindequist praised him as "a hard working, faultless, SA man, and who also enjoys the support of His Ministry President and Senior General Göring."[25] During Schneider's tenure, the performers received no pay and lived in deplorable conditions – a consequence, no doubt, of the racial animus he expressed toward them.[26] His descriptions of the performers, whom he referred to as *Neger*, bristle with radical racist language. In his report to the Propaganda Ministry, for instance, he employed some of the more vulgar racist stereotypes, arguing that "because of the particular racial characteristics of the Negroes, their pronounced lust and their tendency to sexual excess, scandals often occurred, and there were unfortunately always white women who shared intimacy with them, shamed their own race, and brought bastards into the world."[27] As a consequence, he believed "The Negroes [should] be enclosed in a tightly sealed community [Gemeinschaft], which is kept under constant surveillance and whose accommodation is arranged for maximum control."[28]

State recognition of the Africa Show can be interpreted in this context as an attempt to carve out an "appropriate" space for blacks in Germany. Some of the troupe members were in fact former colonial soldiers, and since "the Mandate governments refused to accept" their return, so the logic ran, they could not be sent back to where they "belonged."[29] Indeed, since some officials intended to use performers as future Nazi propagandists, the Africa Show represented a kind of "temporary camp" for displaced colonial subjects. As the National Socialist Party continued to consolidate its control over public life, the colonial space that the revisionists had carved out for the Africa Show became increasingly dominated by questions of race purity and race-political supervision. This brought the show under more intense surveillance. One of the reasons that skeptical party members permitted the show to exist before 1940 was that they believed that the troupe members were Vollblutneger (full-blooded Negroes).[30] Their status as such was important to party members, for the principal target of race anxiety was interracial mixing and the supposed degeneracy that it caused. An August 3, 1939, meeting between the show's administrators and representatives of the Reich Colonial Association (Reichskolonialbund) offers a case in point. The Reich Colonial Association had voiced a variety of objections, one of which was that some of their members had seen a "scandalous" exhibition, believed to be the Africa Show, "in which mostly half-breeds (Mischlinge) were engaged." In the same meeting one representative asked if the "natives" couldn't be administered in some other way. Asked in reply if he had a better suggestion for other modes of employment, he admitted that he "once had the intention of employing a native as a chauffeur, but this indeed posed difficulties, due to the close living quarters with others."[31]

The concept of the Vollblutneger (a term often used synonymously with "natives," or Eingeborenen) was closely tied to both the fact of and the memory of German colonial conquest. In order to qualify as "full-blooded," one had to be able to demonstrate one's origin in a colonized territory (preferably a former German one). In National Socialist praxis, the non-Aryan "pure races" were therefore those that had been conquered in the past and could potentially be conquered again in the future. In the realm of political memory, that is, they remained conquered. They thus "belonged" in the Nazi state (if at all) as constant signs of the fact and rectitude of Nazi racial domination. By extension Mischlinge described those people who had not been adequately conquered in the past, be they Jews, Roma-Sinti, or acculturated blacks. Mischlinge posed a threat not solely because of their perceived racial difference, but also because they had historically been allowed into the body politic, in some cases as legal equals, and hence had become irretrievably corrupted. The fact of their presence in Germany as citizens or resident foreigners was interpreted as a sign of their internal racial confusion, the consequence of which was their inability to appreciate purity and their supposed biological drive to destroy Germany.

Officials debated whether or not some of the Africa Show performers were *Mischlinge*. Opponents were apparently troubled by the difficulty in defining and identifying the performers as "of pure race." Paul Aßmann, a former district leader for the German Labor Front, thus complained to the Foreign Office that Africa Show members had told the audience, "We are the only authorized, officially permitted Africa Show – and that with only one *Askari* [colonial soldier] in our midst. Some others were never in the colonies, one is an American citizen, and some have been here in Germany since childhood."[32] Aßmann singled out for concern, with classic racist paranoia, precisely those Africans who claimed Europe and North America as their homes – that is, those persons he felt were inauthentic and impure due to their corruptive experiences as persons with rights (in his mind) equal to those of other Westerners.

The Nazi category of "Gypsies" (*Zigeuner*), a group that was at once "pure-blooded" and degenerate, offers an interesting point of comparison with the category of so-called "full-blooded Negroes." The Nazi "Gypsy researcher" Robert Ritter, for example, differentiated between "pure-blooded gypsies" (*reinrassige Zigeuner*) and "mixed-race gypsies" (*Zigeunermischlingen*).[33] Heinrich Himmler at one point advocated the "relocation" of the "pure-blooded gypsies" in a kind of reservation, where they could live "according to their customs and traditions (*Sitten und Gebräuche*) . . . and follow their species-specific occupations (*arteigenen Beschäftigung*)."[34] Himmler's suggestion here attempts to reinvent parts of the Roma-Sinti population in colonial terms. Apparently he could countenance the idea of existence for pure-blooded lesser races so long as they were governed in colonial style – separated out, cast into cultural status, and ruled by force. This colonial logic also informed statements about the ultimate target of Nazi racialist violence, Jewish people. Hitler said shortly before the Nuremberg Laws that Jews must be "removed from all professions, ghettoised, restricted to a particular territory, where they can wander about, in accordance with their character, while the German people looks on, as one looks at animals in the wild."[35] One policy proposal, the "Madagascar Plan," brought together Nazi racialist anti-Semitism and colonial models for governance quite literally. The plan, drafted in 1940 by the head of the Jewish Department of the Foreign Office, Franz Rademacher, aimed to completely separate Jews from the "white" world. [36] It stipulated that Jews would be deported to parts of Madagascar, which, once ceded by France, would be put under a police governor directly subordinate to the ss. [37] The Madagascar Plan attracted the interest of Heinrich Himmler, Adolf Eichmann, and Hitler himself. [38] As Alfred Rosenberg put it, "The question is not of creating a Jewish state, but a Jewish reservation." [39]

The plan to send European Jews to Africa, "conceived as a gigantic concentration camp for slow death," seems in part to have been an attempt to fit Jewish people into a colonial logic of appropriately racialized space. [40] In National Socialist race ideology, of course, Jewish people never occupied a "pureblooded" position on a par with the position accorded, however temporarily, to some Roma-Sinti and blacks. Like many racialist anti-Semites before them, the Nazis defined "the Jewish race" as inherently degenerate or "purely mixed," which meant, in the words of the party's high court director, Walter Buch, that "the Jew is not a human being. He is nothing but an agent of decomposition." [41] Here we see the key National Socialist radicalization of colonial-era race-power praxis, one that hinged on the invention of a category between the colonizing Self and the colonial Other that could be blamed for reversals and inversions.

Nazi anxieties about mixing heralded the end of the Africa Show. Despite the surge in popularity that the show seemed to enjoy under its final director, Georg Stock – in September 1937, for example, a total of 27,238 people attended the show's performances in three towns – it started to be constantly harassed by local opponents in 1938. [42] Even its demonstrated colonial propagandistic value could not save it. In the spring of 1940, a few months before it closed, the show generated approximately four hundred new members for the Reich Colonial Association and as many new subscribers to the journal *Kolonie und Heimat* (Colony and home). [43] Around the same time that critics of the show began to join forces, the Office of Race Policy expressed interest in obtaining the names and addresses of all past and present members of the show as well as of other blacks who might potentially be employed by the show. At the office's request, Stock collected a list of thirty-three people, including those who "are not yet with us, but who in time are supposed to join us." [44] The tone of his letter suggests that nobody was forced to join the Africa Show, although the radicalization of Nazi race policies around this time probably pressured many people to do so. Using this list, the Office of Race Policy put together a file of sixty-six "Negroes and mulattos" living in Germany. [45] Although the explicit purpose of this particular file remains unknown, it was probably compiled in the event that the state should decide upon an alternative policy to the Africa Show.

The basis for opposition to the show can be gathered from documents chronicling the state's decision to shut it down in the summer of 1940. Already in 1939 the Labor Front and the Superior Honor and Disciplinary Court had begun to voice concerns about the Africa Show, and especially about the racial status of the show members.[46] Stories of inappropriate mixing between Africa Show performers and female spectators circulated among Nazi Party offices.[47] Although most of the official documents praised the "respectable" way in which members of the Africa Show conducted themselves, complaints were made about a letter exchange, shared conversations, and the public knowledge that some performers were married to white women. A defense of the show written by Lindequist mentions several other occurrences that help explain why the show would be banned.

According to Lindequist, the Sub-District Administration (*Kreisverwaltung*) in Konstanz had complained to the Office of Colonial Policy that a few of the actors had supposedly addressed the audience as "*Landesleuten, deutschen Volksgenossen*," terms that can roughly be translated as "fellow nationals, German Volk-comrades." By then, the term *Volksgenossen* had become politicized and racialized to designate only those people included in the Aryan racial body. In the very last performances, the Africa Show members apparently challenged the prevailing *völkisch* ideology in other ways, too, comparing African dances to Bavarian ones and exhibiting slides of a German farmer boy with a black "boy" (*Kinderboy*) so as to emphasize the "good relationship between white and black in German East Africa." One performer told audiences of his royal family's support of Germany when it first colonized Cameroon and even claimed Gustav Nachtigal, the colonial hero and imperial commissioner for the west African coast, to be his godfather. Finally, young German women reportedly showed great interest in the Africa Show actors and met with them illicitly.[48]

It is unclear from the available documents whether Africa Show members intended these challenges to be open acts of resistance. Using the language of community membership and making comparisons between African and German customs was a stock joke of variety shows and of performances with colonial nostalgia themes. The actors might thus have been employing a standard variety-show or colonial-revisionist language that was no longer tolerated by the Nazi state. Regardless of the intention, the Africa Show performers transgressed the racial boundaries delineated by the National Socialists by suggesting any commensurability between themselves and the proto-Aryan

*Volk.* As one official critic suggested, if non-Aryans were to be tolerated in Nazi Germany at all, they had to be presented as so distant from "Aryans" that they occupied an entirely separate racial universe. He commented that: "Stock's Africa Show . . . led me to certain realizations that are not inconsequential for the reaching of race-political goals and challenges and, above all else, for the awakening of a racial self-understanding, which appears to be of particular importance these days. These realizations all essentially boil down to the same thing: that they [the performances] should serve to increase the distance between African *Neger* and our German *Volk*, not to deaden the feeling for that distance. . . . Furthermore, the very thought is unbearable that some of them are married to German women and have children who serve in the armed forces as *Mischlinge.*"[49] The author of this letter then tied the Africa Show to wider Nazi race policies: "At a time when we must instill self-confidence and a feeling for distance in the German people as against other peoples – for example, in the question of the Polish agricultural workers – the valuation of the circumstances just cited must be strict from a race-political standpoint. Just as we refuse to comply with the Christian demand to recognize baptized *Neger* as our equals, so we also refuse to recognize the fact of military service, achieved by colonial servant groups (*Hilfsvölkern*), as obliging of equal racial treatment." This critic not only challenged the very arguments of state support for the show – that former "colonial comrades" should somehow occupy a "protected" position in the Nazi racial state – but also saw the kinds of mixing that the show encouraged to be inimical to Nazi values. If some racial groups are to be exhibited, he seems to suggest, they should not look like representatives of the Nazi state and they should at least be silent. Another opponent of the show agreed: "Any speaking engagement for the *Neger*," he noted after its cancellation, "is heretofore out of the question."[50]

By 1940 hostility to the show extended even to the Office of Colonial Policy as well as to Martin Bormann at the Deputy Führer's Office.[51] Lindequist would try in vain to keep the show going. It was finally shut down in June 1940 in the town of Horn. After the show had been cancelled, the district head of Lower Austria complained to the Propaganda Ministry that the actors were overtaking his city. "Time and again," he wrote, "it has occurred that individual *Neger* spoke to young women in or in front of taverns and that some wanted to go to the movies, etc. This has, of course, caused displeasure in the population. If it hasn't yet resulted in any incidents, then it is only thanks to the population's discipline."[52]

In the end the state never created a coherent race policy for Africans and other blacks in Germany. The Africa Show's cancellation in 1940 was supposed to be part of a wider prohibition against the public appearance of blacks. Although the Reich Theater Chamber officially forbade such appearances, many Africa Show performers still found jobs in the theater. In October 1940, for example, Propaganda Minister Goebbels attended a special show for war-wounded of the operetta "Die – oder Keine" (She – and no other), in which fourteen black actors appeared on stage. After the show Gregor Kotto and either Sam or Victor Bell, a member of the famous Cameroonian family, were invited into the director's room. There Goebbels is said to have "expressed praise and thanks for the show" and asked them to relate this to the other black actors.[53] Certain party offices, such as the Chancellery of the Führer, were even willing to see the Africa Show reopened after Germany's occupation of France had neutralized the threat of France's colonial troops.[54]

The last known surviving documents relating to the Africa Show are from 1943. The fates of many Africa Show members are still not known. Africa Show performer Juma bin Abdallah survived and worked at the Seminar for African Languages and Cultures in Hamburg in 1948–49.[55] According to Theodor Wonja Michel, Kwassi Bruce and his family were able to emigrate before 1945.[56] Many Africans found parts in state-sponsored colonial nostalgia films that became popular during the war, almost as if UFA, Germany's largest film company, had become an Africa Show without the unpredictability of live performance.[57] Despite the availability of film and theater jobs, many African Germans, especially those categorized as Mischlinge, were forced into concentration camps, and it would be wrong to assume that the Africa Show members escaped this fate.[58] One performer was executed in 1942 for alleged "attempted rape." Another was imprisoned in the Sachsenhausen concentration camp in 1941 for "Rassenschande" (racial pollution). He died there in 1944.[59] The historian Micha Grin estimates that in total about two thousand blacks died in Nazi concentration camps.[60] Despite the space created for Africans in Germany by the Africa Show, the Nazi state still reserved the power to murder them on an individual basis as unwanted race aliens.

## The Africa Show, Colonialism, and Nazism

Until very recently, historians have paid little attention to the ways in which the colonial project changed Germany. This is curious, since many contemporary observers of colonization in Germany saw imperialism as a threat to parliamentary democracy and liberal principles of justice.[61] The philosopher

Hannah Arendt, who already recognized in 1951 that the consequences of the imperial pursuit were not limited to the colonial periphery, was very much a part of this German tradition of colonial critique. She posited the much-debated historical link between imperialism and totalitarianism.[02] In Arendt's work colonial governance encompasses much more than the management of overseas territories and people through discourse and policy. Whatever stand one takes in the debate over theories of totalitarianism, it is hard to disregard Arendt's insight that colonization also concerned the creation of new ideas of governance and new political possibilities that shaped the ways in which some Germans envisioned their world-historical mission and the kind of government that would best reflect it.[03]

The German Africa Show is an example of a new idea of governance opened up by colonization. The National Socialist state used it to concentrate a group of people defined as a "pure race" with the purpose of controlling their contact with the wider population. It was therefore part of the Nazis' larger racial program. Its short history points to ways in which Nazism was tied to the German colonial past. Colonialism seems to have operated in state praxis as a model of race power that seemingly gave order to the "race chaos" of the postwar years, and National Socialists adapted it to their domestic and continental concerns. Once in power, some Nazi leaders gave certain groups provisional "pure race" status because they could be imagined in colonial terms. There were also sporadic efforts to fit those groups deemed extracolonial into colonial policies, such as the plans for "gypsy" and "Jewish" reservations. These examples demonstrate the extent to which Nazi ideas of purity and pollution were based on colonial geography.

The Africa Show is also an example of the disjuncture between colonial and National Socialist systems of governance. Unlike its historical predecessors, the *Völkerschau* in the colonial era and variety shows in the Weimar Republic, the show's existence did not merely raise the threat of racial pollution but was in fact intended to control it.[04] In other words, like all other National Socialist race policies, it had a history fashioned by the conscious application of race theory to political praxis and governance. German colonial policy was never organized around the centralized application of race theory to practical politics. The racism of imperialists at home and abroad was usually tied to their sense of the political threat that colonial subjects posed to German sovereign claims. Even the Pan-Germanists rarely spoke of direct mass murder, preferring instead the idea that unwanted subjects of a Germanic "tribal empire" would "die out" through a coercive policy of sterilization. The genocidal potential of colonization was limited in the metropole by parliamentary institutions and humanist traditions.[65] No one group was identified as Germany's sole obstacle to world power, whose annihilation was the only path to regeneration. Indeed, one of the reasons blacks in Germany could be given the absurd status of "full blooded Negroes" is that the central state had never identified blacks as cosmic race enemies. The Nazis radicalized imperial concepts of race power by linking them to anti-Semitic theories of a "Jewish World Conspiracy" and casting Jewish people as the master puppeteers of the world's races, a role they supposedly used to destroy the integrity of Aryan blood. Race power, when applied to the racialized category of "the Jews," was – as we know – a "governance" aimed at mass murder, at annihilation. Once the Nazis gained power, they applied their visions of race power with new tools of subjugation that stretched the possibilities for political violence and human suffering further than anyone in the *Kaiserreich* could ever have imagined.

The German Africa Show is thus much more than a well-documented example of Nazi policy towards blacks in the Third Reich. The show's archival record offers us rare access to official comparisons of race categories and thereby gives us a vantage point from which to analyze the interaction of these categories in Nazi thought and practice. The show demonstrates the enduring effect of colonial ideas on right-wing German thought and praxis as well as the radicalization that took place within the framework of these ideas. The history of Africans in Germany, like the history of the German Africa Show, gives us an entrée into the continuities and changes in official German race praxis. As this history becomes better documented, we will no doubt gain a deeper understanding of the nodal points in a colonial "boomerang effect" that affected German political culture.

### NOTES

This essay is based on my "Spaces of Memory, Spaces for Survival: The German Africa Show and Nazi Racial Discourse, 1935–1940" (MA thesis, University of Pennsylvania, 1994). An early draft was deposited at the Holocaust Memorial Museum's archives at the request of the late Robert Kesting, who was avidly collecting documentation of blacks in the Third Reich before his untimely death. My initial research on the Africa Show was published as " 'Die große Negertrommel der kolonialen Werbung': Die Deutsche Afrika-Schau 1935–1943," *WerkstattGeschichte* 9 (1994): 25–33. I would like to thank the editors of this volume and especially Eric Ames for his insightful comments and careful editing of this essay. Thanks are also due to Scott George, Michael Katz, Robert Kesting, Gesine Krüger, Matt Ruben, and Michael Zuckerman for their invaluable advice regarding an early draft of this paper. Research trips that contributed to the paper were funded by fellowships from the Fulbright Foundation, the SSRC, and the MacArthur Foundation.

1. Elisa von Joeden-Forgey, "Nobody's People: Colonial Subjecthood, Race Power and the German State, 1884–1945" (PhD diss., University of Pennsylvania, 2004).

2. The impetus for my research was a brief reference to the Africa Show in Wolfe W. Schmokel, *Dream of Empire: German Colonialism 1919–1945* (New Haven: Yale University Press, 1964), 243–44. For an overview of the show's history, see my "Die große Negertrommel." Since the early 1990s, the subject of Africans in Germany has inspired much research. See especially Katharina Oguntoye, May Opitz, and Dagmar Schultz, eds., *Farbe bekennen: Afro-deutsche Frauen auf den Spuren ihrer Geschichte* (Berlin: Orlanda Frauenverlag, 1991); Susann Samples, "African Germans in the Third Reich," in *The African-German Experience*, ed. Carol Aisha Blackshire-Belay (Westport CT: Praeger, 1996), 53–69; Tina Campt, Pascal Grosse, and Yara-Colette Lemke-Muniz de Faria, "Blacks, Germans, and the Politics of Imperial Imagination, 1920–60," in *The Imperialist Imagination: German Colonialism and its Legacy*, ed. Sara Friedrichsmeyer, Sara Lennox, and Susanne Zantop (Ann Arbor: University of Michigan Press, 1998), 205–32; Paulette Reed-Anderson, *Rewriting the Footnotes: Berlin and the African Diaspora* (Berlin: Die Ausländerbeauftragte des Senats, 2002); Clarence Lusane, *Hitler's Black Victims: The Historical Experience of Afro-Germans, European Blacks, Africans, and African-Americans in the Nazi Era* (New York: Routledge, 2002); Marianne Bechhaus-Gerst, ed., *Die (koloniale) Begegnung: AfrikanerInnen in Deutschland 1880–1945: Deutsche in Afrika* (Frankfurt a. M.: Peter Lang, 2003). Marcia Klotz discusses the Africa Show in terms of a "racialized globe" in her forthcoming book, *The Life and Death of the White World: Germany and the Making of the Racialized Globe.*

3. See especially Klaus Wagner, *Krieg: eine politisch-entwicklungsgeschichtliche Untersuchung* (Jena: Costenoble, 1906); Josef Ludwig Reimer, *Ein pangermanisches Deutschland: Versuch über die Konsequenzen der gegenwärtigen wissenschaftlichen Rassenbetrachtung für unsere politischen und religiösen Probleme* (Berlin: Friedrich Luckhardt, 1905); Heinrich Class [Daniel Frymann], *Wenn ich der Kaiser wär* (Leipzig: Dieterich, 1912).

4. Lora Wildenthal, *German Women for Empire, 1884–1945* (Durham: Duke University Press, 2001); Marcia Klotz, "Global Visions: From the Colonial to the National Socialist World," *European Studies Journal* 16, no. 2 (1999): 37–68.

5. Joeden-Forgey, "Nobody's People."

6. Adolf Hitler, *Mein Kampf*, trans. Ralph Manheim (1925; Boston: Houghton Mifflin, 1971), 629. On the Rhineland occupation see Campt et al., 205–14; Gisela Lebzelter, "Die 'Schwarze Schmach': Vorurteile – Propaganda – Mythos," *Geschichte und Gesellschaft* 11 (1985): 37–68; Daniel Morrow, " 'The Black Shame': German Reaction to the French Deployment of Colored Troops in the Occupied Western Zones, 1918–1923 (MA thesis, University of Virginia, 1967); Keith Nelson, "The 'Black Horror on

the Rhine': Race as a Factor in Post World War I Diplomacy," *Journal of Modern History* 42 (1970): 606–27.

7. Alfred Rosenberg, *Der Mythos des 20. Jahrhunderts* (Munich: Hocheneichen, 1935), 647.

8. Foreign Office to the Minister of Finance, August 28, 1940, Bundesarchiv-Koblenz (hereafter abbreviated as BA-Koblenz) R2/11632.

9. On Bruce's citizenship and military service, see Bundesarchiv-Berlin (hereafter abbreviated as BA-Berlin) R901 26046.

10. Staatsarchiv Hamburg 132–1 I Senatskommission für die Reichs-und Auswärtigen Angelegenheiten I 2096: Gesuch des aus Kamerun gebürtigen Mandenga Dick um Verleihung der Reichsangehörigkeit.

11. BA-Berlin R1001 6383, p. 29. The newspaper article is undated and the location only ascertainable from the text. The reporter inadvertently included Samoa in his list of African "natives." While the Africa Show did in fact occasionally perform skits related to Germany's non-African territories, such as Samoa, his slippage is both indication of widespread ignorance of the details of Germany's colonial history as well as the high-profile role Africa was seen to play in this history. For many people, a show about Africa evoked the larger (and in most minds vaguer) history of Germany's imperial greatness.

12. BA-Koblenz R2/11632, p. 244A.

13. Elisa von Joeden-Forgey, "Defending Mpundu: Dr. Moses Levi of Altona and the Prince from Cameroon," in *Mpundu Akwa: The Case of the Prince from Cameroon* (Hamburg: Lit, 2002).

14. Brückner had already tried to find work for Africans from the former German colonies. He had secured employment for Kwassi Bruce at a German zoo a few months prior to the 1935 meeting. Brückner to the Office of Colonial Policy, March 29, 1935, BA-Berlin 1001 7562.

15. Brückner to the Office of Colonial Policy, November 18, 1935, BA-Berlin 1001 6382.

16. Klaus Hildebrand, *Vom Reich zum Weltreich* (Munich: Wilhelm Fink, 1969).

17. Unites States Holocaust Memorial Museum Archive (hereafter abbreviated as USHMM), Record Group 1996.A.350, "Die Deutsche Afrika Schau."

18. Woodruff D. Smith, *The Ideological Origins of Nazi Imperialism* (New York and Oxford: Oxford University Press, 1986), 250.

19. Brückner to the Office of Colonial Policy, November 18, 1935, BA-Berlin 1001 6382. The show had possibly already appeared without the notice of the authorities.

20. Kwassi Bruce described the effects of National Socialism on Africans in Germany in an August 1934 letter to Edmund Brückner from BA-Berlin R1001 7562. The letter has been partially reproduced in Reed-Anderson, *Rewriting the Footnotes*, 63–66.

21. Alon Confino, "The Nation as a Local Metaphor: Heimat, National Memory

and the German Empire, 1871–1918," *History and Memory* 5, no. 1 (Spring/Summer 1993): 46.

22. Note from Dr. Seger of the Foreign Office, October 10, 1936, BA-Berlin 1001 6383.

23. Lindequist to the Reich Propaganda Leadership (*Reichspropagandaleitung*), June 28, 1940, USHMM Archives, Record Group 1996.A.350, "Die Deutsche Afrika Schau."

24. Lindequist to the Foreign Office, December 7, 1936, BA-Berlin 1001 6382.

25. Lindequist to the Foreign Office, December 7, 1936, BA-Berlin 1001 6382. The director, although praised by Göring and even gaining an audience with Hitler on February 18, 1937, would be imprisoned for unpaid debts only three months after taking over the show. Foreign Office to the Minister of Finance, June 18, 1937, BA-Koblenz R2/11632.

26. Society for the Study of Natives to the Foreign Office, June 24, 1936, BA-Koblenz R2/11632.

27. Alfred Schneider to the Cultural Expert of the Berlin Office of the Propaganda Ministry, December 11, 1936, BA-Koblenz R2/11632.

28. Alfred Schneider to the Cultural Expert of the Berlin Office of the Propaganda Ministry, December 11, 1936, BA-Koblenz R2/11632.

29. BA-Koblenz R2/11632, note by the Minister of Finance, February 18, 1937.

30. Lindequist to the Office of Colonial Policy, May 20, 1939, BA-Berlin 1001 6383.

31. BA-Berlin 1001 6383, report from August 3, 1930, p. 338.

32. Paul Assmann to the Foreign Office, BA-Berlin 1001 6383. The letter was undated but received at the Foreign Office on March 29, 1938. For a photo of the African American actor, whose name was Clarence Walton, see Reed-Anderson, *Rewriting the Footnotes*, 72.

33. Wolfgang Wippermann, *Wie die Zigeuner: Antisemitismus und Antiziganismus im Vergleich* (Berlin: Elefanten Press, 1997), 143. The existence of a "pure-blooded" category in Nazi race science meant that many Roma and Sinti soldiers would not be excluded from the German armed forces until 1943. All Jews had been forced out of the military by 1941. Wippermann, *Wie die Zigeuner*, 165.

34. Wippermann, *Wie die Zigeuner*, 166.

35. Michael Burleigh and Wolfgang Wippermann, *The Racial State: Germany 1933–1945* (Cambridge: Cambridge University Press, 1991), 82.

36. He apparently got his ideas from the writings, published in 1920, of a Dutch anti-Semite. Christopher R. Browning, *The Final Solution and the German Foreign Office: A Study of Referat D III of Abteilung Deutschland, 1940–1943* (New York: Holmes & Meier, 1978), 38. Certain Polish circles, too, according to Philip Friedman, exhibited interests in the island, at first as an immigration site for impoverished peasants and later, in 1937, for Jews. Philip Friedman, "The Lublin Reservation and the Madagascar

Plan: Two Aspects of Nazi Jewish Policy During the Second World War," YIVO *Annual of Jewish Social Science* III (1953): 151–77.

37. Browning, *The Final Solution*, 38.

38. Browning, *The Final Solution*, 40; Friedman, "The Lublin Reservation," 173.

39. Quoted in Friedman, "The Lublin Reservation," 154.

40. Friedman, "The Lublin Reservation," 173.

41. Helmut Krausnick, "The Persecution of the Jews," in *Anatomy of the SS State*, ed. Hans Buchheim, Martin Broszat, Hans-Adolf Jacobsen, and Helmut Krausnick (London: Collins, 1968), 22.

42. Report by George Stock, BA-Berlin R1001 6383, p. 22; Lindequist to the Foreign Office, September 16, 1938, BA-Berlin 1001 6383.

43. Wilhelm Soller of the Africa Show to the Society for the Study of Natives, June 25, 1940, USHMM Archives. Record Group 1996.A.350, "Die Deutsche Afrika Schau"; Labor Front to Georg Stock, July 1, 1940, USHMM Archives, "Die Deutsche Afrika Schau."

44. Stock to the Labor Front, March 21, 1938, BA-Berlin 1001 6383.

45. Office of Race Policy to the Foreign Office, October 18, 1938, BA-Berlin 1001 6383. There were certainly many more people of African descent in Germany at the time, yet there is no way of gauging the exact number.

46. Herr Peitsch to the Foreign Office, April 14, 1939, BA-Berlin 1001 6383.

47. See, for example, Sub-District leader of Tulln to the District Office of Lower Austria, July 29, 1940, USHMM Archives. Record Group 1996.A.350, "Die Deutsche Afrika Schau."

48. Lindequist to the Office of Colonial Policy, May 20, 1939, BA-Berlin 1001.

49. Lower Danube Office of Race Policy to district heads, May 13, 1940, USHMM Archives Record Group 1996.A.350, "Die Deutsche Afrika Schau."

50. USHMM Archives Record Group 1996.A.350, "Die Deutsche Afrika Schau."

51. USHMM Archives Record Group 1996.A.350, "Die Deutsche Afrika Schau."

52. Herr Goger to the Propaganda Ministry, June 29, 1940, BA-Berlin 1001 6383.

53. Herr Dustert of the Office of Colonial Policy to Lindequist, October 23, 1940, BA-Berlin R1001 6383. Lindequist was apparently collecting information of this sort to launch a campaign to have the show reinstated.

54. Tiessler of the Propaganda Ministry to the District Propaganda Leadership of Lower Austria, April 23, 1941, USHMM Archives Record Group 1996.A.350, "Die Deutsche Afrika Schau." The show was never reinstated.

55. Hilke Meyer-Bahlburg and others, eds., *Afrikanische Sprachen in Forschung und Lehre: 75 Jahre Afrikanistik in Hamburg, 1909–1984* (Berlin: Dietrich Reimer, 1986), 90.

56. Theodor Wonja Michel, telephone conversation with the author, December 7, 1999.

57. For a discussion of the life of the well-known Cameroonian film actor Louis

Brody (M'bebe Mpessa), see Tobias Nagl, "Kolonien des Blicks," *Jungle World* 20 (May 8, 2002).

58. Oguntoye, Opitz, and Schultz, "African Germans," 75–76.

59. Reed-Anderson, *Rewriting the Footnotes*, 72; Marianne Bechhaus-Gerst,"Der Schwarze Stern: Vom Schicksal deutscher Afrikaner im Nationalsozialismus" (lecture, November 29, 1995).

60. Bettina Schäfer, afterword, in Michèle Maillet, *Schwarzer Stern* (Berlin: Orlanda Frauenverlag, 1993), 188.

61. See, for example, Helmut Walser Smith, "The Talk of Genocide, the Rhetoric of Miscegenation: Notes on Debates in the German Reichstag Concerning Southwest Africa, 1904–1914," in *The Imperialist Imagination: German Colonialism and its Legacy*, ed. Sara Friedrichsmeyer, Sara Lennox, and Susanne Zantop (Ann Arbor: University of Michigan Press, 1998), 107–24.

62. Hannah Arendt, *Origins of Totalitarianism*, new ed. (New York: Harcourt Brace Jovanovich, 1973).

63. On theories of totalitarianism, see Wolfgang Wippermann, *Totalitarianismustheorien: Die Entwicklung der Diskussion von den Anfängen bis heute* (Darmstadt: Primus, 1997).

64. For examples of Weimar-era variety shows criticized for racial inversion, see Peter Jelavich, *Berlin Cabaret* (Cambridge: Harvard University Press, 1993), 174–75; Brandenburgisches Landeshauptarchiv (BLHA), Pr. Br. Rep. 30, Berlin C-Pol. Prs. Tit. 74 Nachttnze Ballet "Lola Bach," 1921–23; Nancy Nenno, "Femininity, the Primitive, and Modern Urban Space: Josephine Baker in Berlin" in *Women in the Metropolis: Gender and Modernity in Weimar Culture*, ed. Katharina von Ankum (Berkeley: University of California Press, 1997), 145–61.

65. On the potentially genocidal legal category of *Eingeborene* ("native"), which defined the state's relationship to its colonial subjects, see Elisa von Joeden-Forgey, "From 'Territorium Nullius' to 'Personum Nullius': German Colonial Law and the Invention of African 'Eingeborene'" (paper presented at the African Studies Association Annual Meeting, Houston, Texas, November 2001).

ROBERT GORDON AND DENNIS MAHONEY

# Marching in Step

## German Youth and Colonial Cinema

"While the mode of imperialism as a policy is economic, its historical energy is profoundly cultural," writes Bill Ashcroft.[1] One of the most powerful means for injecting cultural energy into imperial policies consists of fantasies encouraged and embellished by institutions such as the cinema or organizations such as youth groups. One of Susanne Zantop's major legacies is her wonderful – one is tempted to say, masterful – book *Colonial Fantasies*, in which she examines the German colonial imagination on precolonial terrain.[2] In this essay we explore a particular cinematic manifestation of such fantasies, one drawn from the German *postcolonial* presence in Africa after 1919.[3] We investigate Karl Mohri's *Deutsches Land in Afrika* (German land in Africa), a seventy-minute portrayal of a film expedition to the former German colonies of Tanganyika and South-West Africa. Released in 1939, it was also available in a shorter version as *Der Traum von den verlorenen Kolonien* (The dream of the lost colonies). Both versions of the film, together with their supplementary materials – a study pamphlet by Walther Günther and a picture book illustrated by Mohri himself – lobbied for the return of Germany's colonies so effectively that Mohri returned to southern Africa in order to make a sequel. However, the outbreak of the Second World War and Mohri's subsequent internment in South Africa intervened.[4]

Our analysis of Mohri's film concentrates on two mutually reinforcing issues: the depiction of the former colonies and the film's historical context as both relate to Mohri's representation of organized youth groups. A distinguishing characteristic of Mohri's hardbound and silver-screen adventures is their obsessive fascination with German youth, whose mere presence on African soil ostensibly guarantees their eventual incorporation into the newly expanding German Empire under National Socialism. In Mohri's words, "Whether young lady, or teenager, or little rascal, German is written all over their faces. And when one has come in close contact with this youth in South-West, then one knows: it will never be lost to the Reich."[5] This theme runs throughout many other films of the period, yet recent scholarship on German activities in their former colony, the Mandated Territory of South-West Africa, largely ignores such youth movements, and local accounts celebrating the German contribution to Namibia also typically overlook this phenomenon. The *Pfadfinder* (Pathfinders), the German equivalent of the Boy Scout movement, served as a substitute for illegal Nazi youth groups in South-West Africa during the 1930s. The German youth movement is unique in this context, for it was the only organization to be banned by the Mandate administration not once but twice, in 1934 and 1939. [6] It is one of the oddities of Namibian history that the South African authorities felt more threatened by the emergence of a well-organized youth movement than by indigenous revolt or even brigandage. The copious literature on Namibian colonial resistance ignores German resistance to what Germans themselves perceived to be colonialism. Mohri's film thus represents more than a relic of the interwar period; a close ethnographic reading of it provides visual clues to the manufacture and distribution of what Pierre Bourdieu terms "cultural capital" – those cultural and linguistic competencies that would either physically or symbolically threaten the South African colonial authorities administering the Mandate. To understand *Deutsches Land in Afrika* and its representation of cultural capital, we first provide an analysis of the film and its supplementary materials and then locate the film within the context of the sociomaterial conditions in Namibia. In so doing we aim to show how this film served as a link between colony and homeland, thereby reinforcing local German-settler symbolic capital. In other words the engineering of the visual can both underwrite the (German) imperialist enterprise and undermine the (British and South African) colonial one.

## The Construction of an Imaginary Africa

In order to finance his expedition, Mohri sold the film footage to the National Socialist Propaganda Ministry, whose assembly of this raw material underscores its intent to create the illusion of authenticity in the service of Nazi imperialism. [7] Although Mohri's book makes it clear that his journey began in the British dominion of South Africa and ended in the former east African colony of Tanganyika, *Deutsches Land in Afrika* reverses this route. It makes no mention of South Africa, and devotes the entire second half of the film to South-West Africa. The importance of South-West Africa is underscored by the film's opening review of colonial history. This part of the film features archival photographs of German colonial politicians such as Adolf Lüderitz, the Bremen venture capitalist who first succeeded in having some African land placed under German imperial protection in 1884, as well as photographs of landscapes there, such as the desolate and isolated coast around Germany's port of entry into its imperial adventure in Africa, the town of Lüderitzbucht. The film idealizes the colonial period as a time of cultural development until 1919, when Germany was – in the narrator's words – forced to relinquish its colonies due to allegations that it had mishandled the native population. It makes particular mention of the so-called Blue Book produced by the South-West Africa Administrator's Office in 1918, which documented German colonial atrocities, and seeks to disprove this book with a combination of visual images, musical accompaniment, and voice-over commentary.[8] As waves crash onto the beach at Lüderitzbucht to the accompaniment of stirring martial music that will be repeated at a key scene in the film's conclusion, the narrator states that Deutsches Land in Afrika will document the truth about German accomplishments in Africa, accomplishments that endure into the present and that explain why the natives are still attached to their old German friends.

The action begins with a tour of the former east African colony of Tanganyika, where the film documents the efficacy of German economic entrepreneurship with pictures of well-run plantations, harbors, gold mines, and schools. There is a long section on the education of German youth near Kilimanjaro, with an emphasis on physical fitness and shooting skills. The importance of these scenes becomes apparent later, for the film's conclusion likewise focuses on young Germans living in Africa but devoted to the fatherland. Then we see the supposed motor expedition from Tanganyika to South-West Africa, where German ingenuity and teamwork overcome all difficulties. While this part of the film obviously propagates the notion of Africa as a landscape of romantic adventure, it also depicts the continent as a vast, empty space waiting to be developed – indeed, cultivated – by Germans. The narrator's comment that the license plate of the South African Union (SAU – that is, "pig") fits well in this muddy environment suggests that Germans would do a much better job in constructing roads; as the narrator observed earlier in scenes illustrating transportation difficulties for the German planters in Tanganyika, there is not yet a Reichsautobahn in Africa. In this context it is noteworthy that South-West Africa will be explicitly characterized as the Dornröschen of Africa – a Sleeping Beauty that, so the logic goes, German colonizers would restore to life. The intermezzo also develops a visual theme to supplement this assertion. It starts with the "Bushmen," reportedly the primeval inhabitants of South-West Africa, and then gradually moves up a "civilizational level" to the agricultural people on the Kavango River before focusing on the German farmer and his training of native peoples, including Bushmen, to become productive workers.

German colonial history in South-West Africa is discussed while picturing the German cemetery at Waterberg (the scene of a pivotal German victory over the Herero) and the monument in Windhoek commemorating German colonial cavalrymen. This is not "Deutschland," but it is depicted as "Deutsches Land" in Africa, where the blood and toil of past and present Germans have established a claim to the soil. Even as the voice-over commentator informs the viewer that the NSDAP was banned here in 1933, the image track shows a tombstone decorated with a Nazi flag, thereby establishing a visual link between past and present, Africa and Germany, while demonstrating that gallant Germans will even defy the law in order to honor the graves of their forefathers. A scene of African men making bricks under German supervision suggests that despite restrictions imposed by the Versailles Treaty, the German colonial mission has indeed continued into the present. The narrator quotes the Boer leader Paul Krüger, who noted that if the Germans were given a rocky parcel of land, they would have a garden growing there within a year. He also quotes an allegedly old native saying, "Germans have a hard hand but a soft heart, whereas the English have a soft hand but a hard heart," which has since achieved the status of urban legend among German speakers in Namibia. Images of a young African child receiving medical attention suggest and reinforce the notion that the hardworking Germans also have the best interests of the natives in mind, while the British are inefficient and uncaring colonizers. " *Deutsches Land in Afrika* thus reiterates the eighteenth-century colonial fantasy of Germans as "good" colonizers, while assigning to the English and South Africans the role of villain previously filled by the Spanish. [10]

The notion of struggle is central to National Socialist ideology, and to a certain extent *Deutsches Land in Afrika* is paradigmatic of that concept. It depicts German farmers in South-West Africa who are at odds with an arid and seemingly hostile environment. Within the imaginative subtext of the film, though, this struggle has a fairy-tale ending, as we see how windmills provide not only water for cattle but also a swimming pool for the farmer's children. The narrator informs the viewer that there are (imposed) limits on what the German settlers have been able to accomplish. For example, the diamond mines, which before the war were the riches of the land, had been closed for years under pressure from Jewish–South African interests and had therefore yielded only a fraction of their potential. Likewise, the vast irrigation projects that German colonial administrators had planned shortly before the war were out. Thus it is neither nature nor recalcitrant natives that emerge as the enemy to be opposed, but rather the Mandate administration. Given its climate and soil, we are told, South-West Africa could become the California of Africa. The study pamphlet issued by the film division of the Propaganda Ministry in the spring of 1939 to accompany *Deutsches Land in Afrika* reinforces this designation by placing a lengthy quote from nationalist historian Heinrich von Treitschke's *Deutsche Geschichte im neunzehnten Jahrhundert* (German history in the nineteenth century) regarding unsuccessful Prussian attempts to purchase California from Mexico in 1846 immediately before the pamphlet's discussion of Lüderitz's actual acquisitions in South-West Africa.[11] In other words the wonders that Nazi public-works projects have accomplished in Germany are only waiting to be enacted in this once and future colony – a further underscoring of the film's Sleeping Beauty leitmotif. All that is needed are Prince Charmings, and this is where the film's concluding depiction of German youth plays its role.

After its review of colonial history and present conditions, *Deutsches Land in Afrika* turns attention to the future of South-West Africa, as embodied in German youth. Despite resistance from the Mandate administration, so we are told, Germans have established and maintained schools everywhere throughout South-West Africa. As was true for the parallel sequence at the end of the segment on east Africa, patriotic sentiment and physical fitness receive far more cinematic emphasis than academic or technical training. The musical score by Bernd Scholz plays a key role in providing the requisite emotional underpinning to Mohri's film footage. In a scene outside a German secondary school, for instance, the camera moves in a slow downward tilt from a flagpole above the school to children below, who are seen giving a Hitler salute while the sound track plays the German national anthem. Here, the image and sound tracks interact so as to suggest that "Deutschland" now extends well beyond the nation's borders. In the following sequence we hear the first stanza of the folk song, "[There is] no more beautiful land in this time / than this our own, far and wide."[12] That the voices of children are then joined by those of adults echoes the idea that German youth will lead their elders in claiming South-West Africa as their homeland. A cut to a scene reminiscent of the Wild West, with a large number of horses and youths skillfully engaged in horse jumping, brings the segment on formal education to a close. Logically, this sequence has little to do with the function assigned to it by the narrator, who announces that it is time to return home for vacation; presumably the youths are not going to ride to their distant farms on thoroughbred horses. Within the imaginative subtext of the film, however, several motifs coincide: German South-West as an African California; German youths as the living embodiment of the monumental statue of the German cavalryman in Windhoek; and Romantic horn music as the emotional link between German culture and African landscape.

The film ends where it began – on the coast near Lüderitzbucht, where the German colonial enterprise had commenced in 1884 – with a repetition of the same march music that had accompanied shots of waves crashing on the beach. Now, however, the coastline is populated by *Pfadfinder*, flags in hand, who symbolically take possession of their land. The conclusion of *Deutsches Land in Afrika* amounts to a virtual repetition of the party rallies in Nuremberg, as uniformed youths march in formation to mark the führer's birthday. We see them engaged in literal and figurative construction work (*Aufbauarbeit*), building a house to the accompaniment of a Hitler Youth song. The film ends with a twilight shot of *Pfadfinder* gazing out at the waves; as the final words of the sound track inform us to the accompaniment of a bugle fanfare, it is a vision of Germany's future colonial greatness that inspires these "children of the Land of Thorns." Such a focus on politically committed youth makes clear why *Deutsches Land in Afrika* received the ratings *staatspolitisch wertvoll* (politically valuable for the state) and *volksbildend* (folk forming) and was deemed suitable for showing in school as a *Lehrfilm* (educational film). [13] The study pamphlet that accompanied the film – a teacher's guide for screening and discussing the film in the German classroom – explains why government-sponsored film screenings are, in fact, more necessary than ever before. Such screenings were not to replace political education in the classroom but rather to extend it, advocating through yet another medium the Nazi ideal of enhancing political struggle. As the pamphlet would have it, the age of *Bildungsoptimismus* (educational optimism) is over. The National Socialist revolution has debunked the illusion of the classical concept of *Bildung*, the formation and cultivation of the individual personality through reading, travel, and other experiences – so the pamphlet's argument runs – and replaced that with the idea of the "authentic" German being determined by blood and historical fate and dedicated to real struggle. [14] Within such an educational doctrine, which the émigrée actress and writer Erika Mann characterized at the time as a "school for barbarians," *Deutsches Land in Afrika* registers the difficulties facing Germans in the former colonies while emphasizing the conviction that their heroic struggle will ultimately be successful. [15]

## Nazi Millenarianism at Home and Abroad

What sort of situation did Mohri find in Namibia, and what role did it play in his film? Most visiting journalists to the Mandated Territory (hereafter the Territory) agreed that it boasted one of the most vocal and possibly well-organized Nazi parties outside of Germany prior to the outbreak of the Second World War. Indeed, it was the fear of a putsch on Hitler's birthday that led the South African Mandate administration to abolish the local Territorial Police on April 20, 1939, and to incorporate them into a new police force including some 350 South African police. Given this volatile situation, Mohri's filming activities appealed to the local German establishment and reinforced many of their beliefs and actions.

Local Germans became increasingly militant in their claims for the return of South-West Africa to Germany. Several factors contributed to this. Perhaps most important, at least rhetorically, was the notion articulated by many Germans in the Territory and in Europe that South Africa had not legally colonized the territory. Given South-West Africa's status as a League of Nations Mandated Territory, many Germans saw it as a German colony simply administered by South Africa on behalf of the League of Nations and thus felt that with suitable international pressure it could revert back to Germany. Britain's appeasement policy concerning Austria and the Sudetenland in 1938 certainly encouraged such beliefs. There was also the issue of settler population demographics, coupled with the South African administration policy of encouraging white settlement there. Immediately after the First World War, more than six thousand German nationals were repatriated, yet by 1921–22, nearly eight thousand Germans remained in the Territory and many others were allowed to return or settle – so many, in fact, that when the first elections were held for the Namibian settlers' Legislative Assembly in 1925, German candidates, who were offered automatic dual citizenship in South Africa, won the majority of seats. Domestic relations soon deteriorated, however, as German settlers accused the South Africans of trying to overrun Namibia with poor "Boer" (a derogatory term used to refer to the Afrikaans-speaking South Africans) settlers from Angola and South Africa.

It is in this mélange that the Hitler Youth and *Pfadfinder* movements must be located. While English, German, and Afrikaans youth initially belonged to a multilingual (if English-dominated) Boy Scout movement, the German Pathfinder Society was founded as a separate group in 1928. A scant year later, one commentator noted the ideological impetus for this formation by observing: "When the young boys march through the countryside with their old troop hats and black-white-red cockade, visit the graves of our fallen, fire honor salvos over these graves, when they drill according to the old German orders, make their parade march before German flags and monuments, give all German national holidays the firm setting in stiff discipline – this educates [them] more in the national German thought than the best German curriculum." [16] The formation of the *Pfadfinder* was intimately connected not only to ideals of masculinity and character training but also to German nationalism, grounded as it was in anxieties about the South African faction's new Boer voter power and its recent acquisition of a majority (eight out of twelve seats) in the Legislative Assembly. Though German was acknowledged as one of the official languages, antagonisms escalated rapidly. In 1932 the South African faction, reacting to local German calls for the Territory's return to Germany, proposed closer union between Namibia and South Africa. This further incensed the German faction at a time when Hitler was on the rise in Germany, and his policy on the return of German colonies found a sympathetic ear in South-West Africa. In July 1933 the Nazis sent a special emissary to promote the Nazification of all German institutions there, especially educational and cultural organizations. Similarly, the German consul in Windhoek urged German schools to incorporate Nazi ideas into their curricula, adding that pupils should take a solemn public oath of allegiance to Hitler. In addition Nazi activists had a strikingly well-orchestrated sense of public spectacle that ranged from oath taking in appropriately festooned venues to public marches and the replacement of the South African flag in front of the Administration Building with the swastika.

In response to such public activities, the Namibian administration introduced the Criminal Law Amendment Ordinance, which banned any political organization deemed a threat to public order. In early July 1934, three months after he arrived from Germany, Captain Erich von Lossnitzer, the new Hitler Youth leader, led a march of twelve hundred young people down Windhoek's main street, the Kaiserstrasse, to the government buildings, where, in full Nazi uniform, he demanded a personal interview with the administrator. [17] Shortly thereafter the police raided offices of the Hitler Youth and the Nazi Party, banned the Hitler Youth, and deported its leader. A few months later a similar fate befell the Nazi Party. A year after the Hitler Youth were banned, the administration allowed the German community to create an ostensibly nonpolitical *Pfadfinder* organization, since the English and Afrikaans communities had youth organizations. The leaders of the Hitler Youth anticipated this move.

Already in March 1934, three months before his group was banned, the Hitler Youth Leader for South-West Africa reported to Berlin: "It is absolutely essential that we keep the old uniforms. We must keep the two uniforms so that in case of a prohibition we can put everybody into the *Pfadfinder* uniform. In public we maintain the fiction that a *Pfadfinder* organization still exists. This the government cannot prohibit so easily, seeing that there are also Afrikaner and English Pathfinders. . . . Please confirm this dual uniform."[18] Though the political ban was enforced, there were numerous loopholes in it, as the Mohri film vividly illustrates. While ostensibly nonpolitical, the *Pfadfinder* closely followed prescribed Hitler Youth activities. Patrols were named after Nazi notables such as Göring's wife, Karin, and the nationalist "martyr" Albert Leo Schlageter, a German officer executed by the French in the Ruhr in 1923 for sabotage. Camp-outs commonly featured a group reading of a chapter of *Mein Kampf*. A combination of bureaucratic ineptitude and political constraints prevented the Mandate administration from closely policing the *Pfadfinder*. There were also a number of legal loopholes that were exploited; thus, while youth were not allowed to wear the uniform or emblem of a political organization, the ordinance did not prevent German juveniles from attaching swastika emblems to their bicycles. In addition the film's audience – from settlers in Namibia to spectators in Germany – would have known that the many flags depicted in the conclusion to *Deutsches Land in Afrika*, such as the three-pronged thorn and the old Imperial Navy flags, merely substituted for the Nazi regalia, ironically giving added visibility to that which had been banned from sight.

Indeed, this is where Mohri's film becomes particularly valuable, for its ethnographically revealing depiction of *Pfadfinder* activities shows them to be almost identical to those of the Hitler Youth in Germany. As in the film, *Pfadfinder* clearly were a major focus of attention for settlers. At the time of the film there were some twelve hundred *Pfadfinder* in the Territory, ranging in age from ten to seventeen and organized in about thirteen groups called *Horsts* (eyries). Very few German youths were not members of either the *Pfadfinder* or its female equivalent, the *Bund Deutscher Mädel* (League of German Girls). The *Pfadfinder* were well financed and organized, as evinced by the full array of their activities. Apart from weekly meetings, their calendar was filled with weekend marches and survival-skill contests. On even the most insignificant occasions they marched through town, usually accompanied by a fife-and-drum band. They served as honor guards for almost any German event in Namibia and even did so in the *Heimat* itself, for example appearing at the 1936 Berlin Olympic Games. Apart from weekly activities like those scenes filmed at Lüderitzbucht and Windhoek, they also took extended excursions to destinations such as South Africa, the Kavango River, or the Zambesi, during which time they behaved very much as Mohri portrayed them in the Kalahari segment of his film.

Mohri's film transported firsthand images between Namibia and Germany, thereby making them common visual property for Germans in both locations. Like film, other modern technologies also promoted ties between metropole and periphery. Radio Zeesen, the powerful German shortwave radio station, played an important ritual role in 1930s Namibia. For example, after the famous youth march in Windhoek in July 1934, the Hitler Youth returned to their camp in a torchlight procession and then listened to a special radio broadcast by Hitler, which symbolically linked them to the greater German Reich.

*Deutsches Land in Afrika* did have consequences both in Namibia and in metropolitan Germany. We recently managed to interview several former *Pfadfinder*. They recalled how Mohri was one of several travelers from Germany who filmed and photographed their activities. Apart from the pride and excitement of being filmed, they felt that this also made them part of a vast emergent German Empire, and they found encouragement in their perception that their activities were appreciated in Germany. Being *Pfadfinder* had other benefits as well, including the possibility of all-expenses-paid trips to Germany to attend special leadership courses. [19] Engaging in such *Pfadfinder* activities also made them feel superior to the English and Afrikaans groups, who were simply dismissed as inferior and lazy "Boers." The activities filmed by Mohri encouraged a strong sense of camaraderie that extended beyond the *Pfadfinder*, as when informal gangs of youths prowled the streets of Lüderitzbucht at night and threw rotten eggs at Jewish businesses and offices.

*Pfadfinder* were an intrinsic part of the Nazi hegemonizing process. As Major Weigel, the leader of the Namibian Nazis, wrote in August 1934: "South-West is yearning for Germany. It wants to be German South-West Africa again. South-West has to have Germany, otherwise it will be dead soon. And the saddest part of it is that a portion of the second generation of Germans, the German youth, is in danger of becoming Afrikaners." [20] Yet within eight months he was reporting remarkable success: "I regard South-West not as a foreign country but as a part of Germany. Our youth is awakening and realizing that their life ideal is their German nationality and the German nature of their home country." [21]

The film demonstrates how the metropole and the periphery depended upon each other for framing identity. But that dependence was not equal. The colonials needed the metropole more than the latter required the former. The Third Reich's preferred policy for regaining the former German colonies was through international negotiation in Europe, and so top-level Nazi leaders viewed the more public activities of colonial Nazis and Pfadfinder with embarrassment. But the cultural domain, as distinct from that of international relations, richly rewarded the local incompetence of the Mandate administration. The more tribulations and harassments the colonial Germans endured, the more they were extolled in Germany and their persecution was attributed to the global Jewish-run capitalist conspiracy.[22]

In Germany, too, the film's impact only reinforced the prevailing Nazi policies aimed at strengthening the "New Youth." German youth was particularly receptive to the notion of Volksgemeinschaft (national community). In its claim to rejuvenate Germany, Nazi propaganda offered comradeship and a pioneering role to youth. As Hitler proclaimed at the decisive September 1934 Nuremberg Party Rally, "What we look for from our German youth is different from what people wanted in the past. In our eyes the German youth of the future must be slim and slender, swift as the greyhound, tough as leather, and hard as Krupp steel. We must educate a new type of man so that our people are not ruined by the symptoms of degeneracy of our day."[23] Especially for youth audiences in Germany, those scenes of Pfadfinder actually using their skills in pioneering situations must have made their fantasies seem realizable. Scenes of physically fit young Germans abroad swearing allegiance to Germany must have had a significant propagandistic impact on the prime audience of these films – youth in Germany. For instance the official Handbook for Schooling the Hitler Youth, issued to more than seven million German youth in 1937, has a key chapter on the "German Culture Area." This chapter examines the situation of Germans abroad, especially in the former German colonies. It claims in tones strongly reminiscent of Deutsches Land in Afrika that these

> colonies were built up by great sacrifices on the part of the Reich. After profiting from the first experiences, the colonies blossomed forth mightily and soon demonstrated that they were profitable. Their soil was not only moistened with the sweat of German planters and laborers, but watered with the blood of German soldiers. In spite of that, the German people were denied the right to colonies at Versailles. The lie regarding colonies, which is refuted by the German successes and by the natives themselves, was intended merely to veil and to excuse the robbery. . . .

The German Reich will at all events never cease to demand the restoration of its colonies. [24]

These claims are given added emphasis in the concluding three chapters of the *Handbook*, which reinforce the claim for regaining the German colonies and the importance of the "Soil as a Source of Food Supply" and as a "Support for Industry." As the study guide makes clear, *Deutsches Land in Afrika* encouraged schoolchildren in Germany to identify with their overseas contemporaries by showing the overseas children doing activities that were similar to those of children in Germany yet took place in a more exotic, even adventurous setting. It made them aware that there were millions of people residing outside of their fatherland who were striving to be good Germans. Karl Mohri's film *Deutsches Land in Afrika*, in short, helped maintain the illusory importance of what Hitler called the "eternal value of race and blood." [25]

## NOTES

1. Bill Ashcroft, *Post-Colonial Transformation* (New York: Routledge, 2001), 211.

2. Susanne Zantop, *Colonial Fantasies: Conquest, Family, and Nation in Precolonial Germany, 1770–1870* (Durham: Duke University Press, 1997).

3. By 1942 Germany had produced more than 150 films on Africa, most of which advocated the return of Germany's lost colonies. See Gerlinde Waz, "Auf der Suche nach dem letzten Paradies: Der Afrikaforscher und Regisseur Hans Schomburgk," in *Triviale Tropen: Exotische Reise- und Abenteuerfilme aus Deutschland 1919–1939*, ed. Jörg Schöning (Munich: edition text + kritik, 1997), 98.

4. Walther Günther, *Deutsches Land in Afrika* (Berlin: Der Reichs- und Preussische Minister für Wissenschaft, Erziehung und Volksbildung, 1939); Karl Mohri, *Afrikanische Reise* (Berlin: Horst Siebert Verlag, 1938).

5. "Ob junge Dame, ob Backfisch, ob Lauselümmel, das Deutsche steht ihnen allen auf dem Gesicht geschrieben. Und wenn man mit dieser Jugend in Südwest näher zusammengekommen ist, dann weiss man: Sie geht dem Reich nimmer verloren." Mohri, *Afrikanische Reise*, 88.

6. Even after the Second World War, when influential members of the German community approached the administration with a request to restart the movement, they were turned down again.

7. For a treatment of the cinema of the Third Reich as "a totalitarian state's concerted attempt to create a culture industry in the service of mass deception," see Eric Rentschler, *The Ministry of Illusion: Nazi Cinema and Its Afterlife* (Cambridge: Harvard University Press, 1996), 16.

8. This book has recently been reprinted. See Jan-Bart Gewald and Jeremy Sil-

vester, eds., *Words Cannot Be Found: German Colonial Rule in Namibia: An Annotated Reprint of the 1918 Blue Book* (Leiden: Brill Academic Publishers, 2003).

9. In her discussion of the 1943 feature film *Germanin*, which develops this contrast between the humanitarian Germans and the inefficient and uncaring British more fully, Sabine Hake points out that "cultural" films such as *Deutsches Land in Afrika* "anchored the feature films that followed them as part of a continued reflection on identity and spatiality that established the reading formation necessary for their actualization as colonial and, by implication, hegemonic texts. See Sabine Hake, "Mapping the Native Body: On Africa and the Colonial Film in the Third Reich," in *The Imperialist Imagination: German Colonialism and Its Legacy*, ed. Sara Friedrichsmeyer, Sara Lennox, and Susanne Zantop (Ann Arbor: University of Michigan Press, 1998), 163–87; here, 164. For a further discussion of the motif of the benevolent German colonizer in postcolonial and Nazi films see Alain Patrice Nganang, "Koloniale Sehnsuchtsfilme: Vom lieben Afrikaner deutscher Filme der NS-Zeit," *Welfengarten: Jahrbuch für Essayismus* 11 (2001): 111–28.

10. For the eighteenth-century contrast between "good" and "bad" colonizers, see Zantop, *Colonial Fantasies*, 39–40.

11. Günther, *Deutsches Land in Afrika*, 11–12.

12. "Kein schöner Land in dieser Zeit / als hier das unsre weit und breit."

13. See Helmut Regel, "Der Schwarze und sein 'Bwana': Das Afrika-Bild im deutschen Film," in Schöning, *Triviale Tropen*, 70.

14. Günther, *Deutsches Land in Afrika*, 29–30.

15. For contemporary critiques of National Socialist educational manipulation, see Erika Mann, *School for Barbarians: Education under the Nazis* (New York: Modern Ages Books, 1938) and Gregor Ziemer, *Education for Death: The Making of the Nazi* (Oxford: Oxford University Press, 1941).

16. Quoted in Daniel J. Walther, *Creating Germans Abroad* (Athens: Ohio University Press, 2002), 150.

17. There were many precedents for the use of Nazi uniforms in public, such as when Willy Meyer-Donner, the contact person for the German Foreign Office in Sweden, spoke to local Germans in his SA uniform in 1931. See Donald McKale, *The Swastika Outside Germany* (Kent OH: Kent State University Press, 1977), 28. The twelve hundred participants in the march represented a spectacular increase from the previous year, when the largest march, on the occasion of the visit by the German aviatrix Elly Beinhorn, had attracted only four hundred. At that time fewer than thirty thousand European settlers occupied the Territory, and Germans constituted less than a third of the total number. Throughout the Territory there were approximately fourteen hundred children enrolled in German schools, which meant that practically every German child was a card-carrying member of the Hitler Youth.

18. Quoted in Barron L. Smythe, ed., *The Nazis in Africa* (Salisbury NC: Documen-

tary Publications, 1978), 81. See also Benjamin Bennett, *Hitler Over Africa* (London: T. Werner Laurie, 1939), 173, which cites an airmail letter to Berlin dated March 4, 1934.

19. Indeed, a copiously illustrated volume celebrating the German colonial achievement, while silent on the *Pfadfinder*, does have a group photograph taken in 1936 of German Namibians in Germany. It features some 350 youths, quite a remarkable assemblage – more than half of whom were to later die during the Second World War on the eastern front. See Klaus Becker, Jürgen Hecker and Sigrid Kube, eds., *Vom Schutzgebiet bis Namibia, 1884–1984* (Windhoek: Interessengemeinschaft Deutschsprachiger Südwester, 1985), 396–97.

20. Bennett, *Hitler Over Africa*, 166; McKale, *Swastika Outside Germany*, 94.

21. Bennett, *Hitler Over Africa*, 176.

22. On anti-Semitism in South-West Africa, see McKale, *Swastika Outside Germany*, 95.

23. David Welch, *The Third Reich: Politics and Propaganda* (New York: Routledge, 1993), 61.

24. Fritz Bennecke, *The Nazi Primer: Official Handbook for Schooling the Hitler Youth*, trans. Harwood L. Childs (New York: Harper & Brothers, 1938), 170–71.

25. McKale, *Swastika Outside Germany*, 188.

# PART 5

# Colonial Legacies: The Racialized Self

NINA BERMAN

# Autobiographical Accounts of
# Kenyan-German Marriages

## Reception and Context

Since the late 1960s Germans have been traveling to Kenya in ever-increasing numbers. Visa requirements were lifted for Germans in the early 1980s, which made travel to Kenya significantly easier, and by the mid-1990s German tourists outnumbered British tourists; on average they spent a longer period in Kenya than did their British counterparts.[1] In spite of a general drop in tourism in recent years due to political and economic factors and aggravated by the impact of natural catastrophes such as El Niño, Germans continue to travel to Kenya in large numbers. In 1999, for instance, 152,589 Germans departed for Kenya, and in 2000 the figure had grown to 163,168.[2] In addition to the German visitors, Swiss and Austrians also travel to Kenya, and, although there are relatively few of them, they tend to stay much longer in the country, book more nights, and vacation almost three times longer than, for example, the average American, Italian, or French tourist. Because Germans, Swiss, and Austrians vacation mainly on the coast, German-speaking tourists are the most visible group in this area and book more than 30 percent of all overnight stays.

The presence of tourists – in particular the repeat visitors who frequently establish friendships or romantic relationships with Kenyans – has had repercussions on the social fabric of the country. A study I conducted in the summers of 1998, 1999, and 2000 sheds light on the nature and extent of these interactions, which also include marriage and sex tourism.[3] Although such relationships make up only a small percentage of the overall interactions between German-speaking tourists and Kenyans, they have inspired the imagination and become popular topics of best-selling autobiographies in the German language, contributing to an established and variegated tradition of German writings about Kenya. Two recent autobiographical accounts of marriages between Kenyans and German-speaking tourists, Corinne Hofmann's *Die weisse Massai* (The white Masai, 1998) and Miriam Kwalanda's *Die Farbe meines Gesichts: Lebensreise einer kenianischen Frau* (The color of my face: The life journey of a Kenyan woman, 1999), have enjoyed outstanding popularity in Germany. These accounts highlight the complexities and dilemmas inherent in the cross-cultural interactions that result from the presence of tourists in Kenya as well as document the social changes under way there.

In this essay I begin by outlining the parameters of tourism in Kenya. I then evaluate Hofmann's and Kwalanda's autobiographies by focusing on the ways in which these authors present the stories of their cross-cultural marriages to a German audience. In addition I present aspects of their stories that are central to understanding gender relations in Kenya in order to shed light on the ways in which German-language autobiographical accounts of intercultural marriages correspond to specific social and material conditions in Kenya. In so doing I uncover dimensions of the accounts that are, for the most part, unfamiliar to German-language readers. In the process of considering such historical and cultural knowledge, which Kenyan audiences might readily draw on, both Hofmann's and Kwalanda's texts acquire a new significance.

## Interaction between German-speaking Tourists and Kenyans

German-speaking tourists and Kenyans interact extensively as a result of the high level of repeat tourism in Kenya; German-speaking tourists return to Kenya more frequently than to other areas they visit. Twenty to 40 percent of German-speaking guests are repeat visitors, with some hotels drawing more returning visitors than others. Over the years repeat tourism in Kenya has generated a number of developments and has had a significant impact on the local infrastructure. Tourists venture beyond the traditional boundaries of the tourist ghetto and develop ongoing relationships with the local population. Along the Diani coast south of Mombasa, for example, which was the focus of the study I conducted, signs of a German presence are ubiquitous. Language schools teach German to locals, while Swahili is offered to Germans at the pools of some of the hotels. The weekly newspaper the *Coast* features a page of articles in German. German-language posters announce special events; bulletin boards at the supermarkets are filled with ads in German for yoga and massage classes and used cars for sale. One advertisement put up by the German owner of a small restaurant catering especially to Germans read: "Wir kochen für Euch! We are cooking for you! Am Freitag, den 25.6. ab 19:00 / on Friday evening / Sauerbraten mit Rotkohl und verschiedenen Knödeln / Pudding mit Vanillesosse."

Some repeat visitors and individuals who work in the tourism industry have bought houses on the south coast and no longer stay in hotels. Real-estate business involving Germans has been very lucrative since the early 1990s, when it became legal for foreigners to own land in Kenya (previously, a Kenyan citizen had to cosign legal transactions). Landownership in turn guarantees the right to become a Kenya resident. One company sold over 250 homes to Germans by 1999, a large number of which (possibly up to 60 percent) are owned by residents of the former East Germany. Home ownership has encouraged many repeat visitors to spend even longer periods in Kenya. Some repeat visitors and others who came to work have become residents; in 1999 a German Residents Association Kenya was formed, composed mainly of German residents living on the Diani coast, but the organization disbanded within a year.[4] In addition a small group of Germans, Swiss, and Austrians who came to work in Kenya during the first wave of tourism have lived on the south coast for many years. Many of them have become permanent residents of Kenya. They operate a number of the stores along the Diani-coast beach road, such as clothing boutiques, a telecommunications store, a butcher store, a general store, a discotheque, and restaurants.

These developments are comparable to those observed by Tamara Kohn, who studied a small Inner Hebridean island off the west coast of Scotland, and by Jacqueline Waldren in her analysis of Mallorca, Spain. Kohn's study demonstrates that "tourists over time may possibly become part of and thus create the host community."[5] Waldren shows that the high level of interaction between visitors and their hosts can enable a particular community "to gain full advantage from the economic opportunities opened up by foreigners without losing the fabric of social relations, the meanings and values of their culture."[6] Whether this last claim is applicable to the current situation along the Kenyan coast remains to be explored in future studies.

My study of the interaction between Kenyans and German tourists reveals that a large group of German repeat visitors develop different types of relationships with Kenyans, challenging the widespread notion that the dominant form of close interaction between local Kenyans and visitors to the country involves sex tourism, as suggested in popular German magazines such as *Der Spiegel* and *Stern*, which feature regular articles on the subject. Many German couples and individuals entertain close relationships with, and provide concrete support to, Kenyan families living on the Diani coast. This support takes the form of paying for education, housing, and medical needs and is mostly geared toward enabling Kenyans to support themselves long term; it amounts to a kind of informal development aid.[7]

In addition to long-term interactions that are not motivated by sex tourism, serious romantic relationships, however motivated, appear to be on the rise. Data on marriage patterns shows that significantly more tourists and other foreign-born individuals marry Kenyans today than was the case before the mid-1990s.[8] The age gap between marriage partners is less than common wisdom would have it. In addition the social makeup of those entering marriages reveal that Germans who are marrying Kenyans come from all social backgrounds and that such marriages are no longer limited to the domain of high-society tourism with which Kenya was associated until recently.[9]

Most interesting in this context, the number of Germans and Swiss who marry Kenyans is higher than that of other foreign-born visitors. In 1994, 97 German-Kenyan couples were married; by 1997 this figure had doubled, to 192 couples, and it increased again by 46.9 percent, to 282 couples, in 1999.[10] In comparison, marriages between Swiss and Kenyan citizens occurred less often: 27 Swiss-Kenyan couples were married in 1994; the number increased by 65.8 percent, to 41 couples, in 1999; in 2000 the number dropped to 35; and 36 marriages were registered for 2001.[11] Although these figures seem low, it is worth noting that most of the encounters occur in one place – along the Mombasa coast. The presence of 264 Swiss-Kenyan couples (1994–2001) and 1,161 German-Kenyan couples (1993–99) who were married in the course of only a few years is certainly felt in the closely knit communities along the coast.

Based on an evaluation of marriage licenses for the years 1994–98 kept at the Registrar of Marriages in Mombasa, over 73 percent of all foreigners who marry Kenyans are German-speaking (59.8 percent Germans, 12.3 percent Swiss, and 1.7 percent Austrians).[12] Interestingly, the number of Swiss-Kenyan marriages registered in Mombasa was higher than the total number of Swiss-Kenyan marriages registered per year in Switzerland. This discrepancy might indicate that marriages registered in Mombasa or at other locations in Kenya are not registered concurrently in Switzerland (and other countries). Kenyans benefit locally from registering the marriage – for example, being able to obtain a passport. The fact that Swiss and others do not register the marriages in their home countries suggests that they deem this step unnecessary or perhaps that they are disinclined to make their marriages public. In any case these discrepancies suggest that the total number of marriages is even higher than what is indicated by the official figures recorded in Germany or Switzerland.

There is no reason to believe that cultural attitudes have changed dramatically overnight; therefore, the most convincing explanation for the increasing Kenyan-German marriage rate has to do with the pressing economic situation in Kenya. Most likely, the number of Kenyan-German marriages is greater today because Kenyans are pursuing marriage more vigorously than before, often with the goal of leaving the country, and Germans are responding positively to the situation. The greater number of Kenyan-German unions relative to marriages between Kenyans and other foreign nationals can be attributed, among other things, to the absence of a German colonial legacy in Kenya, the different behavior of Germans abroad and at home, and the interrelatedness of xenophilia and xenophobia, all of which deserve a broader discussion than the one I can provide here. In light of these developments, the two autobiographies under discussion here document a significant trend in recent years toward closer and more extensive interactions between German-speaking tourists and Kenyans.

## The Works of Corinne Hofmann and Miriam Kwalanda

The enormous success of Hofmann's *Die weisse Massai* and Kwalanda's *Die Farbe meines Gesichts* both reflects and feeds the public's interest in relationships between Kenyans and German-speaking travelers; translations of similar texts coming out of other cultural contexts are also available to Germans.[13] Hofmann's autobiographical text gives an account of a German woman's relationship with and marriage to a Samburu man. (Although she holds a German passport, the woman had been living in Switzerland; the man is presented as a Masai, but in fact he is a member of the Samburu society.)[14] The book, published in August 1998, is a simply written but evidently enticing mix of romance and adventure themes. Beginning in the spring of 1999, it held the first or second spot on German best-seller lists for several months.[15] By September 2001, 1.3 million copies of the book had been sold, including 700,000 paperback copies; by March 2003, paperback sales had increased to more than 1 million copies. Assuming that some copies of the autobiography were read by more than one person, it is quite likely that a significant portion of the German-speaking population showed interest in the book. *Die weisse Massai* has been translated into Dutch, Danish, Swedish, Finnish, Norwegian, Estonian, Polish, Hebrew, Italian, French, Spanish, and Japanese. Its striking popularity speaks to the significant interest in cross-cultural relations existing in German-speaking and other countries.

Kwalanda's autobiographical work, *Die Farbe meines Gesichts*, published in 1999, looks at German-Kenyan relations from the point of view of a Kenyan woman who married a German tourist and moved to Germany. Sales figures for the book were not available from the publisher, but in most bookstores it is placed right next to Hofmann's account, and it surely has received attention simply by association with that best-seller. The autobiographies are particularly noteworthy in a comparative context because they allow us to explore the portrayal of the interaction between German-speaking tourists and Kenyans from different perspectives. On the other hand, in terms of how they are received in German-speaking countries, they face similar pitfalls because both texts speak to social issues in Kenya, issues that are typically overlooked by the general German-language reading public but would be compelling to a Kenyan audience.

Hofmann's narrative is rendered in the present tense, which lends it an air of urgency and suspense, successfully drawing the reader into the flow of events. Her encounter with Kenya begins in December 1986, on a vacation with her boyfriend, Marco. During an excursion to the city of Mombasa, an hour's bus ride from the tourist centers on the south coast, Hofmann spots a stunning man: "It hits me like lightning. A tall, dark-brown, very beautiful, exotic man sits on the railing of the ferry, relaxed, and looks at us, the only whites in this bustle, with dark eyes. My God, I think to myself, he is beautiful, I have never seen anything like this before." [16] This chance meeting on the ferry sets in motion a series of events that lead to the end of Hofmann's relationship with Marco and bring her back to Kenya in July 1987. She then becomes romantically involved with the Samburu man, whose name is Lketinga.

Based on her three-week stay, Hofmann decides to sell her business, a secondhand clothing boutique that includes a bridal section; let go of her apartment; sell her car; and move back to Kenya within a period of less than three months. After some dramatic back-and-forth movement between Lketinga's village and the coast, the couple settles down in the Samburu village. They initially live in the traditional village, called the manyatta, which is a group of huts made of mud, cow dung, and wood that stand approximately 160 centimeters (5 feet 2 inches) tall. Over the next couple of years Hofmann and Lketinga get married, move into a shop, and finally open a business on the coast. The account chronicles their marital problems; the many instances when Hofmann gets sick; her pregnancy and the birth of their daughter, Napirai; aspects of life in Kenya, such as the struggle with bureaucracy and the life-threatening obstacles that are a reality of life in the bush. When the marital problems become unbearable, Hofmann, pretending to depart for only a short vacation, leaves everything behind but her daughter and returns to Switzerland. [17]

Which features of this narrative are relevant to our discussion of cross-cultural representation? The text chronicles a circular movement, from Hofmann's home in Switzerland to Kenya and back to Switzerland. Hofmann's story affirms the irreconcilable cultural differences between Kenya and Switzerland and thus serves to strengthen in the reader the abiding sense that the divide between Africans and Germans is unbridgeable and permanent. Her account achieves this result by employing narrative strategies that convey specific legitimizing messages and bolster her view of the situation. These features of the text deserve a critical look.

First, Hofmann claims that her judgments are based on a genuine effort to immerse herself in Samburu culture. Initially, she indeed makes an effort to live according to the community's traditional way of life. Yet her actual stay in the traditional Samburu setting is hardly substantial, made shorter by extended stays in hospitals and in Switzerland, and quickly ends when the couple moves into the shop and then later to Mombasa. Despite the claims on the back cover of the book that the author lived for four years in the Kenyan bush, in fact she experienced the traditional Samburu life-style only briefly, several weeks at a time, after which she recuperated in hospitals and in Switzerland. According to the logic of the text, however, the "fact" of her life in the bush entitles her to the critical attitude she developed after her initial enthusiasm for Samburu culture faded away.

Second, Hofmann presents the reader with a logical succession of events that point to her need for a change and ultimately her return to Switzerland. When she first encounters the Samburu way of life, she is entirely enthusiastic about embracing this new culture; she speaks about "my home," "my country," and "my people."[18] Her positive attitude, however, is gradually replaced by a critical view of practices she cannot tolerate. Whether it is circumcision, the nature of the relationship between men and women, the dirt in the manyatta, the eating and spitting habits, the lack of cleanliness, the boredom she feels because of the Rumhängerei (bumming around), or the jealousy of her husband, in time these aspects of the pastoral way of life she has chosen become unacceptable.

As a result, after only a few weeks in the Samburu village, Hofmann begins to reclaim the life-style she had led in Switzerland. From the moment she decides to buy her first car, the narrative chronicles her struggle to recreate her old life, until she finally leaves the country. Even geographically, her stay in Kenya comes full circle when the family moves back to the coast, where Hofmann had originally met her Samburu husband. It is from there that she finally returns to Switzerland. She recounts the different phases of this struggle in ways that make her choices appear logical. The purchase of a car, for example, buys her mobility and access to food items and other aspects of her former life that she feels she needs most urgently. When Hofmann and Lketinga decide to live in the shop, this move puts her back into a bed and close to a water closet. The opening of the shop, discotheque, and restaurant, and later a boutique at the coast, allows her to resume her former life as a businesswoman. Every enterprise she invests in thrives; the last one, which is closest to the type of business she was running in Switzerland, is also the most successful.

Ultimately, Hofmann attempts to change the structures of the Samburu community that took her in by involving it in new economic enterprises, and when she does not succeed in affecting the general way of life, she leaves for good. Her various initiatives are presented to the reader as sensible responses to the experience of living among the Samburus.

Another message conveyed by the text is that Hofmann's material and technological resources – she spends thousands of dollars on her various projects – buy her independence and power. At the same time her account of the scarcities of Samburu life and the incompetence she observes among Africans confirms German preconceived notions about African ineptness, while whites are presented as successful and superior businesspeople.[19] In light of the nature of African work ethics and the lack of economic initiatives, the account legitimizes and necessitates control exerted by Europeans. Although Hofmann relies to a great extent on the skills of two Italian priests who continue to fix her car and help her out in other ways and on the support she receives in terms of medical care, these factors only stress the achievements of Europeans and their superiority over Africans. In addition Hofmann's numerous illnesses and their gravity reinforce the notion that Africa is dangerous, diseased, and life threatening to Europeans. The fact that Hofmann lived under extreme circumstances in terms of the physical challenges but at the same time did not take any precautions is lost on the uninformed reader.

Ultimately, Hofmann's account defines Africans through their bodies and represents them as intellectually inferior. Her attraction to Lketinga is primarily physical, and her descriptions of his body, smell, skin, and gait depict him as exotic. Occasionally, Hofmann points out favorable aspects of his character. In a couple of instances she praises his courageous and responsible behavior. Unlike other Masai, for example, Lketinga helps in the shop and does not shy away from physical labor. He also does not hesitate to jump into the wild current of a river to save two children who have been stranded on a rock, and, when Hofmann and Lketinga come across a party of Italians whose fellow traveler has fallen off a cliff into a gorge, Lketinga and a companion risk the dangerous climb down to retrieve the body. The nature of the communication between Hofmann and Lketinga (both speak only rudimentary English) limits the degree to which they can understand each other or the situation in which they find themselves. The narrator sees the failure of the relationship as related primarily to her husband's jealousy and his drinking habits and use of *miraa*, a stimulating herb that is chewed. The fact that Hofmann turns her husband's entire life upside down is never acknowledged or questioned.

A scene toward the end of the account is emblematic of the relationship, and it highlights the areas of conflict. Lketinga returns from an initiation ritual in his home area. No longer belonging to the warrior caste, he is not required to wear the traditional Samburu clothes. His long red hair is cut off, he wears less jewelry, but most of all it is his clothing that Hofmann finds appalling: "He is wearing an old-fashioned shirt and dark red jeans that are much too tight and too short. His feet are stuck in cheap plastic low-shoes, and his usually floating gait seems wooden and stiff." After Lketinga explains his reasons for the change in appearance, she expresses her dismay: "I ask him to consider that most Masai in Mombasa still wear their traditional clothes, their jewelry and long hair, and that this is also better for our business, from which he concludes that I am more attracted to all the other Masai. But I just hope that he exchanges again at least shirt and jeans for kangas, because this simple clothing suits him much better" (291).

Lketinga has become a commodity whose traditional appearance benefits the sales volume of his wife's store. Just as Hofmann has hired other helpers in the store on the pretext that their Masai looks will benefit the business (282, 285), she reduces her husband to a promotional ploy. This passage expresses most clearly that Hofmann's relationship to her husband is primarily based on his exotic appeal and her fascination with a traditional life that she cannot live.

This feature of the relationship between Hofmann and Lketinga paradigmatically represents the German relationship to Africa, a relationship oscillating between desire and disgust. Hofmann is at once attracted to and appalled by Masai/Samburu life. The African who mimics the European life-style is rejected and ordered to resume his place in the traditional African world. The European, however, who has learned that she cannot abide in this African world, draws the line of separation. At the very end of the account, in a letter that she sends to Lketinga, Hofmann states repeatedly that her marriage could not have worked out because of the differences between them. She even advises Lketinga not to marry another white woman but, rather, to choose a Samburu.

The circular narrative derives its legitimacy from the claim to an authentic experience and draws the reader into a sequence of events that make the final departure a logical response to irreconcilable cultural differences. It should be pointed out that there is no recourse in the account to political history. Neither colonialism nor current political events are mentioned. The state appears only in the form of repressive and arbitrary bureaucracy, and the economy, regardless of its difficult circumstances at the time, is what enables Hofmann to recover her independence. The reader who lacks historical and other background information is left to interpret the events through the lens of cultural differences.

Miriam Kwalanda's *Die Farbe meines Gesichts: Lebensreise einer kenianischen Frau* also tells the story of a German-Kenyan marriage and divorce, but this time the subject is approached from the perspective of a Kenyan woman. The text is narrated in the past tense, which makes for a more reflective tone and avoids the suspense-driven style of Hofmann's narrative. As opposed to *Die weisse Massai*, Kwalanda's text covers not only the story of her marriage to a German but also her childhood and her life as a prostitute.

The section on her childhood portrays a painful life of deprivation and abuse. Rejected from the beginning by a violent father who eventually sends her mother away, Kwalanda moves back and forth between various refuges and her abusive home, winds up on the streets of Nairobi, and finally ends up in juvenile detention. She escapes from this institution and moves to the coast, where she is reunited with her mother. After working as a prostitute and sustaining a series of relationships with tourists, Kwalanda marries a German man, Heinz, and moves to Germany. The specific situation of Heinz, an ethnic German from eastern Europe (*Spätaussiedler*) who himself experienced abuse and discrimination, mirrors that of Kenyan men in Kwalanda's life who act out their own frustrations by being abusive toward women. While Heinz is initially attractive to her because of his material power, Kwalanda becomes increasingly critical and then intolerant of his actions. Their marriage also ends in divorce, and the autobiography clearly represents an attempt by the author to come to terms with her life and the situation she and her three children face in the new country.

Ultimately, the text depicts Germany as a place that gives Kwalanda a chance to build a new life. There Kwalanda begins to get a sense of her own worth as a woman and an individual.[20] She develops new opinions and a sense of resistance to accepting her dependent situation (271). In her gradual emancipation from an increasingly abusive and unbearable marriage, Kwalanda moves back and forth between homes for battered women and her life with Heinz. Around the time of the birth of their first child, Kwalanda begins therapy. Slowly, she builds a new life inside of herself. This eventually leads to a permanent separation from Heinz, who wanted a submissive wife and is irritated with Kwalanda's newfound independence. Her self-discovery also enables her to develop a different relationship to her body. At the age of thirty Kwalanda has a boyfriend from Cameroon and experiences her first orgasm (291). Finally, after the death of her mother, she finds the courage and strength to leave her husband (299). The book closes with Kwalanda's expressed desire to learn a vocation. She wants to become a midwife, she says, "[b]ecause I love happy endings. Even if the birth of a child is always painful and exhausting, it is a happy ending to put this child, this new life, into the arms of a mother" (303).

The narrative, cowritten with the help of Birgit Theresa Koch, a journalist and psychologist (but not the one overseeing her therapy), is a coming-of-age story. It describes Kwalanda's development from complete dependence on men and subjection to abuse and violence to a self-determined life. Violence against and oppression of women is thus the pervasive theme of the narrative, whether it occurs in Kenya or in Germany.

What messages does this autobiography relate to the German reader? First of all, the account portrays Kenyan men as violent and abusive. Kwalanda's descriptions of Kenyan men include hardly any positive characters; almost all men are portrayed as violent, reckless, lecherous, and greedy, and their status is defined by material and social power. The consistent abuses that Kwalanda experiences characterize Kenyan society as violent. [21] Even though the reader encounters in Kwalanda's husband, Heinz, an example of a German man who regularly demonstrates the unpredictable behavior of an alcoholic, Kenyan men come across as more abusive and disrespectful toward women than their German counterparts. Her account includes a description of female circumcision rituals, one of the most frequently cited examples in Western discussions of the endemic violence against women in African societies. Kwalanda is spared the ordeal because her parents comply with government regulations that outlaw the practice (34); nevertheless, the general German reader's assumptions about Africans as violent and abusive are confirmed through Kwalanda's firsthand account.

As the mirror image of Kenyan men, many Kenyan women featured in this autobiography are prostitutes who are not interested in establishing loving relationships but, rather, are primarily trying to earn money. Women are entirely dependent on men, and they learn to be manipulative in order to survive. Kwalanda's story conveys a sense that no options apart from prostitution are available to women who do not obey oppressive family structures. She describes her life as a prostitute as a logical response to her dismal situation and asserts that her body is like a wallet (122). Widespread notions about Africa as a place of sexual license are confirmed through Kwalanda's lengthy description of the sexual practices of men from different cultures.

Kwalanda's story, as it is narrated with the help of a German woman, ultimately validates views about Africa that are commonly held by the German public. Kenyan society, as described by Kwalanda, is abusive toward women, and both men and women are primarily driven by a lust for sex and money. The fundamentally different nature of German society is underscored by the fact that Kwalanda is able to begin a more self-fulfilling life in Germany. There Kwalanda can thrive and develop, regardless of her background, and leave her abusive Kenyan past behind.

Because of its authenticity, readability, and narrative coherence, Kwalanda's story conveys the illusion of giving full access to Kenyan society. This feature mirrors Corinne Hofmann's account, which succeeds in explaining away the complexities of Kenyan society through her coherent narrative and seemingly logical argumentation. Thus far, I have focused on the accounts' effects on the German reader in light of their narrative features and thematic foci. In my further discussion I consider the question of reception through an overview of aspects that both Kwalanda and Hofmann leave out but which are crucial for a meaningful understanding of the texts – namely their relation to Kenyan society. Framing the texts in this manner shows that a historicized reading of the stereotypical images contained in both accounts shifts our understanding of these images.

## The Kenyan Context

It is quite likely that many German readers will not be knowledgeable regarding three interrelated areas that I consider significant to situating the texts. First, neither text addresses the fact that the situation currently facing Kenyan women is a result of colonization and modernization processes and does not resemble that of the precolonial period. Second, the texts do not provide information that would enable the reader to historicize the social dimensions of Kenyan women's current situation. Third, the German reader does not learn about the history of the political and economic struggles of women in Kenya, who are highly organized and visible in the public sphere. Let me elaborate on these three points.

First, the autobiography addresses the effect that colonial history had on Kenyan society only tangentially. In contrast to Hofmann's narrative, Kwalanda's account does contain occasional references to politics, the power dynamics between white and black, and the legacy of colonialism.[22] Male-female relations, however, are the focus of the narrative and are discussed in ways that transcend the cultural context in that both Kenyan and German men are portrayed as abusive.

Absent from this approach is an understanding of the impact of colonization and modernization on Kenyan societies. Scholarship on women's situation in contemporary Africa, however, demonstrates consistently that the precolonial situation was markedly different from the current one. Although most Kenyan societies were traditionally patrilinear and polygynous, the communal mode of production employed a distribution of labor that assigned formal and informal areas of control to women.[23]

One key area that allows us to glean the changes in gender relations in Kenya is trade.[24] In a study of the roles played by Kikuyu and Kamba women in trade, Claire Robertson details the changes that have occurred during the past century. In precolonial times women participated to a great degree in long-distance and local trade and wielded a considerable amount of power, though the right of women to control their own profits was a contested area and did not exist universally.[25] At the end of the nineteenth century Kenya's integration into the long-distance caravan trade led to the commodification of women as objects of the slave trade and suppliers of provisions. The Swahili-European caravan trade upset the previous balance between male and female traders, brutalized gender relations, displaced members of communities, subjected populations to epidemics due to the introduction of new illnesses, increased demands for labor, and stratified relations both between the sexes and within male and female groups.[26] As Robertson shows, the "segregation of women's trade from men's trade was implemented under colonialism," so that "[w]omen increasingly were confined to local trade only and gender segregation was more pervasive in markets."[27]

It is important to note that in their struggle to control women's labor and sexuality (and particularly prostitution), colonial administrators and local men collaborated consistently from the period before World War I until Kenya's independence in 1963. Urban trade in particular afforded women new opportunities outside of the traditional areas of economic activity, in which they had been marginalized. Urban trade thus posed a challenge to Kenyan men in their efforts to exert control over women, which was presented increasingly as a matter of national or ethnic pride among men; these men cooperated with colonial administrators in setting up market and taxation systems that put women at a disadvantage.[28] As one critic described it, with the advent of colonialism "the dynamic tension between formal patrilineal domination and both formal and informal female power has been snapped, and partilineal domination has united with Victorian and Christian notions of male domination."[29]

Into the 1960s these attempts at controlling women's labor and sexuality were carried out in multiple ways, and, according to Robertson, "[w]omen traders pursuing their usual rounds found that much of what they were accustomed to doing was becoming criminalized as regulations proliferated."[30] During the period of the Emergency (1952–60) the traditional division of labor was further altered, and the relations between the sexes became more antagonistic and divided. The gendered stratification of labor put women at a further disadvantage no longer because of their sex alone but because their access to "training, capital, loans and trade sites" was infinitely weaker than that of their male counterparts.[31]

During the struggle for independence many Kenyan women participated in political activism. Numerous biographies of women who were active in the Mau Mau rebellion, which initiated the path to independence, document their efforts.[32] Urban markets, where women worked alongside men, were also hotbeds of political resistance. Nevertheless, the arrival of independence did not advance women's political and social emancipation. As in many other postcolonial societies, in Kenya men reacted to the new political order by asserting the power they had gained over women during the colonial period, whereas women wanted social change in addition to the political transformation, and those who had been active in the Mau Mau rebellion were not willing to give up the status they had achieved in fighting colonization. Their dissatisfaction is reflected in the common lament of Kenyan women that since decolonization men have "gotten lazy," are not interested in social change, and have abandoned the causes of women.[33]

Since independence the scope of women's involvement in trade has continued to grow, largely out of necessity, as it enables them to escape increasingly abusive marriages and to acquire the means to raise children.[34] Kenyan women are currently more vulnerable to abuse and poverty, because they have lost the benefits of the former system; their current struggle centers on creating new institutions that would give women appropriate rights and protections, acknowledging their significant contribution to the economy and their worth as human beings. This leads us to the second point.

Kwalanda's story indeed addresses problems that affect a large segment of the female Kenyan population. [35] The story of her mother, for example, is representative of that of many women traders, whose "struggle over . . . control of their own labor, produce, and profits" is especially noticeable in Nairobi, where trade "became a survival strategy for women seeking independence from men." [36] The life stories of individual traders recorded over the last few years by various scholars resonate with aspects of the situation Miriam and her mother experienced, from a lack of support to outright abuse at the hands of men. Only a few women collaborate successfully with the men in their lives, and these few cases validate such cooperation; the outcome is overwhelming positive, with increased prosperity for the entire family. [37] The struggle for economic independence is also related to reproductive rights. By not marrying, women are granted undisputed rights over their children. [38]

Kwalanda's narrative contributes another chapter to the history of prostitution in Kenya, a topic most intriguingly explored by Luise White in *The Comforts of Home: Prostitution in Colonial Nairobi*. White attempts to avoid the moralizing narratives that dominate many public and scholarly discussions of the subject in Kenya and elsewhere; rather, she analyzes the ways in which colonial Kenyan women have attained economic power through prostitution.

> Not all Nairobi prostitutes acquired urban property. Some subsidized their families' farms, others bought livestock (precapitalist wealth in East Africa), while others – fewer in the past than today – just managed to get by. Even women who never managed to acquire real property spoke of the value of self-reliance and having a few material possessions; women saw prostitution as a reliable means of capital accumulation, not as a despicable fate or a temporary strategy. Indeed, whether a woman invested in urban real estate for herself or bought goats for her father did not seem to have been a personal or a cultural decision. The work of prostitutes was family labor. [39]

Kwalanda achieves economic power through prostitution in postcolonial Kenya, a distinctly different context from the one analyzed by White. Yet, although her experience is now rendered within the framework of the German view of prostitution, she clearly addresses the same issues that White does. (White assigns prostitution a far greater social respectability than it has in Kenya, at least in the contemporary period. The wealth attained through prostitution has been a product of necessity but does not imply that this route to wealth is officially condoned by society, especially given the high level of control over women that existed in Kenya throughout the twentieth century.) Nevertheless, the pride Kwalanda takes in having achieved a high standard of living through prostitution is tangible throughout her book. Hers is a success story – a survivor's story.

It is also significant, in seeking a more differentiated understanding of the situation, to place Kwalanda's as well as Hofmann's experiences within the context of developments occurring in the 1970s, 1980s, and 1990s. Their stories document the effects of continued urbanization, the gendered nature of poverty, and, last but not least, the effects of globalization. International loans given to Kenya in the course of the 1980s and 1990s made the country more dependent on foreign investment, with profits disappearing into accounts abroad and the pockets of corrupt Kenyan officials. The economy faltered, and poverty rates increased drastically, effecting or aggravating some of the social woes described especially in Kwalanda's account. As a result, violence against women increased.[40] Although younger Kenyan women tend to be less tolerant of abuse (older women are more accepting of a husband's right to use physical punishment), the instances of abuse have increased for them as well. Even in terms of political representation, women fared better in the 1970s than they do today.[41] The nature of Hofmann's various enterprises, the bureaucratic obstacles she encountered, but also the success of these different projects are all clearly associated with the system of foreign investment in Kenya.

The third point is that Kenyan women are active in a range of political and social organizations and occasionally female politicians, such as Charity Ngilu, have played a significant role at the national level.[42] Their involvement is a legacy of the traditional gerontocratic organization of Kenyan women. In a 1982 survey the Women's Bureau recorded 14,635 women's groups, with over 500,000 members.[43] These women's organizations play a significant role to this day, for example, by turning the public's attention in the 2002 elections to the contested issue of violence against women, focusing particularly on instances of rape by employers and husbands.[44] The high level of political organization is especially noticeable in the realm of trade, where women hawkers, within informal and formal associations, are more well organized than their male counterparts.

Neither Kwalanda's nor Hofmann's account acknowledges the current social and political debates under way in Kenya. In Kwalanda's case we should not assume that the absence of references to Kenyan social and political situations reflects the limited insights of a prostitute with little formal education; on the contrary, interviews I conducted in Kenya demonstrate a high level of awareness among uneducated people about these issues. The fact that Kenyan women are highly organized across social strata proves that political activity is not restricted to upper- or middle-class women. It is possible that references to social, historical, and political issues in Kenya were erased in the process of composing the text with Koch, Kwalanda's German cowriter, who might be unaware of these dimensions. In addition the uninitiated German reader might not be aware of the ongoing discussions among African intellectuals who have articulated distinctly original feminist positions for themselves. This is evident in the discussion of the term "womanism" as an alternative to "feminism" as well as in the sophisticated discussion of gender relations one finds in the works of African writers such as Nurrudin Farah, Ben Okri, and Mariama Bâ.[45] The image conveyed through Kwalanda's story is that of an abused African woman who has learned to express herself with the help of a German therapist. The fact that Kenyans have formulated their own emancipatory positions is not acknowledged; one could even argue that it is incompatible with the approach pursued in the narrative.

Hofmann's account also speaks to current gender issues in Kenya. Although her account is presented as a conflict between different cultures, we can alternatively read it as one over control of resources and labor. Against the background of Kenya's historical developments, Hofmann's story acquires a new dimension. While she presents the clashes with her husband as being rooted in differing cultural norms, a review of the changes Kenya's gendered economy underwent over time exposes these clashes as having resulted from a complex history of colonization and modernization. Like Kwalanda's narrative, Hofmann's account documents the battle over economic independence and control of female bodies in contemporary Kenya. With regard to the Masai, Dorothy L. Hodgson has argued that aspects of today's Masai gender hierarchies are reactions to modernization and development, in particular to colonial as well as postcolonial strategies that attempted to confine the Masai to their pastoralist tradition.[46] Because of the Masai's status as Kenya's "noble savages," they (particularly Masai men) have come to be regarded as exotic and sexualized people.[47] In this regard Hofmann's tale provides evidence of the ongoing struggles related to the situation of the Masai/Samburu community in Kenya.[48]

In light of the social, economic, and political changes that Kenya's society underwent beginning with colonization, Kwalanda's and Hofmann's stories can be understood in a framework that considers this legacy of colonial history and modernization. Both stories are authentic, reflecting the situation of many women in Kenya who fight for equality in a stubbornly male-dominated society. A Kenyan audience might be able to appreciate these texts as relevant commentaries on the struggle over resources and women's rights in contemporary Kenya. This audience would be able to evaluate Kwalanda's and Hofmann's accounts within the larger framework of gender relations and the economy, and distinct segments of Kenyan society (men versus women, Masai versus other ethnic groups, prostitutes versus other social groups) would react differently to various aspects of the texts. Awareness of certain historical dimensions touched on in the two accounts may be less pronounced among some individuals or groups, but the centrality of current debates about gender relations and the control of resources would likely encourage a critical reading.

Unlike this supposed Kenyan readership (so far, the texts have not been translated into English), the German audience who engages with Hofmann's and Kwalanda's accounts typically does not have the background to evaluate either of the texts fully and very likely draws on stereotypes to make sense of the narratives. As a result the texts end up confirming existing clichés without acknowledging the historical dimensions of the conflicts they seek to describe. Historical knowledge and awareness would allow the reader to engage his or her own historicity. After all, the situation of women in Europe has improved significantly only over the past one hundred years. A story such as Kwalanda's could occur in a number of cultural and historical contexts – in fact it might be typical for a certain stage of modernization in which, for example, high numbers of impoverished women come to the metropolis in search of a better life. In turn-of-the-century Germany the number of prostitutes in Berlin was "thought to be 40,000" and in the nation as a whole "as high as 350,000" as a result of modernization, urbanization, and migration from the countryside. [49] An uninitiated German reader, however, might read Kwalanda's and Hofmann's accounts as a testimony to the superiority of German society over African culture, without considering the relatively recent emergence of prevailing ethics and rights in European cultures.

Kwalanda's and Hofmann's texts ignore the impact that modernization and colonization have had on Kenyan society, and both fail to address the historicity of the situation. While these gaps can be filled in, at least in part, by different kinds of Kenyan readers, the typical German reader will be less able to situate the accounts in similar ways. For the German audience cultural difference remains a timeless and unbridgeable divide between Germany and Kenya.

NOTES

1. Unless indicated otherwise, data regarding tourism are based on publications by the Kenya Association of Tour Operators (KATO), the Kenya Tourist Board, the Kenya Association of Hotelkeepers and Caterers (KAHC), and the Mombasa Coast Tourist Association (MCTA). The data were published in 1996 to 1998 or compiled for the author in 1998, 1999, and 2000.

2. Figures according to Statistisches Bundesamt, Wiesbaden, prepared for the author in 2001 and 2003.

3. See the chapter "Tourism: Repeat Visitors Turned Aid Workers in Kenya" in my book *Impossible Missions? German Economic, Military, and Humanitarian Efforts in Africa* (Lincoln: University of Nebraska Press, 2004), 175–212.

4. The founding of the association was announced in one of the national newspapers, *Daily Nation*, July 12, 1999, 4.

5. Tamara Kohn, "Island Involvement and the Evolving Tourist," in *Tourists and Tourism: Identifying with People and Places*, ed. Simone Abram, Jacqueline Waldren, and Donald V. L. MacLeod (Oxford: Berg, 1997), 15.

6. Jacqueline Waldren, *Insiders and Outsiders: Paradise and Reality in Mallorca* (Providence RI: Berghahn, 1996), x.

7. See the discussion of the results of my study in Berman, *Impossible Missions*, 195–204.

8. Berman, *Impossible Missions*, 204–8.

9. My study challenges views presented in earlier analyses such as Philipp Bachmann, *Tourism in Kenya: A Basic Need for Whom?* (Bern: Lang, 1988); Eva Kurt, *Tourismus in die Dritte Welt – Ökonomische, sozio-kulturelle und ökologische Folgen: Das Beispiel Kenya* (Saarbrücken: breitenbach, 1986); Wilhelm Englbert Pompl, *Der internationale Tourismus in Kenia und seine Implikationen für die sozio-ökonomische Entwicklung des Landes* (Munich: Frank, 1975).

10. Figures according to Statistisches Bundesamt, Wiesbaden, prepared for the author in 2001 and 2003. The Embassy of the FRG in Nairobi recorded 141 marriages between Kenyans and Germans in the year 2000 and 284 in the year 2001.

11. Figures provided by the Swiss Office Fédéral de la Statistique, prepared for the author in 2001 and 2003.

12. See Berman, *Impossible Missions*, 206, 226.

13. One of the earliest accounts in this genre is Marguerite Mallett's memoir *A White Woman among the Masai* (New York: Dutton, 1923).

14. "Masai" is technically a linguistic term for speakers of this Eastern Sudanic language, including the pastoral Masai, who range along the Great Rift Valley of Kenya and Tanzania; the Samburu of Kenya; and the semipastoral Arusha and Baraguyu (or Kwafi) of Tanzania. Because the Masai are more widely known internation-

ally and have acquired a reputation as mysterious warriors and "noble savages," the publisher might have opted to use this term in the title to attract more attention to the book.

15. The novel was on the best-seller list of the weekly magazine *Der Spiegel* from January 1999 to March 2000; in spring and summer 1999 it held the second place for fourteen weeks. In the weekly *Die Zeit* the autobiography ranked first for several weeks.

16. Corinne Hofmann, *Die weisse Massai* (Munich: AI Verlag, 1998), 8.

17. Hofmann's return with her daughter is reminiscent of the much more dramatic escape from Iran described by Betty Mahmoody, with William Hoffer, in *Not Without My Daughter* (New York: St. Martin's Press, 1987).

18. Hofmann repeatedly speaks of her feeling of belonging, of being a member of the Masai tribe, of having a new family, and of being a part of their world (compare 32, 40); she also compares Masai country to Switzerland (50, 52).

19. See instances in which Lketinga drinks beer or chews the stimulant *miraa* (253, 280) or ruins the car (267).

20. Miriam Kwalanda, with Birgit Theresa Koch, *Die Farbe meines Gesichts: Lebensreise einer kenianischen Frau* (Frankfurt am Main: Eichborn, 1999), 270.

21. An especially appalling example is given in her account of a botched abortion. The doctor who messes up the procedure requires that she sleep with him as part of the payment (122–24).

22. See Kwalanda, *Die Farbe meines Gesichts*, 5, 24–27, 65–66.

23. Patricia Stamp, "Kikuyu Women's Self-Help Groups: Toward an Understanding of the Relation between Sex-Gender System and Mode of Production in Africa," in *Women and Class in Africa*, ed. Claire Robertson and Iris Berger (New York: Africana Publishing, 1986), 29–34.

24. For case studies focusing on a range of African countries, see contributions to Kathleen Sheldon, ed., *Courtyards, Markets, City Streets: Urban Women in Africa* (Boulder CO: Westview, 1996).

25. Claire C. Robertson, *Trouble Showed the Way: Women, Men, and Trade in the Nairobi Area, 1890–1990* (Bloomington: Indiana University Press, 1997), 67–71.

26. Robertson, *Trouble Showed the Way*, 71–73.

27. Robertson, *Trouble Showed the Way*, 80, 85.

28. Robertson, *Trouble Showed the Way*, 92–96. Regarding the issue of clitoridectomy as a symbol of ethnic identity, see Robertson, *Trouble Showed the Way*, 96, and Carolyn Martin Shaw, *Colonial Inscriptions: Race, Sex, and Class in Kenya* (Minneapolis: University of Minnesota Press, 1995), 65–71.

29. Stamp, "Kikuyu Women's Self-Help Groups," 37.

30. Robertson, *Trouble Showed the Way*, 102.

31. Robertson, *Trouble Showed the Way*, 145.

32. See Muthoni Kilimani, *Passbook Number F.47927: Women and Mau Mau in Kenya* (London: Macmillan, 1985); Cora Ann Presley, *Kikuyu Women, the Mau Mau Rebellion, and Social Change in Kenya* (Boulder CO: Westview, 1992); Wambui Waiyaki Otieno, *Mau Mau's Daughter: A Life History* (Boulder CO: Lynne Rienner, 1998).

33. See *Our Mothers' Footsteps: Stories of Women in the Struggle for Freedom*, ed. Wanjiku Mukabi Kabira and Patricia Ngurukie (Nairobi: Collaborative Centre for Gender and Development, 1997), 2, 31, 65, 73–75.

34. See also Bessie House-Midamba, "Kikuyu Market Women Traders and the Struggle for Economic Empowerment in Kenya," in *African Market Women and Economic Power: The Role of Women in African Economic Development*, ed. Bessie House-Midamba and Felix K. Ekechi (Westport CT: Greenwood, 1995), 81–97.

35. For an analysis of the situation of professional women, see Harriette McAdoo and Miriam K. Were, "Extended Family Involvement of Urban Kenyan Professional Women," in *Women in Africa and the African Diaspora: A Reader*, ed. Rosalyn Terborg-Penn and Andrea Benton Rushing (Washington DC: Howard University Press, 1996), 135–63.

36. Claire Robertson, "Trade, Gender, and Poverty in the Nairobi Area: Women's Strategies for Survival and Independence in the 1980s," in *Engendering Wealth and Well-Being: Empowerment for Global Change*, ed. Rae Lesser Blumberg, Cathy Rakowski, Irene Tinker, and Michael Monteon (Boulder CO: Westview, 1995), 66.

37. Robertson, "Trade, Gender, and Poverty," 78–79.

38. Robertson, *Trouble Showed the Way*, 217.

39. Luise White, *The Comforts of Home: Prostitution in Colonial Nairobi* (Chicago: University of Chicago Press, 1990), 1–2.

40. Robertson, *Trouble Showed the Way*, 205–23.

41. Jean Davison, *Voices from Mutira: Change in the Lives of Rural Gikuyu Women, 1910–1995* (Boulder CO: Lynne Rienner, 1996), 7–9.

42. For an overview, see S. A. Khasiani and E. I. Njiro, *The Women's Movement in Kenya* (Nairobi: AAWORD, 1993).

43. Khasiani and Njiro, *The Women's Movement*, 44.

44. See Regan Good, "Rape Is Prominent Issue in Kenya Elections," posted on June 4, 2002, on http://www.womensenews.org/article.cfm/dyn/aid/864/context/archive; Njue Lloyd, "Women Tell of Rape in Farms," March 9, 2002, http://allafrica.com/stories/200203090138.html.

45. Mary E. Modupe Kolawole, *Womanism and African Consciousness* (Trenton NJ: Africa World Press, 1997).

46. Dorothy L. Hodgson, *Once Intrepid Warriors: Gender, Ethnicity, and the Cultural Politics of Maasai Development* (Bloomington: Indiana University Press, 2001).

47. On the sexualization of the Masai, see Shaw, *Colonial Inscriptions*, 198–201.

48. It would be worthwhile to investigate the perspectives of the two books' men, both Lketinga and Heinz, in a separate study.

49. Volker R. Berghahn, *Imperial Germany, 1871–1914: Economy, Society, Culture, and Politics* (Providence RI: Berghahn, 1994), 71.

PATRICE NGANANG

# Autobiographies of Blackness
# in Germany

*And now I realized that I couldn't return to Mary's, or to any part of my old life. I could approach it only from the outside. –* Ralph Ellison, *Invisible Man*

This essay analyzes the discovery of race in two autobiographies, with particular focus on what is perhaps the greatest consequence of that discovery: the subject must approach himself and his world from the outside. Each of these testimonies – Hans Jürgen Massaquoi's *Destined to Witness: Growing Up Black in Nazi Germany*, and Chima Oji's *Unter die Deutschen gefallen: Erfahrungen eines Afrikaners* (Among the Germans: An African's experiences) – describes the remarkable experience of a black man in Germany.[1] These stories complement each another in many ways. Whereas Massaquoi recounts his life in Germany between 1920 and 1950, Oji explores what it means to be black there after 1968. Born in 1926 in Hamburg, the only son of Al-Haj Massaquoi and Bertha Baetz, Massaquoi lived in Germany throughout the Weimar Republic, the Third Reich, and the Second World War. In 1948, following in the footsteps of his father, he went to Monrovia for two years and then to the United States, where he continues to live. As chief editor of *Ebony* magazine, he took part in the civil-rights movement and interviewed some of the most influential figures of the black world. Chima Oji was born in 1947 in Enugu, Nigeria. In 1967 he left his country, which was embroiled in civil war, in order to study in England, when a brief visit to Münster led him to adjust his plans and settle in Germany. After earning a degree in chemistry at the University of Münster, he went on to medical school. Specializing in dentistry, he studied in Münster, Düsseldorf, and Hannover and completed his training in Freiburg. He practiced medicine for several years in Germany before returning to Nigeria. Today, Oji is the director of a hospital in his native town of Enugu. Massaquoi and Oji each follow a trajectory that ultimately leads away from Germany, to a critical distance from it.

By reading the story of their lives backward – from the end of the story to the beginning – we come to see what both men, in spite of their evident differences, lose along the way: a sense of belonging, indeed, a "home" in every sense of the word. For Oji it is the loss of a nostalgic relationship to his native Nigeria. As Oji describes his return to Enugu, after spending more than fourteen years in Germany: "In Nigeria, I encountered a completely different reality and, like it or not, I had to face it: the extended family, as a place of security and togetherness, had become nothing but a farce."[2] Massaquoi would fare no better with his own "homecoming." Having spent years in Liberia and the United States, he would conclude upon his first return to postwar Hamburg, "you can't go home again" (433).

The experience of losing a home can also be read in terms of self-development, to be sure. Massaquoi and Oji chart the process of their own disenchantment, growing up and out of childhood, while reflecting upon their increasing sense of displacement. Yet these tales of black lives represent much more than narratives of individual development. They highlight the difference between the received idea of a commonly shared humanity, which inspires autobiographies or biographies in general, and the particular discovery of race – the discovery of one's exteriority, of one's own body and blackness – as a very important element of self-definition. The discovery of race, seen in negative or positive terms, offers a key to autobiographies of blackness in Germany.

Massaquoi begins his narrative by quoting Frederick Douglass: "To write of one's self, in such a manner as not to incur the imputation of weakness, vanity, and egotism, is a work within the ability of but few; and I have little reason to believe that I belong to that fortunate few" (xi). In so doing he offers his book as a continuation of both "classical" autobiography (of which such declarations of humility are typical) and the "canonical" genre of African American slave narratives. At the same time he situates his autobiography in the tradition of fictional and nonfictional African American first-person narratives, alongside The Autobiography of Malcolm X, Richard Wright's Black Boy, and Ralph Ellison's Invisible Man, to name only a few. Philippe Lejeune has defined autobiography as a narrative of self-exposure written in prose, the ultimate form of literature in which an individual's life and history are made public.[3] Even if we accept that definition, we must make certain readjustments to it when reading the autobiographies of Massaquoi and Oji, for each one demonstrates that the discovery of blackness represents a turning point in the course of self-exploration, a point from which there is no turning back. This moment of self-discovery – not simply as a man or as a human being, but as a black man in particular – also marks the loss of home. From that point onward each writer, each speaker enters into what Massaquoi calls the "game" of survival, waging a permanent struggle to maintain his dignity and reclaim his humanity (xiv).

In their rhetorical composition, autobiographies obviously take the figure of the "I," the position of the first-person narrator, as given. Let us insist on this evident subject and its inscription in our respective narratives. Here is how Massaquoi begins: "One beautiful summer morning in 1934, I arrived at school to hear the third-grade teacher, Herr Grimmelshaeuser, inform the class that our principal, Herr Wriede, had ordered the entire student body and faculty to assemble in the schoolyard" (1). Compare Oji's beginning: "There I was, back in Germany – I knew that when, in September 1986, after four weeks of vacation in Nigeria, I had gone through the passport control at Frankfurt airport."[4] In each instance the beginning is really an end, for all autobiographies are written, of course, in hindsight. More specifically, however, for these two men, each of whom has already experienced a lifetime of racism, we might say in Ralph Ellison's words that "the end [is] in the beginning."[5] The end is the beginning, because the "I" of the storyteller is already marked as black at the first moment of its enunciation; it is never the subject of a history to be discovered. Moreover, it is the witness of a lifelong struggle over self-definition inside and outside concepts of race.

When the subject has been caught by racism, it becomes impossible to restore its neutrality and originality without taking blackness into consideration, for such narratives are in the broadest sense descriptions of the ways in which concepts of race (for example, everyday racism, Nazism, structural racism, paternalism) come to be imbricated in the most "neutral" structures of the environment and sometimes even threaten the subject's existence. What makes these autobiographies interesting, though, is that they articulate how the lives of Oji and Massaquoi come to be subordinated to such concepts of race, while showing the different ways in which the authors free themselves from these concepts in order to regain their essential humanity. The position of a life before racism is emblematic here: it is the idyllic life in Nigeria, which Oji describes at the beginning of his book, and the peaceful life of Enugu, to which he later returns; it is the childhood of dreams that Massaquoi unfolds in his tale – a beautiful, peaceful childhood without racism, where the only imposing figure is that of his grandfather, Momolu. Images of a quiet, harmonious subjectivity – an autobiographical "I," prior to racism and to its racialization – show that, for Massaquoi and Oji, being black is anything but self-evident. Rather, it is constructed as a "fact" in at least three ways: in the act of being publicly seen, in the awareness of having a fragmented body, and in the uncanny experience of being someone else.

To represent the discovery of the "fact" of blackness is to identify the phe-

nomenological violence that takes place when the black body is publicly transformed into an object – such as the object of vision, of manipulation, of possession – and the original self, the original quest, the original will of the "I" gets
lost in the process. Thus the black body is experienced as a body in pieces: there
are the legs, for example, which run like those of an athlete. For Massaquoi his
legs are those of Jesse Owens: "With all the publicity showered on Jesse Owens,
some of my playmates could not resist calling me Jesse, the way a short while
earlier they had called me Joe" (123). There are also hands, shoulders, and fists.
In Massaquoi's case these become the hands, shoulders, and fists of Joe Louis,
who roundly defeated the German boxer Max Schmeling. For his playmates
constructing a figure of blackness, names are as interchangeable as the black
body parts. The fragmentation and interchangeability of the black body goes
along with its multiple transmutations, for the imaginary world in which it
is constructed does not set itself any boundaries. If at one moment the black
body is located in the training arena, at another it becomes the body of the first
black man ever seen. In a very moving scene, Massaquoi recalls how, after the
war, his body had suddenly become that of an "American soldier" wandering
in the bombed-out city of Hamburg:

> "There's one of them!" a woman shrieked. Screaming hysterically at the
> top of her lungs, a woman of Valkyrian proportions pointed straight at
> me. "There's one of the murderers!" she continued. "Kill that American
> swine! Let him find out how it feels to burn alive!" Summoned by the
> woman's screams, people came running from every direction to investi-
> gate. Within a minute, I was surrounded by an angry, cursing, and wildly
> gesticulating mob. At first, I was at a total loss as to the meaning of
> the commotion. Then, looking down on the welding goggles around my
> neck, my grease-splattered blue coveralls, and – more to the point – *my
> brown hands*, the ironic truth hit me. They were mistaking me for a black
> U.S. pilot who, they believed, had bailed out after his plane had been shot
> down. (235; italics added)

In its unstoppable transmutation, the black body here takes on a life of its own,
quickly going from the realm of pure imagination to one of violent madness
– indeed, the fragmentation and transmutation of his body nearly costs Massaquoi his life at the hands of the mob. The only rule that could be applied
here is that of *fiction*, for the "brown hands" described here could also be those
of any dominant black fictional figure. As Oji describes: "Naturally, in the
course of the many years I spent in Germany, derogatory comments were often

shouted at me on the streets and elsewhere; for example, when the television series *Roots* was screened for the first time, I heard 'Kunta Kinte', 'Kunta Kinte' on every street corner."[6] It is clear that the black body, fragmented as it is, unseen as it is, is perpetually lost in the realm of imagination and invention, in the social grammar of fiction. Its physical presence does not withstand its permanent recomposition as somebody who it is not, or even as something which it is not. It is estranged from itself, because it is definitively somebody or something else. This loss can explain why at another juncture in Oji's life, his body is seen and described by others as the body of *an animal*: "A German family crossed the street and walked some steps behind us. Suddenly, the father said to his son (and not the other way around), 'Look, a gorilla'. The boy laughed loudly about the joke his father had made."[7]

The discovery of the "I" as being somebody or something else (a perfect doppelgänger) is profoundly marked in autobiographies of black men. Let us follow the young Massaquoi as he and his parents visit Hagenbeck's Zoo in Hamburg. Standing alongside other children, he observes one of Hagenbeck's ethnographic exhibitions, an "African Village," where African performers are displayed adjacent to wild animals:

> Suddenly, something happened that I had feared from the moment I caught sight of the exhibit. Despite the fact that I had carefully tried to stay in the background in order to see without being seen, one of the Africans spotted me in the crowd. All at once the entire village took notice of me. The two women stopped pounding and the men stopped puffing. As if they had seen a long-lost relative, they were all pointing and grinning at me. Desperately, I tried to hide behind one of the spectators, but to no avail. Tipped off by the African's finger-pointing, one of the zoo visitors spun around and, after realizing what the Africans' excitement was all about, pointed his own stubby finger at me. "Look," he alerted his female companion. "Here's one of their kids." This set off a chain reaction among the rest of the spectators until everyone, both African and German, was looking at me. (25–26)

Here, one can almost see his embarrassed face, as the young Massaquoi seems to ask both the Africans and the Germans: Why are you looking at *me*? His reaction would seem to assert his profound humanity, and with it, the fact that he, Massaquoi, is *not like and does not belong to these Africans*. Let us imagine that he quickly looked around, assuming primarily that he could not be the object of everyone's gaze, for he is indeed not an object. If his fear when approaching the cage ("something happened that I had feared the moment I caught sight of the exhibit") testifies to his initial acceptance of his racialized, fragmented, and estranged body, it also highlights his quick refusal to belong to these Africans on display, as if they were animals – his refusal to be identified with *them*. However shocking this scene at the zoo is, it demonstrates the "fact" of blackness as it is experienced by and simultaneously foisted upon him – a "fact" that means the public construction of a body, indeed a discourse of racial differences that the subject must constantly either accept or reject. The "fact" of blackness, as it appears in this scene, inadvertently exhibits the process by which the body of the young Massaquoi is publicly constructed as being black, as being "African," and this only through an interplay of gazes: the gaze of the Germans looking at the "African Village," that of the Africans looking at him, and that of the Germans looking at him. Caught at the intersection of these multiple and contradictory gazes, Massaquoi is initially defined as somebody he does not see himself as being but who he has otherwise yet to become, namely, a black man or, on this occasion, a black boy. Only at the intersection of gazes do the fragmented parts of his body become unified by a single color and identified with a continent he does not yet know, "Africa," as if testifying to his indisputable blackness.

An unexpected exchange of gazes likewise serves to construct Oji as a racialized subject. Recalling an episode that took place in his Münster apartment building, he writes: "A door opened and a young woman dressed in uniform and carrying cleaning utensils came out. When she saw me, she abruptly stopped in her tracks; she stared at me with wide-open eyes, and her face turned white as chalk before she dropped her things and, with a piercing scream, hastily stormed away. I was deeply shocked by the unbelievably frightening effect of my mere appearance. Later, after we had both regained our composure, the young woman confided in me that today she *had seen* a black man close up for the very first time."[8] In this case the gaze negates Oji's subjectivity by rendering him an object of horror. The phenomenology of such a public negation has been described by Jean-Paul Sartre in terms of *chosification* (thingification), as a moment in which the perceived subject is suddenly caught in his very presence and thus robbed of his freedom, negated by the violent and humiliating gaze of the Other. Drawing on Sartre's phenomenology, Frantz Fanon writes: "Sealed into that crushing objecthood, I turned beseechingly to others. Their attention was a liberation, running over my body suddenly abraded into nonbeing, endowing me once more with an agility that I had thought lost, and by taking me out of the world, restoring me to it. But just as I reached the other side, I stumbled, and the movements, the attitudes, the glances of the other fixed me there, in the sense in which a chemical solution is fixed by a dye."[9] Thus the white gaze both constructs and annihilates the black body at the same time. As Fanon says, "I am overdetermined from without."[10] His treatment of subjectivity, situated as it is in the tradition of Sartre's philosophy, emphasizes three particular aspects of the black body's discovery: namely, its public display, its objectlike relationship to the gaze of the Other, and the inferiority complex that derives from such a discovery.

Whereas Fanon traces the genealogy of blackness in negative terms, Jacques Lacan's notion of the subject allows us to describe an alternative lineage of the racialized subject.[11] Lacan's notion suggests a private experience of racialization that is a consequence of public discovery. Analyzing the general experience of the subject's constitution, Lacan locates the beginnings of one's socially recognized identity in the mirror stage of childhood development:

We have only to understand the mirror stage as an identification, in the full sense that analysis gives to the term: namely, the transformation that takes place in the subject when he assumes an image – whose predestination to this phase-effect is sufficiently indicated by the use, in analytic theory, of the ancient term imago. This jubilant assumption of his specular image by the child at the infant stage, still sunk in his motor incapacity and nursing independence, would seem to exhibit in an exemplary situation the symbolic matrix in which the I is precipitated in a primordial form, before it is objectified in the dialectic of identification with the other, and before language restores to it, in the universal, its function as subject.[12]

The mirror stage complicates and enriches Fanon's analysis of racism by exploring an "earlier" moment in the subject's formation: namely, when the child sees his image as it appears in an actual mirror, *not as it is reflected in the eyes of others.*

The immateriality, or better, the fictional nature of this appearance in a mirror is itself as constitutive of the subject as the white gaze that haunts the liberatory theory of Fanon. If Massaquoi's zoo scene, with its public display of the black body as a body being seen by others, corresponds to Fanon's phenomenology of blackness, the discovery of one's subjectivity in front of the mirror, as described by Lacan, applied to our analysis, also introduces a less public moment, which is as fundamental to the constitution of the subject as its public display. That is, the constitution of the "I" of our autobiographies *as* being the "I" of a black man appears to take place as much in the void between multiple gazes as in front of one's mirrored self-image, for it is here that the subject truly confronts his fictional doppelgänger. The transitory function of the mirror is essential in such a process, as Massaquoi recalls:

> After a girl I had been playing with told me that I looked better with my cap on, I rushed home and did what I had avoided doing for some time, namely taking a long, probing look in the mirror. To say I didn't like what I saw would be putting it mildly. The boy who looked back at me, I decided with brutal objectivity, was plain ugly. His nose was much shorter and wider than that of "normal" boys, and his skin, although smoother-looking than the skin of other boys, was several shades too dark to pass for a tan. Worst of all was the kinky hair. . . . There were two aspects of my appearance, however, that I not only appreciated but was actually rather proud of, *despite the fact that they were probably racial traits.* One was my physique. Although I was of average height, I had a well-proportioned, athletic body with well-muscled legs and arms. The other was my teeth, which earned me many compliments, especially during dental examinations in school. (93–94; italics added)

In other words, standing in front of the mirror, the young Massaquoi gathers together his publicly fragmented physique (that is his hair, skin, legs, arms, teeth) and accepts not only the complexion of his body but also the fundamental "fact" that his subjectivity is racially defined. He becomes one with the fiction of himself, with his black doppelgänger. In so doing he starts constructing his subjectivity *from inside the fiction, from inside the void of multiple gazes.* If, standing at the crossroads of different and contradictory gazes in the zoo, he experienced the public distortion and deconstruction of his body, then alone in front of the mirror he intimately accepts his black image in an effort to make sense of his torment. Indeed, one might say that he has no other choice than to accept being black.

Massaquoi's self-presentation as black creates a relationship between the autobiographical subject of his narrative and the "fact" of his blackness. Only then does the status of the narrative subject become unambiguous, for only from inside the accepted fiction of his racialized body can he say: "I am a black person in Nazi Germany" (xii). This sentence entails both a solution to an internal fight with a racial construct of himself and the recognition of his race as a social fact. In a further parallel between the autobiographer's self-definition as black and Lacan's mirror stage, Massaquoi's acceptance of his mirrored body opens up a new space of subjectivity. In accepting his reflected image, Massaquoi defines the "I" of his autobiography – which is, strictly speaking, that of somebody else, that of a black man – as his own, thus opening himself to the "game" of black survival in a white world, in Nazi Germany. Here it is important to emphasize that when Massaquoi identifies with his mirror image, he simultaneously locates his subjectivity inside a discourse on race, one that is admittedly positive, insofar as it is self-defined and self-centered, but racist nevertheless. His discourse on race, which evolves into a politics of race relations, will ultimately lead him back to the Africans at Hagenbeck's zoo, to black American soldiers in postwar Hamburg, to his paternal roots in Liberia, to the civil-rights movement in the United States, to the staff of Ebony magazine, and to many African leaders. In so doing he defines, as would Oji, the autobiographical subject, the "I" of his book as the subject of a discourse on race.

This discourse on race has several implications, one of which is literally vital: in order to survive after the war, Massaquoi must strategically accept his life-threatening status as an *outsider* in Germany: he must accept the "fact" of his blackness. In contrast to Oji, whose outsider position in Germany is clearly indicated by the terms *Ausländer* (foreigner) and *Gastarbeiter* (guest worker) despite the fact that he lived and worked there for years, Massaquoi has a more ambiguous relationship to Germany, for he is German by birth and, at the same time, he is black.[13] It is the "fact" of their blackness that, in one way or another, positions both autobiographers as outsiders and insiders at once. As Massaquoi writes: "Alex [Haley] felt that because I was both an insider in Nazi Germany and, paradoxically, an endangered outsider, I had a rare perspective on some of the Third Reich's major catastrophic events" (xi–xii).

The position of black autobiographers as insider/outsiders has a direct bearing on their respective narratives. Whereas Massaquoi's autobiography is more or less a love letter to his courageous and caring German mother, Bertha Nikodijevic (to whom the book is also dedicated), Oji's text, though dedicated to his German wife, Barbara, is also at times less personal in tone, more openly polemical. Massaquoi and Oji's relationship to the German language becomes a kind of field where the "game" of survival also takes place, where they negotiate their dual position as outsiders and insiders – as inhabitants of what Massaquoi calls "a nationality twilight zone" (335). A native speaker of English, Oji enters the German language through a different syntax. His struggles in the German-language classroom represent more than a rite of initiation into a foreign culture. They also describe a long and tortuous exercise in reworking the German language to "fit" his own subjectivity. At the beginning of his narrative he writes: "For a long time, I did not feel really sure of myself in the German language, and for that reason, I once missed the stopping time of an examination. Our work had been scheduled to stop at 3:30 p.m. [*halb vier*]. I stumbled over the language transfer between German and English."[14] Working his way through the German grammar, he soon realizes that before he can begin to use the language effectively, he must deconstruct its very relationship to things – in particular, its relationship to the "fact" of his own blackness. He realizes that the multiple gazes that publicly see in him merely a black body are also formed inside the very structures of the German language. He realizes that, as with the gazes around him, the language that everybody around him uses – the very language he must master in order to be able to study – also constructs and determines his fictional body as a black man in Germany. Thus the language student quickly becomes not only a linguist, but also a philosopher, indeed, a teacher of German:

> Everyday language deserves particular attention, for two reasons. First, it has an enormous impact on everyday consciousness, and second, it serves as the best mirror of that consciousness, for everyday language is not critical; rather, it confirms that which is unclear and blurred, that which is known and therefore cannot be questioned. In common forms of expression such as proverbs, it offers an impressive picture of foreign cultures, from which nobody can remove himself or herself. This happens, for instance, when a teacher asks his students not to "behave like niggers" [literally, "stage a Negro revolt"] or when parents say to their children at the lunch table that they should not "eat like kaffirs."[15]

Oji's experience in the language classroom echoes the words of Fanon: "To speak means to be in a position to use a certain syntax, to grasp the morphology of this or that language, but it means above all to assume a culture, to support the weight of a civilization."[16] For Oji, however, to "assume a culture" is also to critique it, for his autobiography concludes with an extended and sometimes vehement commentary on the structure of the German language, on what it means to say the word "black" in German, and on the significance of speaking and writing in German as a person deemed black. For him, that is, speaking German as a black person means adopting a deconstructive position toward the German language and people. He chooses to write his autobiography in German because the discourse of race that he employs and critiques is deeply connected to the primordial acceptance of his blackness *inside* the German language and *inside* Germany. As Oji explains:

> First of all, I would like to tell other foreigners, especially Africans, who have not yet set foot on European soil, what it is like to be a black man there. . . . My second concern in writing is to help enlighten people in Germany and elsewhere on everyday racism in this country. . . . For it is different to experience Germany when one has black skin. And for this reason – last but not least – I am also of the opinion that I owe it to myself, after more than twenty years of silent persistence in this country, for once to speak out in public, to let out everything that I have had to swallow during my life in Germany, simply because I had no other choice.[17]

Oji's autobiography thus represents a scream, voiced in German, of a man caught in a black body.

The position of the outsider/insider is not only one of reflection, as we see in Oji's autobiography; it is also a position of negotiation and translation. Witness the young Massaquoi learning English in Nazi Germany, secretly listening to BBC programs during the war, negotiating multiple personalities, playing the black American GI in postwar Germany, selling cigarettes on American ships in order to survive, and serving as a translator between Germans and Americans. Here the autobiographer recalls some of the most refreshing parts of his life, concluding his truly breathtaking tale of adventure on a joyous and poignant note. Yet Massaquoi rejoins his fellow Germans after the war only to realize that, once again, they have made someone else out of him:

> It dawned on me that in one fell swoop I had ceased to be what I had always considered myself – a German. But somehow, the thought didn't bother me. The Germans never let me fully share in their happy past. Now I didn't need any part of their miserable present. . . . For the first time in years I felt totally free of the paralyzing fear that my pride had never permitted me to admit to anyone, not least of all to myself, but that had stalked me relentlessly by day and by night. It was not an ordinary kind of fear, such as the fear of being killed in a bombing raid or in a Nazi extermination camp. Instead it was the fear of being humiliated, of being ridiculed, of being degraded, of having my dignity stripped from me, of being made to feel that I was less a human being, less a man than the people in whose midst I lived. Suddenly, that fear was lifted from me like a heavy burden I had carried without being fully aware of it. (257–58)

NOTES

1. Hans Jürgen Massaquoi, *Destined to Witness: Growing Up Black in Nazi Germany* (New York: Harper Collins, 1999); Chima Oji, *Unter die Deutschen gefallen: Erfahrungen eines Afrikaners*, (Munich: Ullstein, 2001). All translations are mine unless otherwise indicated.

2. "Ich traf in Nigeria auf eine völlig veränderte Wirklichkeit, und ich musste ihr wohl oder übel ins Auge sehen: die Grossfamilie als ein Hort der Geborgenheit und des Zusammenhaltes war nur noch eine Farce" (265).

3. Philippe Lejeune, *Le Pacte autobiographique* (Paris: Le Seuil, 1986), 13.

4. "Ich war wieder in Deutschland – das wusste ich, als ich im September 1986 nach vier Wochen Ferienaufenthalt in Nigeria die Passkontrolle im Frankfurter Flughafen hinter mich gebracht hatte" (7).

5. Ralph Ellison, *Invisible Man* (New York: Vintage, 1995), 571.

6. "Natürlich sind mir im Laufe der vielen Jahre, die ich in Deutschland verbracht habe, auf der Strasse und anderswo oft abfällige Bemerkungen nachgerufen worden; so hiess es zum Beispiel in der Zeit, als die Fernsehserie 'Roots' zum ersten Mal ausgestrahlt wurde, an jeder Strassenecke 'Kunta Kinte,' 'Kunta Kinte' " (318–19).

7. "Eine deutsche Familie überquerte die Strasse und lief dann ein paar Schritte hinter uns. Plötzlich sagte der Vater zu seinem Sohn (nicht etwa umgekehrt) 'Sieh mal da, ein Gorilla.' Der Junge lachte laut über den Scherz, den sein Vater gerade gemacht hatte" (319).

8. "Da wurde eine Zimmertür geöffnet, und eine junge Frau im Kittel mit Putzutensilien in den Händen kam heraus. Als sie mich erblickte, hielten ihre Schritte plötzlich inne; mit weit aufgerissenen Augen starrte sie mich aus einem Gesicht heraus an, das im Nu kreidebleich geworden war, bevor sie ihre Sachen fallen liess und mit einem grellen Aufschrei fluchtartig davon stürmte. Ich war tief betroffen von der unglaublichen angsterregenden Wirkung meines blossen Anblicks. Später, nachdem wir beide unsere Fassung wiedergewonnen hatten, vertraute mir die junge Putzfrau an, dass sie heute zum ersten Mal einen schwarzen Mann von nahem *gesehen* hatte" (74; italics in the original).

9. Frantz Fanon, *Black Skin, White Masks*, trans. Charles Lam Markmann (London: Pluto Press, 1993), 109.

10. Fanon, *Black Skin, White Masks*, 116.

11. As Fanon contends, "consciousness of the body is solely a negating activity" (110).

12. Jacques Lacan, "The Mirror Stage as Formative of the Function of the I as Revealed in the Psychoanalytic Experience," in *Ecrits: A Selection*, trans. Alan Sheridan (New York: Norton, 1977), 2.

13. In a series of extraordinary passages, Massaquoi describes his battle to be

accepted in key arenas of everyday life in Nazi Germany, including his unsuccessful attempt to enlist in the *Wehrmacht*. See 195–96.

14. "Ich fühlte mich noch lange nicht wirklich sicher in der deutschen Sprache, und einmal verpasste ich deswegen die Stoppzeit einer Klausur. Unsere Arbeitszeit wurde bis auf halb vier (15.30 Uhr) begrenzt. Ich stolperte über den sprachlichen Transfer zwischen dem Englischen und dem Deutschen" (102).

15. "Beachtung verdient . . . die Alltagssprache, und zwar in doppelter Hinsicht: zum einen hat sie eine enorme prägende Kraft auf das Alltagsbewusstsein, zum anderen ist sie gleichzeitig auch dessen bester Spiegel, denn sie ist nicht kritisch, sondern bestätigt ganz selbstverständlich das Unklare und Verschwommene, das als bekannt gilt und deshalb nicht in Frage gestellt wird. In geläufigen Ausdrucksformen wie Sprichwörtern und Redensarten vermittelt sie ein eindrucksvolles Bild fremder Kulturen und Gesellschaften, dem sich niemand entziehen kann, sei es nun, dass ein Lehrer seine Schüler auffordert, bloss 'keinen Negeraufstand' zu machen, oder dass Eltern ihren Nachwuchs beim Mittagstisch ermahnen: 'Friss nicht wie ein Kaffer' " (61–62).

16. Fanon, *Black Skin, White Masks*, 17–18.

17. Indeed, Oji's discourse only makes sense in German: "Zum einen möchte ich anderen Ausländern, besonders Afrikanern, die ihren Fuss bisher noch nicht auf europäischen Boden gesetzt haben, erzählen, wie es einem Schwarzen dort tatsächlich ergeht. . . . Mein zweites Anliegen beim Schreiben ist es, zur Aufklärung der Menschen in Deutschland und anderswo über den alltäglichen Rassismus hierzulande beizutragen. . . . Es ist eben etwas anderes, Deutschland zu erleben, wenn man selbst in einer schwarzen Haut steckt. Und deshalb – last but not least – bin ich auch der Meinung, dass ich es mir nach mehr als zwanzig Jahren geduldigen und oft schweigenden Ausharrens in diesem Land selber schulde, mich einmal in aller Offenheit auszusprechen, einmal all das herauszulassen, was ich während meines Lebens in Deutschland schlucken musste, weil ich keine andere Wahl hatte" (11–13).

# Contributors

VANESSA AGNEW is assistant professor of German at the University of Michigan.

ERIC AMES is assistant professor of German at the University of Washington.

NINA BERMAN is associate professor of German at Ohio State University.

ROBERT GORDON is professor of anthropology at the University of Vermont and research associate at the University of the Free State, South Africa.

PASCAL GROSSE is a historian and a neurologist on the faculty of the Humboldt University, Berlin, Germany.

SUSANNAH HESCHEL is the Eli Black Associate Professor of Jewish Studies in the Department of Religion and chair of the Jewish Studies Program at Dartmouth College.

ELISA VON JOEDEN-FORGEY is a graduate student at the University of Pennsylvania.

MARCIA KLOTZ is lecturer in English and women's studies at Portland State University.

KRISTIN KOPP is assistant professor of German at Harvard University.

SARA LENNOX is professor of German at the University of Massachusetts at Amherst.

DENNIS MAHONEY is professor of German at the University of Vermont.

BRADLEY D. NARANCH received his PhD in history at the Johns Hopkins University.

PATRICE NGANANG is assistant professor of German and French at Shippensburg University of Pennsylvania.

DAVID SIMO is professor of German at the University of Yaoundé, Cameroon.

WOODRUFF D. SMITH is professor of history at the University of Massachusetts at Boston.

LORA WILDENTHAL is associate professor of history at Rice University.

# Index

In the **Texts and Contexts** series

**Germany's Colonial Pasts**
Edited by Eric Ames, Marcia Klotz, and Lora Wildenthal

**Affective Genealogies**
*Psychoanalysis, Postmodernism, and the "Jewish Question" after Auschwitz*
By Elizabeth J. Bellamy

**Impossible Missions?**
*German Economic, Military, and Humanitarian Efforts in Africa*
By Nina Berman

**Sojourners**
*The Return of German Jews and the Question of Identity*
By John Borneman and Jeffrey M. Peck

**Serenity in Crisis**
*A Preface to Paul de Man, 1939–1960*
By Ortwin de Graef

**Titanic Light**
*Paul de Man's Post-Romanticism, 1960–1969*
By Ortwin de Graef

**The Future of a Negation**
*Reflections on the Question of Genocide*
By Alain Finkielkraut
Translated by Mary Byrd Kelly

**The Imaginary Jew**
By Alain Finkielkraut
Translated by Kevin O'Neill and David Suchoff

**The Wisdom of Love**
By Alain Finkielkraut
Translated by Kevin O'Neill and David Suchoff

**The House of Joshua**
*Meditations on Family and Place*
By Mindy Thompson Fullilove

**Inscribing the Other**
By Sander L. Gilman

**Antisemitism, Misogyny, and the Logic of Cultural Difference**
Cesare Lombroso and Matilde Serao
By Nancy A. Harrowitz

**Opera**
*Desire, Disease, Death*
By Linda Hutcheon and Michael Hutcheon

**Man of Ashes**
By Salomon Isacovici and Juan Manuel Rodrìguez
Translated by Dick Gerdes

**Between Redemption and Doom**
*The Strains of German-Jewish Modernism*
By Noah Isenberg

**Poetic Process**
By W. G. Kudszus

**Keepers of the Motherland**
*German Texts by Jewish Women Writers*
By Dagmar C. G. Lorenz

**Madness and Art**
*The Life and Works of Adolf Wölfli*
By Walter Morgenthaler
Translated and with an introduction by Aaron H. Esman in collaboration
with Elka Spoerri

**The Nation without Art**
*Examining Modern Discourses on Jewish Art*
By Margaret Olin

**Organic Memory**
*History and the Body in the Late Nineteenth and Early Twentieth Centuries*
By Laura Otis

**Book of the Sphinx**
By Willis Goth Regier

**Crack Wars**
*Literature, Addiction, Mania*
By Avital Ronell

**Finitude's Score**
Essays for the End of the Millennium
By Avital Ronell

**Herbarium / Verbarium**
The Discourse of Flowers
By Claudette Sartiliot

**Atlas of a Tropical Germany**
Essays on Politics and Culture, 1990–1998
By Zafer Şenocak
Translated and with an introduction by Leslie A. Adelson

**The Inveterate Dreamer**
Essays and Conversations on Jewish Culture
By Ilan Stavans

**Budapest Diary**
In Search of the Motherbook
By Susan Rubin Suleiman

**Rahel Levin Varnhagen**
The Life and Work of a German Jewish Intellectual
By Heidi Thomann Tewarson

**The Jews and Germany**
From the "Judeo-German Symbiosis" to the Memory of Auschwitz
By Enzo Traverso
Translated by Daniel Weissbort

**Richard Wagner and the Anti-Semitic Imagination**
By Marc A. Weiner

**Undertones of Insurrection**
Music, Politics, and the Social Sphere in the Modern German Narrative
By Marc A. Weiner

**The Mirror and the Word**
Modernism, Literary Theory, and Georg Trakl
By Eric B. Williams

Printed in the United States
69600LVS00004B/253-255

9 780803 248199